PRAISE FOR *THE FURIES*

"*The Furies* is a glorious excavation of women's rage. But it is also a cautionary tale of how the world treats women who dare to fight back, to assert their rights, to scream into the dark void of endless discrimination and inequality. These three women will fill you with hope, despair, and yes, fury."

—Rachel Louise Snyder, author of *Women We Buried, Women We Burned* and *No Visible Bruises*

"Arresting, deeply reported . . . a patient reporter who embeds with her subjects long enough to write about their inner worlds with authority and nuance. . . . *The Furies* is deeply respectful of its subjects' autonomy, including their self-justifications and mistakes. Flock largely withholds judgment, and her work is richer and more troubling because of it."

—*Washington Post*

"Sensitively reported. . . . There is a deep compassion in Flock's account."

—*The New Yorker*

"*The Furies* is a remarkable and important exploration—reported with deep rigor and care—of what justice looks like for women who have been stripped of power and are trying to reclaim it."

—Rachel Aviv, author of *Strangers to Ourselves*

"Intricately reported."

—*New York Times Book Review* Editors' Choice

"A captivating examination of violence and power. . . . Flock has a novelist's knack for creating suspense, her reporting is thorough, and her ll stick with readers."

—*Publishers Weekly* (starred review)

"Readers of Chanel Miller's *Know My Name* and Jon Krakauer's *Missoula* will be familiar with the shocking ways police departments, medical centers, and courts sometimes treat rape victims. *The Furies* adds to that conversation, demonstrating how the justice system seems completely stacked against people who aren't 'ideal victims' . . . a powerful reminder not only of the difference individuals can make in larger struggles for justice but also of the limits of their success."

—*Minneapolis Star Tribune*

"Incisive. . . . In the hands of a less adept journalist, *The Furies* might read as a predictable, even formulaic feminist exposé. But Flock acknowledges the women's fallibilities as readily as she does their strengths. . . . Flock clears space for opposing truths, demonstrating how many women embody myriad, simultaneous contradictions to survive. . . . Though Brittany, Angoori, and Cicek ultimately fall prey to systemic patriarchal forces, Flock's work feels hopeful, even rebellious. Because just as women confront similar challenges, so too can they stage analogous forms of resistance."

—*Los Angeles Review of Books*

"These stories of women's vengeance are both harrowing and thrilling. Rosa Parks's defiance was a carefully planned political act; these begin as the opposite—sheer rage. This gripping, inflaming book, itself an act of fury, shows how revenge can transmute into politics or be crushed by it."

—Larissa MacFarquhar, author of *Strangers Drowning: Impossible Idealism, Drastic Choices, and the Urge to Help*

"Women around the world are fighting back against their oppressors, and these powerful stories—conveyed with rigor and compassion—will leave readers fired up, furious, and raring to join the cause."

—Kirsten Miller, author of *The Change*

"Flock notes that the Furies of ancient Greek mythology, who tormented Orestes, were hideous and pitiless—the stuff of nightmares. Flock makes a compelling argument that women who stand up for themselves are still seen in this same light. . . . The women are drawn in shades of gray, and that is what makes *The Furies* so powerful. Brittany, Angoori, and Cicek are not mythical figures, but ordinary, flawed humans who fight for their lives, their dignity and justice—despite the cost."

—*BookPage*

"Three women pursue justice in this powerful account of what happens when institutions do not protect them. Journalist Flock brings the gripping stories of Brittany Smith, Angoori Dahariya, and Cicek Mustafa Zibo to life with vivid detail and in-depth research. . . . Her compelling narrative will resonate with those who seek to live in a more feminist, egalitarian society."

—*Booklist*

"Drawing on in-depth interviews over many years, Emmy Award–winning journalist Flock, author of *The Heart Is a Shifting Sea*, creates vivid profiles of three women who responded to abuse with violence and vengeance. . . . Stirring narratives of defiance."

—*Kirkus Reviews*

THE FURIES

WOMEN, VENGEANCE, AND JUSTICE

ELIZABETH FLOCK

HARPER PERENNIAL

NEW YORK • LONDON • TORONTO • SYDNEY • NEW DELHI • AUCKLAND

HARPER ● PERENNIAL

A hardcover edition of this book was published in 2024 by Harper, an imprint of Harper-Collins Publishers.

HarperCollins books may be purchased for educational, business, or sales promotional use. For information, please email the Special Markets Department at SPsales@harpercollins.com.

FIRST HARPER PERENNIAL EDITION PUBLISHED 2025.

Photograph of Brittany Smith by Elizabeth Flock, January 2020. Photograph courtesy of Elizabeth Flock.

Photograph of Angoori Dahariya by Gayatri Ganju, January 2019. Photograph courtesy of Gayatri Ganju.

Photograph of Cicek Mustafa Zibo by Delil Souleiman, May 2021. Photograph courtesy of Delil Souleiman.

"Gunpowder & Lead" (Miranda Lambert and Heather Little) © 2007 Sony Music Publishing LLC, Nashville Star Music and Publisher(s) Unknown. All rights obo Sony Music Publishing LLC and Nashville Star Music, administered by Sony Music Publishing (US) LLC, 424 Church Street Suite 1200, Nashville, TN 37219. All rights reserved. Used by permission.

"For Inez Garcia" by Marge Piercy. Copyright © 1974 by Marge Piercy and Middlemarsh, Inc. From *Living in the Open*, Alfred A. Knopf, 1976. Used by permission of Robin Straus Agency, Inc.

Library of Congress Cataloging-in-Publication Data has been applied for.

ISBN 978-0-06-304879-9 (pbk.)

24 25 26 27 28 LBC 5 4 3 2 1

To the ones who defended themselves
and the ones who could not

Ni Santas, ni putas, solo mujeres / Neither saints, nor whores, only women.

—Feminist protest slogan used by women in Mexico, Spain, Italy, Canada, and the United States

CONTENTS

PREFACE

Just before turning twenty-one, I saved up enough money to visit Rome with a few friends, thinking of nothing but the Spanish Steps and rigatoni. One of us had an idea to do a guided tour of the city, and we found one advertising a day trip to the monuments, followed by a night jaunt to the tourist bars. Our guide was a little older than us, a stocky man in his mid-twenties with a bristly beard. Two of my friends flirted with him as we visited the Colosseum. I can't remember having an opinion of him at all.

On the night tour, I took a shot at the first bar. Everybody did, including the tour guide. It was a tacky American-owned establishment, the kind that serves soggy sliders and greasy chicken wings, with liquor bottles backlit at the bar. I don't think I had anything else to drink that night, although I have second-guessed my memory a few times over. Afterward, we went to the Trevi Fountain and threw pennies over our shoulders, a local superstition to ensure that one day we'd return to the city. It's the last thing I remember about that tour. The next is waking up in a dimly lit room somewhere in Rome, being raped by the guide, who, I later realized, had slipped me Rohypnol—a roofie.

It was an unnerving lesson to learn, that fight or flight are not the only two responses a person can have to threats. Another is: freeze. I was passive, I let it happen, I dissociated, and I was gone. I did not go to the police, because I did not think they would help me. For years afterward,

I was angry: angry at him for doing it, my friends for not saving me, and myself for not fighting back. Like most women, I have been violated at other times and in other ways. But the Rome incident was formative. I have spent the last fifteen years not at home in my body, in the skin that I once saw as protection. Often, I've wondered how that morning, and my life since, might have been different if I'd had access to a knife or a gun.

But this fantasy only led to more difficult questions. If I had shot him that morning, would it have helped anything, or only made it worse? If I had fought back, would the authorities have believed me, or would I have been arrested and jailed? Most painful of all, how many more women did he go on to hurt because I stayed quiet and did nothing?

In the spring of 2016, almost a decade after it happened, I decided to find him. I knew only his first name and the name of his tour company, but as an investigative journalist, it took only an hour to find his full name, social media accounts, and where he lived. He looked just as I remembered him, though a bit less stocky, with the same red drinkers' skin. His LinkedIn mentioned that he ran a furniture store, and his current location—the city where I lived at the time. My stomach turned and my skin itched. I blinked rapidly to ensure I was reading it right. Maybe he lived in my neighborhood. Maybe I had wandered into his business, looking for a couch or a chair.

Soon, I found myself fantasizing about burning down his store. For months I thought about how I would do it, the materials I'd use, and how to cover my tracks. Over Facebook, I eventually sent him a message, asking if he remembered what he did to me, how many other women he'd hurt, and if he ever lost sleep at night, as I did. He did not reply, or maybe he didn't see the message. But I was on the hunt now, for answers and for women who had followed their instincts to fight.

Vigilante women are easy to find in media, fiction, and across cultures: *The Girl with the Dragon Tattoo, Kill Bill, Watchmen, Lady Vengeance,* "Goodbye Earl," the Furies, Kali, and Athena. We are drawn to these figures, perhaps because we wish we could be them. These tales fascinated me, and I spent years diving into the stories of violent women in mythology and history, some of whom are in these pages. It was only later that I realized there were so many living versions.

• • •

It was August 2008, a sweltering day in Mumbai, India, where I got my first job as a reporter at a business magazine. I kicked up small clouds of dust behind me as I walked, the sun baking the road iron hot. A placard in the median, the kind that usually bears the faces of politicians or historical heroes, stopped me. This one showed a slight woman with a round face and penetrating stare. The text below her image read: *Phoolan Devi, the "Bandit Queen."*

Curious, I typed her name into my phone. I learned that Phoolan Devi was a low-caste woman who fled her child marriage, became a bandit, and spent years avenging crimes against women and the poor. She died in 2001, less than a decade before. My stomach churned with the nervous thrill of finding someone you didn't know you'd been looking for, and the realization that there were undoubtedly others like her—women who'd defended themselves in places where institutions failed to protect them.

This book is the product of that continued search for women who took matters into their own hands: a study of three real-life women who, like alchemists, took their stories of pain and transmuted them into power. It is also a study of how women sometimes cross the line.

In small-town Alabama, I found a woman facing trial for shooting and killing a man she said had raped and attacked her in her home. I met a female guerrilla fighter in northeast Syria battling jihadists and their reign of rape and terror. And in northern India, where the Bandit Queen was born, I encountered a new female vigilante leader who wielded bamboo canes against abusers and treated the police with as much impudence.

All three of these women handled matters on their own because the cops, courts, and state had failed to safeguard them. All three live in places with cultures of honor, where deeply ingrained ideas about masculinity and women helped breed the violence they faced. As scholar Nimmi Gowrinathan argues in *Radicalizing Her: Why Women Choose Violence*, a woman who takes up arms does so "because she is the target." The women in this book were the targets, as were their communities.

They wielded violence to survive, using a revolver, canes, and a Kalashnikov to protect themselves and other women. They broke the law and social norms, and risked jail time and death. My questions persisted: Did their actions ultimately help or hurt them? And did anything systemically shift as a result?

This book is a work of nonfiction. I relied on extensive interviews with these three women, and all other available subjects, to reconstruct events where I was not present. Wherever possible, I checked events, memories, and biographical details against a wealth of supporting documentation: medical records, court files, police reports, diary entries, emails, texts, letters, news articles, academic studies, book-length accounts, and more. For all historical and contemporary accounts in this book that go beyond the three women, and all epigraphs, I made every effort to rely on primary sources, local voices, and respected scholarship. Ultimately, though, this book reflects these women's stories.

To report the stories of Brittany Smith, Angoori Dahariya, and Cicek Mustafa Zibo, I got to know them over the course of years. I learned of Brittany's case in April 2019 after reading an online news article in *The Appeal* that said a woman in Alabama was facing a life sentence for killing a man who allegedly raped her. The story left me with more questions than answers, so I flew down to Alabama shortly after to meet Brittany's mom. Together, we visited Brittany in a psychiatric hospital in Tuscaloosa, where a judge had sent her and a nurse told me she didn't belong. Brittany was claiming self-defense for the shooting, while others in her community saw it as an act of reprisal. I wrote a feature about her case for the *New Yorker*, but its gray areas kept me reporting long after the piece was done. I ultimately followed Brittany's story for four years, visiting her hometown of Stevenson, Alabama, almost a dozen times, including for a documentary we made on her case for Netflix, whose interviews are included in this book. When I wasn't in Alabama, I spoke to Brittany regularly over jail calling apps or by letter, hers sometimes enclosed with plucked clovers.

My reporting in India began in Mumbai all those years ago, when I first learned about Phoolan Devi. After that, I kept an eye out for present-day Bandit Queens, and I finally found Angoori in 2018 in the small town of Tirwa, in the northern Indian state of Uttar Pradesh. I learned of Angoori from a short online news article, which said that a low-caste woman in Tirwa had formed a gang that "thrashed" domestic abusers with bamboo canes. When I contacted the local journalist who wrote the piece, Saurabh Sharma, he agreed to take me to meet Angoori. I met Angoori at her home in Tirwa in the winter of 2018, where she was seated and surrounded by her gang of women. As she narrated her life story, the women listened closely, laughing when she laughed and crying when she cried. Other Tirwa residents saw Angoori more skeptically. I wrote about her and her gang for the magazine *California Sunday,* but given Angoori's cultlike figure, I knew there was far more to tell. Angoori and I spoke for years with the help of Saurabh—who knows the region intimately and translated the Hindi dialect of Bundelkhandi that Angoori speaks—along with his late wife, Dipali, who brought so much care to these stories.

The female guerrilla fighter Cicek (*Chee-czech*) and I first spoke over WhatsApp in 2020, chatting back and forth from the U.S. to her military base in the fertile plains of northeast Syria. For years, I had read news reports on the exploits of her all-female militia, the YPJ, a sister force to the larger YPG. Both are led by the Kurds, an ethnic minority native to the region. Since 2013, YPJ female fighters had battled ISIS militants, and were now fighting the Turkish state in defense of their new autonomous region, Rojava. The story of the region was complicated, but I wanted to tell a sliver of it by extensively interviewing one YPJ fighter, and asked several local journalists for help. Syrian journalist Solin Muhammed Amin ultimately made the introduction and translated my conversations with Cicek. Solin, who is a force, has been reporting this book alongside me ever since. I interviewed Cicek in person during two reporting trips to northeast Syria, in May 2021 and 2022, making the crossing from Iraq into Syria with the help of local journalist and jack-of-all-trades Majd Helobi, and reporting with the assistance of Solin and two other brilliant Syrian producers, Kamiran Sadoun and Obeid Sheikhi, who translated many hours of Arabic and the Kurdish dialect Kurmancî. Some towns and cities have both Arabic and Kurdish names; I used the names the fighters did.

I am not a war correspondent, so reporting in Syria took months of preparation, including enrolling in a hostile environment training course that involved a fake kidnapping as well as instructions on how to handle suicide bombings, crossfire, and IEDs. I created proof-of-life documents in case of abduction and snapped photographs so people could identify my body. Once in Syria, my main safety goals were to avoid the regime, ISIS sleeper cells, and Turkish drone strikes. The local journalists who cover the region do not have the luxury of all this preparation, and some have been arrested, tortured, or killed for their coverage.

Reporting in northern India and Stevenson, Alabama, came with its own set of challenges, which local journalists face every day. Angoori's area is so unsafe to report in as a woman that Saurabh insisted we stay in Lucknow, two and a half hours from Tirwa, and commute back and forth daily. In Alabama, it was also unsafe to meet some sources, though transparency was my greatest obstacle—it was difficult to pin down good data on domestic abuse in Brittany's county, for example, because of how police were recording assaults. All these places were costly to report in, especially over the course of years. I owe thanks to the International Women's Media Foundation and the Pulitzer Center on Crisis Reporting for their support, plus the *New Yorker*, the *California Sunday Magazine*, *Foreign Policy*, the *Guardian*, Lemonada Media, and Tripod Media for putting out these kinds of stories.

There is a short story by Lesley Nneka Arimah that I thought about often while in the field, called "What It Means When a Man Falls from the Sky." In the story, a "grief worker" has the mathematical formula to suck the grief and sadness out of people, "like poison from a wound," but she has to die in the process. Many days, I felt the poison of covering domestic and sexual violence—violence I myself had faced—and also complex trauma, conflict, and war. Then I felt the guilt of knowing I wasn't healing anyone only by listening, and that I would be just fine. Over the course of my reporting, I developed chronic fatigue and stomach pain, my body's way of telling me it was overwhelmed. But then I finished writing this book about agency, power, and survival, and—foolish as it sounds—my body healed. After years of internalizing the harshness imposed on traumatized women, these days I am gentle with myself, and with others' stories.

This book is a tribute to the women who have fought back, who have rewritten stories of disempowerment into stories of resistance, today and yesterday and tomorrow, in real life and in our wild imaginings.

Elizabeth Flock
Los Angeles
October 2022

PRELUDE

Justice goes by many names.

It goes by the name Athena, whose story began with a prophecy that she would one day overthrow her father. After her father took her mother without consent, Athena sprang from his skull with a ferocious war cry, fully grown and clad in armor, holding weapons likely fashioned by her mother. While her brother Ares represented war and bloodlust, Athena would use wisdom, valor, and cunning to defend and protect her people—and do whatever it took to get justice.

Justice also goes by the name Durga, who was born with many arms to fight demonic forces. In the Hindu text the *Devi Mahatmya*, Durga was said to have been merciful of mind but fought with fierce cruelty in war. She rode atop a tiger or a lion and wielded a shield, club, spear, and sword. The weapon of choice did not matter. Durga was protector and destroyer in equal measure.

And justice goes by the name Inanna, who once unleashed plagues upon her rapist. She released raging storms and water turned to blood against those who committed wrongs. The Sumerian goddess was sometimes symbolized as a dove, but she was more often depicted as angry. In the "Hymn to Inanna," poet-priestess Enheduanna writes: "Inanna sits on harnessed lions, she cuts to pieces him who shows no respect."

In Greek and Roman mythology, vengeance was also three women: the Furies, fearsome goddesses with hair that writhed with snakes. They punished crimes against the so-called natural order: Tisiphone was the "voice of vengeance," Megaera "grudging," and Alecto the "unceasing one." When the prince Orestes murdered his mother, in retaliation for the death of his father, the Furies endlessly tormented him for his crime.

"And so, gorged on human blood, so as to be the more emboldened, a revel-rout of kindred Furies haunts the house," wrote Aeschylus, the Greek tragedian. "Lodged within its halls they chant their chant . . ."

Orestes Pursued by the Furies, William-Adolphe Bouguereau, 1862

BOOK I

BRITTANY

GUNPOWDER

His fist is big but my gun's bigger
He'll find out when I pull the trigger.

—From "Gunpowder & Lead," a country music song released
by singer Miranda Lambert in 2008

The town of Stevenson, Alabama, and what happens there, is easy to overlook. It sits in the northeast corner of the state, close to the border with Tennessee and Georgia, but is nestled deep in the overgrowth of the region. It is only five square miles, population 2,000 or so. Antique stores occupy the downtown, as if it is frozen in the past. The town's roller rink caved in long ago. Many of the houses and double-wides are vine-covered and crumbling, and residents complain of nothing to do.

Stevenson has no shortage of natural—many in town would say *God-given*—beauty. The light at dusk is salmon pink over the old oak trees in rich shades of green. Children ride bicycles through empty streets, shrieking over the sound of the cicadas' insistent drone. Teenagers drive four-wheelers up mountain roads and fish in the nearby Tennessee River using chicken drumsticks on a string. But as a person ages, there is less to do. As an adult, Stevenson holds only the promise of sweet tea, high bills, and losing lottery tickets.

From town, it is an hour's drive northeast to Chattanooga or southwest to Huntsville. If a person has enough gas money to make it to one of the bigger cities, they might drive to the movies or the bowling alley on the weekend. But if they get stuck in Stevenson, that means getting caught up in the drama, like a fly on flypaper. Like many small towns, everybody knows everybody else, and word of trouble travels fast.

Some wake up in the morning and check the jail roster first thing to see who the police arrested the day before. Often, the arrests are for drugs. Sand Mountain, a plateau that many call "meth mountain" because of how much methamphetamine has been manufactured there over the years, is just a short ride from town. Pills and meth wrapped their determined fingers around Stevenson's neck years ago and never let go. If not for drugs, the arrests are often for domestic violence, or both. Nearly every woman in Stevenson has a love story she'd rather forget, a deepening bruise, or an ex of whom she is still afraid.

But much of this domestic violence is never reported because women in the region generally do not trust the police. In the past, women say, they tried to call and report incidents but got nowhere or somewhere worse than they were before. Sometimes the police knew the perpetrators, or the cops were the perpetrators themselves, and those cases never went far.

For many women in Stevenson, life is lived in preparation for what is just around the corner. Girls learn young from their mothers that when hit, hit back. If not, they'll only keep getting hurt. They learn not to tell anyone what happened because the authorities won't believe them, or will only make it worse. When a girl heads out from home, few people say "Goodbye," or "See you later." Instead, they say "Be safe," or "Be careful."

Be careful of what?
Just be careful.

Brittany Joyce Haley Smith was born in Scottsboro, the county seat and just twenty minutes from Stevenson, on her mother's nineteenth birthday, and her grandmother's birthday before that. When Brittany was young, her family moved all over: across Alabama, to Tennessee and Texas, before finally returning to the Stevenson area for her to go to school. For the most part, Brittany had been in Stevenson ever since, working odd jobs and living with her mother and then her husband— always in other people's spaces.

Now in her thirties, Brittany worried that her body showed her four pregnancies. But everyone else saw her as athletic and younger than her years, with her easy smile and boyish frame. She had soft, mousy blond hair that fell straight past her shoulders and gray-blue eyes that were bright and knowing. Although she was book-smart, she often made silly mistakes—"Dingy," her mother called her with endearment, for being scatterbrained. Still, Brittany was tall and spoke with confidence, wearing worn blue jeans and boyish T-shirts. Many men in the area fell for the combination of her devil-may-care attitude and natural beauty. She could make anyone laugh, often by poking good-natured fun at them.

Brittany recently had split up with her husband of about a decade, this time for good. She'd met him at a party in college, him in a silly outfit, a tiny vest on his brawny frame. That was before he got bad on pills, and got rough with her, she said. They had been on and off for years, and gone back and forth about a divorce, yet somehow it had never gone through. But now they were agreed on a separation, and he'd left the rented house to Brittany. Even if she was only renting it, she felt lucky to have a home of her own in town at last. And she was optimistic that her "babies" could finally come home, all four of them.

It was a two-story red-brick house with grand painted white columns and white shutters. The grass grew thick out front in the summer, and old maple trees with rough bark shaded the house. Inside, the rooms had a 1970s feel, with patterned green tile in the kitchen and wood paneling throughout that Brittany loved. It had four bedrooms so her four children would not all have to share. As she walked through the empty spaces of her new home, she felt more content than she had in a long time.

Nothing troubled Brittany when she was with her babies. Her oldest, a momma's boy, was sensitive and aware; her second son was earnest and wanted to be a paleontologist; her first girl was sassy and a tomboy through and through; and her younger daughter was still a baby but already developing a goofy, fun-loving demeanor. Brittany joked around with her children and listened to their private fears. She wrapped them in big hugs in the morning and sang them "You Are My Sunshine" at night.

It had been five years since Brittany lost custody. After she fell into the deep hole that methamphetamine created in Stevenson, the state removed her older three. They eventually went to live with her uncle in a town over from Stevenson, where Brittany visited them as often as she could. When she gave birth to her youngest in 2017, the state took her, too, citing Brittany's substance abuse history. She knew that she'd become an erratic mother after substances took over. She had been arrested several times, all on petty charges related to her drug use.

But she was clean now, and confident all that was behind her. Separating from her husband had helped. A social worker had recently visited and approved her red-brick house, suggesting she could get increased visitation. Brittany hoped that she would get full custody after that. She was ready for a more peaceful life because she owed it to her babies. To make good on that promise, she had an upcoming interview for a steady job at a flooring company in town, with reasonable hours and good pay, which didn't come around often in Stevenson.

Over the years, Brittany had often done menial, backbreaking work because it was what was available and there were bills to pay. While pregnant her second time, she did heat-setting at a carpet company, which meant being on her feet on concrete in a hot room twelve hours a day. And while pregnant with her youngest daughter, she worked from early afternoon until four in the morning at a local chicken plant, where her job had been to hog-tie chickens, kill them with an air gun to the skull, and cut off their heads. She'd also worked at most of the fast-food restaurants in Stevenson, including Burger King, where she now manned the window six days a week. The flooring company job would be easy in comparison if she got it.

It felt to Brittany like her life was finally coming together after years of upheaval. There was just one hitch, which was how lonely she felt. Her mother and brother lived just down the road, but there were still many lonesome hours in the house without her husband, and an unknown waiting period before her children came home. She could feel the house's yawning space. When Brittany ran into a friend holding a wriggling pit bull puppy at a convenience store that January, she decided she would get one of her own. The puppy would be her companion as she rebuilt her world, and her kids would be so excited to come home to a pet.

Her friend told her that he'd bought the pit bull puppy from Todd Smith, who bred them just across the Tennessee state line. Brittany knew the name. She had met Todd back in high school through a family friend. They'd even hung out a few times, but she had not seen him in years. When she got home, she sent Todd an excited message on Facebook: "I just saw Auntuan'[s] new pup. I want one!!! Please tell me you still have one?!!!!"

She sent the message not knowing the chain of events it would trigger, and that the red-brick home would remain hers for just another week.

When Joshua "Todd" Smith took methamphetamine and Xanax together, the entire neighborhood in Glover Hill, Tennessee, "walked on eggshells," according to his cousin, Jeff Poe. When Todd was not on drugs, Jeff said, he would give a person the shirt off his back. Todd's ex-girlfriend and the mother of his child, Amanda Reed, said the same thing of Todd, that he "would give the shirt off his back to anybody." But the difference between sober Todd and Todd on drugs was so distinct that Jeff thought of him as Dr. Jekyll and Mr. Hyde. He knew instantly from how his cousin walked or talked which version he was dealing with that day.

Many people in Glover Hill knew that Jeff sold drugs and that he and Todd both used them. Jeff found that if he gave Todd meth and Xanax together, "it was almost guaranteed Todd was going to jail that day." Meth can make people more aggressive, while abuse of Xanax can lead to mood swings; together, the results are unpredictable. Todd told Jeff the combination made him feel like Superman, especially when alcohol was in the mix. "He walked around like: 'This is my dadgum county, and I can do whatever I want to with it.'" The cocktail pushed Todd to dark places, making him wild and mean.

Todd was different when they were younger. He had grown up under Jeff's wing. They explored the mountains and woods of Tennessee together, gathering crawdads and minnows from the rivers to bring home and watch swim in a blue plastic pool. Young Todd had a round face, bowl-cut hair, and blue eyes that shined. People said he was a cute kid, and then he grew up to be handsome, like a member of a 1990s boy band. At thirteen, he was confident and calm, which drove the girls in school wild as they developed their first crushes. He stayed that way until meth came to town, his mother got sick, and his father taught him how to fight. Stevenson and Glover Hill are both in the Tennessee Valley, just twenty minutes apart, and so close that residents share the same hopes, the same troubles. Meth arrived as an obvious problem in both places in the 1990s.

According to Jeff, Todd's father put boxing matches on television when they were young teenagers, and made Todd fight him and other grown men in town. Todd was forced to grow up and get tough fast, as boys in Alabama had long been made to do. Jeff said Todd's mother, who had multiple sclerosis, soon retreated from the matches to watch her TV shows in the basement. Drugs were often available at the house, and Jeff and Todd started experimenting with alcohol and pills around that time. When visiting Todd's home in those years, Jeff said, "I knew it was time to put my mask on for drinking, partying, and fighting." Police were often called to the residence.[*]

By January 2018, hard living had caught up with Todd. He was thirty-eight, living with his father, and had been arrested some eighty times. His charges included public intoxication, drug possession, and at least a dozen assaults, some of which were aggravated assaults, and many classified as domestic violence. In the intervening years, he had grown into a stocky man with a red face, goatee, and shaved head. Jeff, too, had been rangy and handsome in high school, but after two stints in prison, wore messy stubble and a haunted look.

At least Todd had his pit bulls. Jeff thought Todd's first pit, Cody, which Todd got at age eleven or twelve, was ugly and told him so. "It's not what he looks like," Todd told his cousin. "It's about the game." "The game" meant fighting them—breeding dogs from the right bloodlines, brawny and fierce enough to fight, and win. Dogfighting was a common underground activity in the area, and police mostly left Todd's

---

[*] Todd's father declined to comment.

pit bull obsession alone, though he was taken in at least once on a charge of cruelty to animals.

In a way, Jeff thought that Todd and the pits were not so different from one another. One minute, they were sweet and shy, while the next, they could tear a creature apart. Cody had once ripped off a cow's jaw. But for Todd and his dogs, their violence was learned, if not forced upon them by their caretakers. In *Culture of Honor*, Richard E. Nisbett and Dov Cohen argue that, in an honor-based society like the South, a major cause of male violence is a man's learned "sense of threat to one of his most valued possessions, namely, his reputation for strength and toughness." For Todd, drugs only exacerbated that sensitivity to threats. "Todd would have been a totally different person if it hadn't been for drugs," Jeff said.

Earlier that January, Todd and his father fought so badly that the police were again called to their residence. Todd was charged with domestic assault, and Todd's father kicked him out of the house. When Jeff went to pick up Todd at a friend's house one night afterward, he could tell something had shifted: Todd, off the cocktail of drugs, was uncharacteristically cruel to him. "If you ain't got no drugs, then get the hell out of here," Todd said. Jeff was concerned. He realized his cousin no longer wanted to be sober, which he thought was the saddest thing in the world.

In recent years, Todd had begun selling his pit bull pups that were less suited for fighting. After Brittany messaged him, he offered her a male and female pup, and told her she could come over to his dad's house and see them. Brittany went to Todd's house twice to meet them—once on the day of a party, with Jeff in attendance—before choosing the female pup, reddish-brown with a plucky attitude, despite her tiny size. Brittany named the puppy Athena. She didn't know why. She just thought the name suited her.

A heavy snow fell over Stevenson on January 15, 2018, as Brittany and her younger brother, Christopher McCallie, drove to McDonald's for a meal. Chris was twenty-six, pudgy, nerdish, with the presence of an amiable bear, a man who often kept to himself. Brittany was his polar opposite, outgoing and effervescent, and she chattered excitedly to Chris as he drove. The flooring company had offered her the job, hiring her on the spot, and she would start orientation the next week. Her cheeks flushed from the cold and her elation.

On their way home with the food, Brittany got a call from Todd. She had brought the puppy Athena home just the previous night. According to Brittany, she left Todd's house in a hurry during a party after Todd got a call from several women who said they were bringing over meth. She knew she couldn't be in those environments anymore. Jeff said Brittany stayed for longer, and that he was certain she and Todd had hooked up.

Either way, text messages show Brittany rejecting Todd's advances after the party was over. When Todd messaged her to say that he had "drunken thoughts" about being with someone like her, Brittany replied that she wasn't interested. She told him she liked him but his "priorities [were] fucked up," and until they got straight, they couldn't regularly hang out. "Because I am actually trying to get my shit together, and I don't need the extra drama," she wrote. She was trying to stay clean, and Todd, as charming as he could be, was not the kind of man she should be around. Todd agreed, but told Brittany that she was "so damn addictive it's crazy," and that he was trying to change his ways.

Now Todd was calling Brittany to see if she and Chris would come pick him up from a city park in Tennessee, not far across the state line. He said he was stranded and freezing in the cold, and no one else had answered the phone. It would snow an inch in the Tennessee Valley that night, which was unusual for the area, and he said he didn't have anywhere to sleep. Neither Brittany nor Chris thought picking him up was a good idea. "I just had a gut feeling that something was going to happen," Chris said. Brittany also knew picking up a fellow addict was a poor decision. Later, her father would say that his daughter's biggest problem was the friends she kept, because "if you want to get bit by a shark, jump in an ocean full of them." Brittany told Todd no and hung up the phone.

But Todd persisted. "Please help this 1 time and I won't ever bother you again," he texted. And then: "Some friend."

Brittany was annoyed. "Some friend . . . ?" she texted back. "I didn't leave you there or I WOULD come get you. Call whoever did. You're not my kid."

Todd called again. As Chris drove toward home, the snow fell in thicker flakes. The temperature was close to freezing. Brittany looked at Chris. Chris told her no. Although Chris was younger than his sister, he had always looked out for her. He'd watched her fall prey to meth—the euphoria came first, then the agitation—and saw it steal her body, mind, and children. She was sober now and trying to leave the old drug crowd behind, which was not easy in Stevenson. But Todd had a way of charming his way into things, and Brittany's insecurities often led her to say yes to things she shouldn't. She told her brother they couldn't leave a person out in the cold to freeze to death, and eventually Chris relented to avoid the argument.

Brittany told Todd they would pick him up but that he had to sleep on her couch. She said her new home was not a "crash house," and that she didn't want him sleeping in the children's beds. Chris reluctantly drove them toward the Tennessee park through the falling snow, hoping he would not come to regret it.

According to Brittany, after Chris dropped them off at Brittany's red-brick house, she and Todd bathed the puppy, then hung out in the living room. Their conversation turned to how meth had spread across the Tennessee Valley and thrown both of their lives off track. Brittany had gotten hooked in 2012, after she'd lost both a baby to a rare congenital disease and her grandmother to cancer. Her baby Will had been born and lived for just a minute before he turned blue. Her grandmother, who she called MawMaw, had been fierce and funny and raised Brittany along with her mother. The grief from the two losses sent her spiraling into a deep depression, until she found meth. The drug eventually made her so skinny her mom started describing her as "a toothpick with a bobblehead on top."

Brittany told Todd that, after a series of relapses, she was finally staying far away from meth, though a family doctor prescribed her Xanax for anxiety, a medication many people abused in the area. Todd, whose face was flushed from drinking beers all night, his eyes a steely blue, told her he was also working hard to change his ways. He said he was upset that he rarely saw his young daughter, who lived with his ex-girlfriend. He was tired of the drugs and wanted a better life, though it would later emerge that Todd took a large amount of meth—a quantity where violent episodes were common—and some Xanax at some point that night. It was unclear when he ingested them, and Brittany was never drug-tested.

Brittany advised Todd in the living room to get his priorities in line, just as she had written him in a text. She said that since she had gotten clean, only good things had followed: a big house, a better-paying job, and custody of her children close at hand. As she spoke, Todd's face hardened, and Brittany realized she sounded like she was bragging. According to Brittany, Todd jumped up and began screaming at her, asking her if she thought she was better than him. Startled, Brittany also jumped to her feet. "You're a bitch," Todd said, and head-butted her to the floor.

Brittany had seen this kind of meth rage before. Frantic, she looked around for an exit. She knew there were dead bolts on her house's front door and locks on the back entrance for security, so she ran upstairs to her room. She slammed the bedroom door behind her, but Todd broke through it and tackled her on her bed. He weighed 265 pounds—about a hundred pounds more than Brittany—and easily overpowered her.

According to Brittany's account, Todd wrapped his hands around her throat and strangled her until she passed out. When she woke up on the bed, her pants were off, she had peed on herself, and Todd was raping her, his hands still tight around her throat. Involuntary urination is a common sign of strangulation, and, according to the Training Institute on Strangulation Prevention, strangulation is one of the top predictors for victims of domestic violence[*] to subsequently become a victim of homicide.

"We're friends," Brittany tried to tell him, but she could barely breathe, and her voice was high-pitched through his grasp, like the

---

[*] This book uses both the word "victim" and "survivor" according to what the speaker or source uses.

squeak of a squirrel. "We're friends," he replied, in a mocking voice. "Don't say a fucking word, or I'll kill you," he said. "If you even breathe wrong, I'll kill you."

Brittany fought back, sobbing and clawing at him until an acrylic fingernail ripped off along with the natural nail beneath it. Todd held her neck against the side of the bed so hard she was sure he would break it. "Is this what you want?" he asked. Brittany managed to flip them both off the bed and onto the floor. Once again, Todd got control and strangled her until she blacked out a second time. As Brittany saw black, she thought: *This is what it's like to die. God, please don't let me die.*

Brittany knew this feeling, the feeling of being desperate to survive. Years before, when she was pregnant with her second son, she said her husband, drunk and high on pills, had thrown her into the couch and then off their nine-foot-high balcony. (Brittany's husband admitted he'd thrown her, but said it was down the stairs and that she had initiated the fight.) That time, her mother, Ramona, had stepped in to put an end to the violence. After dropping Brittany off at the hospital, Ramona went to Brittany's house and punched her husband square in the jaw. And it worked. Brittany's husband had not hurt her again, not like that. This time, though, Brittany was all alone. *God, please don't let me die.*

Brittany said that when she woke up from being strangled the second time, she let Todd finish raping her. Then his face changed and "went back to normal." In a calm voice, Todd told her that if she told anyone what happened, he would kill her and her entire family—her mother, brother, and children—and then himself. Brittany promised him she wouldn't tell. "Everything's okay," she said shakily, trying to deescalate his anger. "It's okay. It's okay."

After a while, Todd said he wanted cigarettes, and Brittany spotted her opportunity. She didn't have a car but said she could call her mother, Ramona, to take them to the store. Todd warned her that if she tried anything funny, like dialing the police or telling her mother what happened, he would kill her. Brittany assured him she would not but had no doubt her mother could help. Ramona had once twirled an unloaded gun to scare off a boy from Brittany when she was just thirteen. Todd held Brittany's phone as she typed in her mother's number.

"Momma?" said Brittany, trying to make her voice sound both normal to Todd and unusual to her mother. She was hopeful that her mom, whip-smart and sturdily built, would notice something was off and come to her rescue. She asked her mom to bring her a pack of cigarettes. "Baby, I don't have any money 'til Wednesday or Thursday," said Ramona, speaking from her apartment in a public housing complex down the road. Ramona often ran out of money before payday, and everyone in the family subsisted on a fast-food meal or two every day. Brittany told her she had money and just needed a ride to the store.

Ramona thought her daughter's voice sounded "funny," and asked Brittany if she'd been crying. There was a long pause. Brittany said she was fine, though Ramona's motherly instinct told her that something was wrong. But she was so tired from work that she ignored it. She worked long hours, her hair was wet from the shower, and it was freezing cold and snowing outside. Plus, this wasn't the first drama with her daughter, whose addiction had led her to chaotic places. So she asked her son Chris, who lived with her, to take Brittany to the store instead.

Chris was no longer concerned about his sister and Todd, because at this point he was irritated. He'd already driven Brittany home earlier, and now it was the middle of the night. He liked to play video games at this hour until he fell asleep. But he got up and drove the five minutes over to Brittany's house, where she got in the front seat and Todd sat in the back. Chris could not see his sister well in the dark, but he noticed that she was unusually reserved, almost as if she'd been crying. Too tired to worry, he told himself that maybe she and Todd had watched a sad movie. Chris made small talk with Todd while they drove to the gas station for cigarettes.

Paige Painter was working third shift at the MAPCO gas station that night, a shift that ran from ten p.m. until seven in the morning. She remembered it being around one a.m. when Brittany walked in. Brittany was a regular customer, whom Painter often joked around with and told funny stories to, as she did many of her regulars. Painter said that when Brittany came in that night, it looked as if she'd been crying, and "like she had gotten into a fight." It seemed like "something was really wrong." Painter was dealing with a customer at the cash register, but Brittany approached her anyway, and asked Painter for a piece of paper and a pen. "Don't look at me, don't talk to me, and, um, pretend like you're talking to her," Brittany said, her voice frantic.

Brittany was there in the convenience store with Painter, but perhaps she was also in a sinkhole of her past. She was four, a small child in a big room. She was calling 911 because, as she remembered it, her father was drunk again and roughing up her mom. She'd seen them physically fight a lot as a kid, with no way to escape and nowhere to run. Ramona told Brittany she'd finally put an end to the abuse when Brittany was five, when Ramona found an old broom with a sawed-off end and beat her husband with it when he came home from work. "Don't you ever hit me again," Ramona told him, "or next time your momma's going to miss you." According to her, he never did.

Brittany needed her mother, but her mom was not there. She needed someone's help—that was the important thing. The cashier stood in front of her. She was finding it hard to think clearly.

Painter was confused by Brittany's request for paper but did as she was told. She handed Brittany a torn-off piece of a receipt and asked her what was going on. Brittany told her that a man had been holding her hostage at home, that he'd beaten and raped her, and that he was sitting outside in the car. "Oh my god," said Painter, who had seen domestic abuse up close with her own parents. "Stay here with me, do not go with him." She offered to blockade Brittany in the MAPCO supplies closet, but Brittany shook her head. She looked anxiously out the window, and said that if she didn't go with Todd, he might do something to her brother. She said he had threatened it already.

Brittany wrote down several phone numbers on the receipt for Painter to call for help, including the number for her mom, Ramona. She also wrote down Todd's name and neighborhood, and told Painter, "If anything happens to me, he did it." She told the cashier she would tell Chris to return to the MAPCO, so Painter could tell him what was going on.

When Chris arrived back at the convenience store after dropping off Todd and Brittany, Painter related what Brittany had said. Chris reddened: "That son of a bitch." He said he was going to get Brittany, but Painter urged him to first pick up Ramona, who would know what to do. Chris didn't listen. "I saw red," he said; he was furious and felt like he should handle it himself. As he peeled out of the parking lot and sped toward Brittany's, in his glove compartment was his gun—a Heritage Rough Rider .22 single-action revolver. Chris had bought it recently and always kept it on him. A man never knew when he was going to need a gun to protect himself and his honor, or someone else's.

As Chris drove back to Brittany's house from the MAPCO, Todd went to the kitchen for a beer. In the living room, finally unaccompanied, Brittany picked up her phone and texted her mother. "Mom Todd has tried to kill me literally," she wrote. "Don't act like anything is wrong . . . He will kill me if he knows." Brittany was sure her mother would rush over after receiving the texts, but Chris had taken the one working car. Ramona tried to reach Chris but he didn't answer.

According to Chris's account, he arrived at Brittany's to find Todd standing alone at the fridge. Chris was afraid but brandished his new .22-caliber revolver and spoke with all the bravado he could muster. "I'm only going to give you one chance," Chris told Todd. "You need to get your shit and leave." But Todd just stood there, unbothered. Chris aimed the gun, cocked it, and fired a shot above Todd's head, into the wooden cabinets Brittany loved. To this day, Chris was not sure if he fired it as a warning or by accident because the gun had a hair trigger. So much of that night would run together in his memory.

Even after the shot, Todd held his beer, unfazed. Perhaps it was the combination of meth and Xanax that made him fearless. Chris, planning to physically remove Todd, put his revolver down on the counter between them. As Chris approached, he said, Todd quickly got him in a headlock. The two men were about the same size, but their bodies were not the same. Chris chain-smoked, ate poorly, and never exercised. Todd was muscular and barrel-chested.

Brittany said she ran into the kitchen after hearing the gunshot and found Todd and her brother fighting on the other side of the counter. Todd was choking Chris in the headlock and punching him in the head with his other hand. Brittany screamed at Todd to stop. She was panicked because violence kept finding her; she was four, she was in her twenties, she was thirteen. In an even tone, Todd replied that he'd kill them both. Brittany picked up the gun. Perhaps she saw images of her mother: Ramona wielding a sawed-off broom, or twirling an unloaded gun, or hitting Brittany's husband in the jaw. "I don't want to shoot you," Brittany told Todd, her voice ragged. "Just let my brother go." But Todd continued choking Chris, just as he'd strangled Brittany, and her brother's face turned ruby red.

Sobbing, Brittany fired. It seemed as if nothing happened, so she shot again. Again, it seemed to have no effect. When she shot the revolver a third time, both Todd and Chris fell to the floor. *Oh my god,* she thought. *I've killed my brother.* But after a minute, Chris sat up, heaving: "Sissy, I'm okay, we're okay." He took the gun, placed it on the counter, and hugged her. He repeated that they were okay, that they were alive. They both looked at Todd, who was taking shallow breaths. Brittany told Chris to find her cell phone, fast, so that they could call 911.

"Jackson County nine one one."

"Someone just got shot at 211 Sharon Drive," Brittany told the operator in a strained voice. "He—he tried to kill me and—"

The operator began asking questions. "Where is the person that shot him?"

"He's right here with me," Brittany said. "He's my brother."

Brittany didn't know why it came out of her mouth that Chris was the shooter. Chris had brought the gun to her house, and Chris had fired the first shot. She was in shock, but she'd soon feel a stinging guilt at how carelessly she threw her brother under the bus.

"[But] he's not going to jail, like, he—he's—like, he was trying to protect me," Brittany told the operator, in a belated attempt to shield her brother from the consequences of her lie. Later, she'd say she lied because she was so close to getting her kids back, and an arrest would mean the end of that. At a gut level, she also knew that in Stevenson, and wider Jackson County, a woman who defended herself would be treated differently than a man. Her mother had always told her that, and women in town had always said so. She thought that both reasons had motivated her, but she could not say for sure, because there had not been time to think. Later, this lie would be the main reason that the police, prosecutor, and judge would doubt Brittany's story. One lie meant there might be others.

The operator continued asking Brittany a slew of questions: *Where is the weapon? Who was shot? In what part of the body?* "I don't know, ma'am," Brittany said. "He just needs an ambulance." The operator assured her the paramedics were on the way. Brittany said she didn't know what to do, that "I've been choked, almost dead, like, raped almost in my bed twice." The operator kept asking more questions. As Todd's face turned blue, Brittany lost her patience. "Just have an ambulance come, please, because I don't want this man to die."

The operator told her again that an ambulance was en route and instructed her to do CPR on Todd while they waited. Chris did chest compressions while Brittany pressed her mouth against Todd's and blew air into his lungs. She begged Todd to stay with them and think of his daughter. She begged him not to die.

A FLY ON FLYPAPER

Life-saving tips to avoid assault and/or abduction, as excerpted from *Immediate, Direct, Explosive! Basic Self-Defense for Women and Girls*, by Carolyn Zengel, published 2005:

> Wear comfortable clothing (to be able to run)
> Avoid alcohol
> Consider a dog
> Don't lead an attacker home
> Be perpetually aware
> If you carry a weapon, know how to use it

In the early-morning hours after the shooting, officers with the Jackson County Sheriff's Office arrested Chris. "Please don't shoot," Brittany had told officers as they arrived at the house, their guns drawn, "because he choked me, he raped me." Todd was rushed away in an ambulance. Both Chris and Brittany said that Chris had fired the gun—his new .22 single-action revolver, only recently out of its case. Brittany was placed in a patrol car to be driven to a sexual assault exam, which the four male police officers at the scene determined she needed. It was January 16, 2018, and the snow had stopped falling over Stevenson.

After several hours of sitting in the patrol car, Brittany was told by police that they were taking her to Crisis Services of North Alabama, based in neighboring Madison County but with a satellite office for Jackson County. It was one of the only nonprofits available to handle domestic and sexual assaults for Stevenson. "I'm not fucking going down there," Brittany said, according to one officer's account. "I've been there before, and I'm not going again." Brittany said she had previously reported being raped and the police took her to Crisis Services, but nothing happened in the courts after that. Local victim advocates said that was a common experience in the area. Often, they said, police took a report and even made an arrest, but it never went any farther than that. Plus, a sexual assault exam was invasive and upsetting, and Brittany didn't want to do one if it wasn't going to help her. Despite her resistance, the officers drove her to Crisis Services, which was housed in a nondescript building to help victims stay anonymous.

The office in Madison County is quiet but welcoming, with deep couches and warm yellow lighting. A patchwork of jeans hangs framed on the bathroom wall, symbolic of a protest by thousands of women in Italy in 1999, after a court there suggested a woman couldn't be raped if she was wearing tight jeans. Bright-colored Post-its stuck to the bathroom mirror reassured clients: "Everything will be okay," "You are braver than you think!," and "Every day is a fresh start."

The sexual assault nurse examiner, Jeanine Suermann, was a kindly woman with a short brunette ponytail and an open face. In less than a year at Crisis Services, she had examined more than a hundred women with sexual assault cases. Brittany came in "very anxious, very agitated," Suermann recounted later. Her account to the nurse included that she "woke up naked in a pool of my own urine" and "a man died in my kitchen." Brittany described the assault in detail and complained of pain all over her body. She said she was having trouble swallowing, and it felt like her neck was swelling. When the nurse asked her to describe the pain of strangulation on a scale of 1 to 10, she said "Ten." She said she'd believed she was going to die.

Suermann documented thirty-three injuries on Brittany's body, including on her neck, chest, breast, arms, legs, and feet. Part of a rape kit exam is reconstructing what took place, and it was clear to the nurse that this assault had been brutal. Abrasions on Brittany's chin and breast appeared to be from bite marks. Bruising around Brittany's trachea and petechiae on her face and chest—little red dots caused by the rupture of capillaries from intense pressure—left no doubt Brittany had been strangled. There were two apparent handprints on her neck, and fingerprints on her forearm that suggested she had been held down. Bruising on her shins indicated she had likely fought back. The nurse also found secretions on Brittany's neck and vagina but no definitive sperm sample. As Suermann would later testify, unfortunately for victims, many sexual assault cases did not have one.

Brittany found the exam invasive, with lots of difficult questions and photographs taken of her in the nude. She understood that it was necessary but found it humiliating to strip down after what she'd just endured. She also worried that she could not keep the precise order of the night's events straight. She knew its broad contours: the assault, the trip to MAPCO, then the shooting, but some of it in between was fuzzy. Suermann would later testify that disordered thinking was common for a woman who had been assaulted. In a court of law, however, disordered thinking could make a person seem less credible.

Brittany's mom, Ramona, saw the rape kit exam several weeks later. The stapled packet of pages included line drawings of the female body, with markings that located Brittany's injuries. Lines pointed to almost every part of her daughter's body. "When I got that rape kit, I just squalled my eyes out like a baby," Ramona said, in the deep drawl she'd gotten from her mother. "I'm just looking at these pictures thinking, 'That's my baby girl on that paper. And she's got all these bruises and bite marks and everything.'"

Ramona blamed herself for not responding to her daughter's strange tone of voice that night. She thought that if only she had noticed something was amiss, none of this would have happened. She would have known how to handle Todd. And she wouldn't have needed a gun to do it.

It was during her senior year of high school that Ramona had gotten pregnant with Brittany. She attended prom with a little bulge beneath her blush pink dress. Her brunette hair was permed and she wore pretty dark eyeliner, and often cheesed for the cameras. Brittany's biological father soon disappeared, and Ramona felt the judgment of others at church for being pregnant and single. But she tried to own it. The truth was that she was terrified of giving birth and did not know what to expect. But then came Brittany, right on time on her birthday, and the birthday of Ramona's mother, MawMaw. As Ramona pushed, MawMaw held her hand and babied her, until Ramona began screaming and MawMaw told her to "hush that shit."

Brittany did not come out pink or pretty, as Ramona thought babies should. She was bloody and purple, and her head was shaped like a cone. When Ramona saw her, she grew distraught, asking the doctor and nurses what was wrong. She insisted she hadn't smoked or drunk alcohol during pregnancy, but everyone in the room, including MawMaw, just laughed. Brittany was fine and strong. And after a few days, when she filled in a little, Ramona thought she looked beautiful, too.

When Brittany was one, Ramona married Ricky, a lanky man with a bushy mustache and a penchant for mischief. Ricky gave Ramona an engagement ring after they'd been dating for only a week. He told her he didn't know with whom he was more in love: her or her baby Brittany. "That's right, she stole my heart, crawling through that room bald-headed as all get out," Ricky remembered later. Brittany saw Ricky as her father, accepting that he sometimes worked and drank too much. Ramona said their fights when Ricky was drunk were partly her fault for "being mouthy," while Ricky called her a "very temperamental woman" who often initiated. Brittany was four when she said she called 911 on her father for beating her mom, and five when Ramona hit Ricky with the sawed-off broom to get him to stop.

As the years passed, Ramona and Ricky grew apart and got divorced but stayed on friendly terms, understanding that they had both been "young and dumb," Ramona said. Brittany stayed close with Ricky. He paid child support, but it wasn't enough, so Ramona worked twelve to sixteen hours a day for years at a local factory, coming home dusty and dirty in her steel-toed boots. She said she "played both mommy and daddy" to Brittany and Chris, though she also relied on MawMaw to do a lot of the childrearing.

Ramona never remarried. The experience of being hit stayed with her, and then she had to watch what Brittany went through with her husband. At first, it seemed to Ramona that he beat Brittany because he wanted to make her submit—because he was the man. Ramona felt that in the beginning her daughter was submissive to him. But one time, after Brittany's husband beat or strangled her, or threw a sewing machine at her—no one could remember which—Brittany did fight back and, according to her husband, stabbed him in the arm with a fork.

As Ramona put it: "When a woman has enough of it, you're going to know it. Because she's gonna snap, or she's gonna hit you, or someone in her family's going to come and do it." It did not escape Ramona's attention that Brittany was now sitting in jail, accused of murder, for doing exactly that.

Todd Smith did not survive the shooting. Three of the rounds Brittany had shot at him entered his left arm, left chest, and right flank. He likely died from the chest wound before making it to the hospital.

Todd's cousin Jeff remembered every detail of the morning of January 16. He was asleep at home when a neighbor came crying and knocking on his door. "She [the neighbor] never could get it out of her mouth," Jeff said. "She just kept on saying: 'Todd, Todd, Todd.'" Jeff realized that he'd been expecting Todd's death, because a person couldn't live that rough for long. At first, Jeff felt rage, the kind that radiated from a man's body with nowhere to land. When he learned that Brittany—the bubbly woman who bought the puppy from Todd, who'd been at that party and maybe slept with his cousin that night—shot Todd, his rage turned vengeful. Despite knowing about Todd's violent tendencies, Jeff could not believe that Todd raped Brittany. "He might have hit her or something like that, but raping her?" Jeff asked, shaking his head. "How can you rape the willing?"

Instead, Jeff dismissed the encounter as rough, meth-fueled sex, as others in Stevenson and Glover Hill would later do. He knew that Brittany was a former meth user, and that she had access to Xanax. Jeff decided that Brittany must have given Todd the drugs that made him unhinged that night, though Brittany denied that.

The night of the shooting, Todd had called Jeff first to ask for a ride, but Jeff had told him no. Sometimes, Jeff had to give his cousin tough love. An hour later, Todd called Jeff again, this time in a good mood. It was the mood of a person who had been looking for his fix and got it—his desperation lifted and transformed into something sickly sweet. Todd had friends around that park, friends who dealt drugs. But Jeff was convinced Brittany gave him something. On that last call, Todd told Jeff he loved him, and Jeff replied that he'd see him tomorrow.

Now that Jeff would never see his cousin again—not in the woods or full of mischief at a party—he was determined to get even.

After she got home to her mother's house from the rape crisis center, Brittany fell asleep, then woke late the next day awash with guilt. She was the shooter, yet her brother Chris had been arrested. She kept picturing him alone in a jail cell. In a small voice, Brittany told her mother, "Momma, I have to go turn myself in." Ramona contacted a local attorney she knew, who advised Brittany to go to the police station and tell the truth.

In an interview with Jackson County Sheriff's Office investigator Eric Woodall, Brittany recounted the night's events for the second time. In the video of the interview, she sits catty-corner from Woodall in a white-walled interrogation room, wearing jeans and an oversized gray zip-up, what is visible of her neck still clearly red and raw. Woodall wears a baseball cap, as if he is doing the interview off-hours. "I wasn't trying to murder anybody," Brittany says through tears, her voice hoarse. "I was just trying to . . . because he had just tried to kill me." Woodall asks why she lied about who the shooter was at first. "We was so scared, we didn't know what to do, you know?" Brittany says. She tells the investigator that she was supposed to get her kids back soon, and that Chris "was just trying to protect me and cover for me. And I was just, I don't know, we should have told the truth to begin with . . . I'm sorry that I lied to you."

The investigator asks where he can find the clothing Brittany wore when the cops showed up that night: an orange T-shirt and baggy pajama pants. Brittany tells him but says these were a different set of clothes than what she was wearing when Todd assaulted her. "Yeah . . . [but] when Todd was shot, you had them on then?" Woodall asks. She did.

Brittany thought it was strange the investigator wasn't interested in the clothes she wore during the rape, but she was no longer the victim. She was the criminal now.

When a different Jackson County investigator interviewed Chris on the day of the shooting—while still believing he was the shooter—the investigator appeared deferential and understanding as Chris explained his version of the night's events.

"Only reason why I had my gun with me is because, after I was told what happened, I felt my safety and my sister's safety was in danger," Chris said. He desperately wanted a cigarette and tried not to think of Todd's body on the floor.

"Right," the investigator replied.

Chris went on: "If that would have been your sister, your mother, your daughter, your niece—"

"Yessir," the investigator agreed.

"I feel you probably would have done the same."

"Yessir."

It hadn't always been easy for Chris to grow up with an older sister four years his senior. When they were kids, Brittany went one way and Chris the other. She was social, while he was the "weird, quiet kid" who kept to himself. He liked video games, surfing the Internet, and taking apart computers. Brittany enjoyed going out with her mother and grandmother and, later on, with her friends. But even though Chris and Brittany sometimes fought, they always had each other's backs. He regretted having brought his gun to Brittany's house that night, but he didn't see what else he could have done. He was sure, because he knew the type, that Todd would have killed his sister if he hadn't shown up. While Todd was choking him, he seemed to have the strength of five men. Then, *bam*, his sister shot him. It was a horrible thing to watch a man die before your eyes. For months afterward, Chris woke up screaming in his sleep.

Several days after that first police interview, Chris faced the same investigator a second time. This time, without knowing Brittany had come clean, because they could not contact one another while Chris was behind bars, he also came forward to say that he and Brittany lied. "Everything I put in my first statement is true except the actual shooting of Todd Smith," Chris wrote in his second statement.

Chris's statement did not address why he had gone along with the lie. It had been a split-second decision to do so. Later, Chris said he'd taken the fall for Brittany mostly because he knew she was trying to get her kids back. If Brittany admitted she'd shot Todd, she might never see her children again, and Brittany's kids were her everything. Also, Chris had always heard the same refrain growing up, from his mom, his sister, and other women in Stevenson—that women were treated as second-class citizens in Jackson County, especially by police. If Brittany had admitted right away that she'd shot Todd, he thought officers would never have taken her to get a rape kit exam. He believed they would have arrested her on the spot.

Chris, on the other hand, could say he was merely standing his ground to protect his sister, as any reasonable man would do. In Jackson County, it was a "good ol' boys club," Chris said, and he was one of the boys.

Yessir.

After her confession, Brittany was immediately arrested and charged with murder. She was taken to the Jackson County Jail in Scottsboro, about a half hour from Stevenson. The jail in Scottsboro is a squat brick and concrete building, one of countless depressing jail facilities around the country. Ads for bail-bond agents hang in the lobby, and screens to chat with the incarcerated on a spotty calling service called GettingOut.com are screwed to the wall. Many women were in for drug offenses or violating probation, while many men were in with those charges, or some for domestic violence. The female unit was perpetually overcrowded, with women sleeping beside toilets on the floor. Like many of the other women, Brittany slept on a thin mat on the ground.

In jail, staff told Brittany she would no longer be able to take her Xanax prescription. It is common for jails to discontinue a person's medicines, especially a substance user like Brittany, because it helps keep controlled substances out of the facility. It is possible Brittany was abusing her Xanax. But it is dangerous to suddenly stop taking a benzodiazepine, and severe withdrawal symptoms can include panic attacks or hallucinations.

Within days, Brittany experienced both. She could not stop thinking about the assault and the shooting and saw images of Todd and his pit bulls while awake. "They took me off [the medication] cold turkey," she said. "And after this traumatic experience, I . . . just had a meltdown." Ramona received a call from Brittany in jail in which "she was talking crazy, and it freaked me out." Brittany told her mother she feared that one of her kids was dead. Staff soon moved Brittany into solitary confinement, describing it as a room for medical observation. Brittany said that two jailers began taunting her there, telling her that the cell had an invisible elevator with a button she could push to see her children.*

A jail therapist who saw Brittany at the time reported that she was dealing with anxiety and depression, but that she "speaks with clarity and logical thought process." On another visit, the therapist wrote that Brittany felt increased anxiety and was finding it difficult "to manage anxiety without medication," though he believed she was likely addicted to it.

As a girl, Brittany had not been so anxious or depressed. She had been confident and funny, and her teachers said she was the brightest girl in the class. Ramona bragged that she could pass any test without cracking a book. In grade school, she wore oversized round glasses, her hair in barrettes, and was a self-professed nerd. That changed after they moved, from Tennessee back to Alabama, and she switched schools to a place where the girls were more advanced. Brittany was not street-smart and knew nothing about kissing or sex. She didn't think she was pretty, skinny, or cool like them either, which made her feel self-conscious. She was also the tallest girl in the class, towering over her petite, well-groomed classmates. Sometimes, the other girls bullied her. Brittany

---

* The Jackson County Sheriff's Office declined to comment on the allegations.

spent most of her time with her mom and MawMaw instead. They were goofy together, once riding bicycles around town wearing pigtails and blackened teeth, pretending they were stereotypical country bumpkins.

But like most teenagers who want to fit in with others, Brittany stopped wanting to spend time with her mom and grandma in high school. She made a circle of friends and began to party, experimenting with drugs and alcohol. She slimmed down and dyed her hair. Everyone knew her as a big "cutup," meaning she joked around nonstop. When Brittany got her first car, a Honda with pop-up headlights, she drew big eyes on them and attached flirty eyelashes. She was charming and vivacious. But inwardly, as she learned that boys in Jackson County roughed up girls, just as her father had roughed up her mother, she began to feel anxious and afraid.

Brittany went away to college in Tennessee with dreams of a degree and supporting herself through graphic design. She hoped for an escape from the small towns of Alabama, whose women were more likely to live in poverty and less likely to have higher education than others in America, according to the nonprofit Women's Fund of Greater Birmingham. But then Brittany met her future husband at a party, a man with a deep, calming voice who made her laugh in his silly costume vest. They married quickly, Brittany got pregnant, and she soon dropped out of school to raise the baby. Then came the pills and his abuse, more babies, and next the loss of Baby Will and MawMaw, both in the same year.

Everything hurtled forward from there, like a train barreling down the tracks: the depression, the addiction, getting clean, and the assault and her shooting of Todd. Now, here she was in jail in Jackson County, stuck and distressed, hoping people would understand it was self-defense. As Brittany tried to sleep on her thin sleeping pad in jail at night, all she could think about was her four earnest, beautiful children she could not see.

With her daughter in jail and no way to reach her in isolation, Ramona sat on her porch in jeans and a big T-shirt, chain-smoking and scrolling obsessively on her phone. By this time, Ramona wore her thick chestnut hair straight and long instead of permed and short. She no longer cheesed for the camera. "I begged them to get Brittany help," she said. "Instead, she has a daggone meltdown, and they put her in a room alone."

For the first week or two after the shooting, Ramona kept the puppy Athena in the bathtub because she could not bear to look at her. Eventually, with so much else on her hands, she gave her away. For one thing, Ramona couldn't afford to bond Brittany out—the bond was set at $250,000—because she lived in public housing and had recently stopped working due to a host of health issues: an ulcer, a kidney stone, gallstones, and a bad back. She called nearly everyone she knew to ask them if they could put up their property as collateral to bond out Brittany, but her friends did not own expensive houses.

Ramona monitored any news stories posted on Facebook about the shooting, most of which provided few details: a brother and sister were arrested in the shooting death of Joshua Todd Smith. Some stories said that Todd had been shot and killed by a woman named Brittany Smith in "a home," not "her home." This outraged Ramona because she felt that one word changed the whole outlook on the case. She also noticed that no journalist had mentioned Brittany's assault or rape, which she felt was critical information. She replied to any fault-finding commenters by telling them that they did not know the whole story.

Throughout that February 2018, Ramona stewed and smoked on her front porch, feeling powerless to help her daughter. With Brittany in solitary, Ramona could no longer talk to her through the jail calling service, so she called the staff instead. She repeatedly warned them not to mistreat Brittany. "Do you hear me?" Ramona said, her voice like a chiding principal's. Or she browbeat them, threatening, "I'm fixing to come up there." If the staff hung up, she called right back and repeated herself, this time louder than before.

She put on a good face for the neighbors and her son, Chris, whom she knew could not stop thinking about the shooting. "People stare at me in town," Chris worried to his mother. His and Brittany's mugshot had made it into the papers by just two days after the shooting, and he said he didn't want to leave the house anymore. "Just go with it, baby," Ramona told him. She joked that he was like a celebrity in town.

But at night, alone in her bathtub, Ramona allowed herself to cry. She sobbed as she soaked in the hot water, then climbed into her big bed piled high with blankets to watch Netflix before a fitful night's sleep. Above her bed sat a row of antique dolls of MawMaw's, and on the wall was a framed photo of Brittany at prom in a baby blue dress—reminders of when life had been simpler.

A grand jury indicted Brittany for murder that March. If convicted, she faced a sentence of twenty years to life. The judge reduced Brittany's bond from $250,000 to $100,000, but that was still an astronomical sum. Ramona could not afford a lawyer either, so the court appointed an attorney for Brittany. No statewide public defender system exists in Alabama, so private attorneys are often assigned to represent the indigent. These court-appointed attorneys are paid poorly for their time and have little motivation to take the cases to trial, which can involve weeks or months of preparation.

For Brittany, the court selected a local criminal defense and personal injury attorney named James Mick. Mick, as everyone called him, was a former police officer with salt-and-pepper hair, a nervous temperament, and a habit of wearing ill-fitting suits. He typically handled low-level drug cases, burglaries, evictions, custody suits, and divorces, and had never been to trial for a murder case. Brittany feared he would not adequately represent her. She said that he advised her to plead guilty to manslaughter, which was better than a life sentence, as it would carry a sentence of between two and twenty years. But Brittany told Mick she would never plead guilty, since she shot Todd in self-defense. She didn't know much about self-defense law, but she knew that she wanted to plead innocent. "I did what I thought I had to do, what I did have to do, no doubt in my mind," Brittany said later. By March, she was out of solitary confinement and her mood had stabilized in jail, so she had no problem articulating to her lawyer that she felt the shooting was justified.

At home in Stevenson, Ramona went online and also scoured a thick law book she had taken from Mick's office to educate herself about self-defense law. That's when she learned about a statute called Stand Your

Ground, which made it legal to use lethal force to defend oneself against threats or perceived threats if necessary, with no duty to retreat. The law exists in dozens of states, including Alabama as of 2006. Its supporters say it allows people to protect themselves in dangerous situations, like the one Brittany had been in, while its critics argue it allows for a kind of vigilante justice.

The law's shortcomings became keenly apparent in 2012, when vigilante George Zimmerman shot and killed unarmed black teenager Trayvon Martin, who had just bought a packet of Skittles from a nearby 7-Eleven, and who Zimmerman falsely perceived to be a threat. Though Zimmerman's attorney didn't explicitly use the Stand Your Ground law at trial, the lawyer might as well have, with jury instructions that read that Zimmerman "had no duty to retreat and had the right to stand his ground." The case set off angry protests across the country, including in Los Angeles, where one woman held up a sign that read: "WHAT ABOUT MY GROUND"? But Wayne LaPierre, the vice president and CEO of the National Rifle Association (NRA), a major proponent of Stand Your Ground laws, argued at a 2013 conference that the statute could, in fact, help women: "The one thing a violent rapist deserves to face is a good woman with a gun," LaPierre said.

Ramona was relieved to find the Stand Your Ground law. She felt it fit Brittany's situation perfectly: "This is her law that's gonna get her out of it." It was the first bright spot she'd had in weeks. After Ramona spoke to her daughter in jail, Brittany asked Mick to enter a Stand Your Ground defense in her case. Doing so would mean she'd have a Stand Your Ground hearing, where a judge would hear the facts of the case from Brittany's defense attorney, the Jackson County prosecutor, and witnesses called by both sides. If the judge agreed the shooting was self-defense, Brittany's murder charge would be dismissed, and she'd walk free.

If she were able to afford him, Ramona would have hired Victor Revill, an Alabama criminal defense attorney who had handled several Stand Your Ground claims, all of them men. Later, after I began covering Brittany's story, I asked Revill to review her case. He said it was "absolutely Stand Your Ground," noting that Todd had been a clear threat to Brittany and Chris, since he had already assaulted Brittany, refused to leave Brittany's home when asked, and apparently choked out Chris. Brittany had no "duty to retreat" that night, Revill told me—she had the right to stand her ground. "And I'm going to tell you," he said, "I would have shot him."

Maybe so, but women have long struggled to win cases like Brittany's, since long before Stand Your Ground became law. In part, this is because self-defense laws in the U.S. and Europe were written by and for property-owning white men. The common law principle of the "castle doctrine," which later came to America, was defined by England's attorney general Sir Edward Coke in 1604 this way: "The house of everyone is to him as his castle and fortress, as for his defense against injury and violence as for his repose." Essentially, Coke meant that white men with property were justified in defending themselves against aggressors.

In her seminal 1989 book, *Justifiable Homicide*, women's rights advocate Cynthia Gillespie argued that, as a result of its origins, self-defense law evolved based on masculine assumptions—that the fight is between people of "roughly equal size, strength and fighting ability" and that it's "never acceptable to kill an unarmed adversary." Both assumptions have made it difficult for women to win self-defense cases because women and men are often different sizes and strengths, and women are more likely to defend themselves with guns or knives, while men more often use hands and fists, as happened with Brittany and Todd.

Gillespie also wrote that, of the two hundred cases she reviewed of women who killed men in self-defense, the outcomes were "depressingly similar": the women were arrested, charged with murder, pled guilty to murder or manslaughter, and went to prison. (She did not review men's cases.)

Among the most damaging aspects of self-defense law is the requirement that the threat of harm be "imminent," or about to happen. A woman cannot say she defended herself because she believed she was about to be killed in a few hours, or that she saw a look in her abuser's eye that suggested serious harm was imminent, even if she was right in assessing that danger. Courts rely on what many victim advocates describe as a "male standard of danger," demanding that a woman defend herself just as violence is initiated against her—as two men might in a fight—even if that's rarely possible in abusive situations.

For victims of abuse, Gillespie wrote, "death or serious injury is always imminent."

Back in 2012, the same year George Zimmerman shot unarmed black teenager Trayvon Martin, protesters sang in court after a black Florida mother named Marissa Alexander was sentenced to twenty years for firing a warning shot at an abusive husband. "We believe in justice and cannot rest until it's won," they sang in perfect harmony, before law enforcement escorted them out. Like Brittany planned to do, Alexander had made a Stand Your Ground claim of self-defense. Her husband had admitted to his abuse under oath, but later recanted it, saying: "I got five baby mamas and I put my hand on every last one of them except one. The way I was with women, they was like they had to walk on eggshells around me. You know, they never knew what I was thinking or what I might do. Hit them, push them." It was only after national outrage and a retrial that Alexander was fully set free in 2017.

The stark disparity between the George Zimmerman and Marissa Alexander cases infuriated women's and civil rights advocates, including University of Miami law professor Mary Anne Franks. In a 2014 paper on gender disparities in the application of Stand Your Ground, Franks wrote that Marissa Alexander should have been an exemplary Stand Your Ground claimant, and the fact that she and Zimmerman were treated so differently "offers reassurance and encouragement to men who would not only initiate violent encounters with strangers in public places, but also those who attack their wives in the privacy of their own homes." Franks argued that Stand Your Ground was not only failing to protect women—it was directly endangering them.

Data supports Franks's argument. A 2017 analysis of Stand Your Ground cases in Florida, conducted by political scientist Justin Murphy and published in *Social Science Quarterly*, examined 237 incidents between 2005 and 2013, and found evidence of both racial and gender bias. The gender bias applied to "domestic" cases, meaning those that occurred on a person's property or in their home. A man's likelihood of conviction in this kind of case was about 40 percent, while for a woman it was about 80 percent, which suggested that Stand Your Ground was working doubly well for men as for women in cases that happened at home.

Still, it's possible that the Stand Your Ground law has helped women in some states. In 2019, before Brittany had her Stand Your Ground hearing, I asked John Roman, a researcher at University of Chicago's NORC (National Opinion Research Center) social research team, to conduct an analysis to see how men fared versus women since the statute had been introduced. Using FBI homicide data, Roman found that, nationwide, Stand Your Ground laws have assisted both women and men in prevailing in justifiable-homicide defenses. But in Alabama, he found zero women who had won justifiable-homicide rulings between 2006, when the state passed its Stand Your Ground law, and 2010, when the state essentially stopped reporting its homicide data to the FBI.

At home in Stevenson, Ramona eventually discovered one promising case: a Huntsville, Alabama, woman named Jewel Battle, who was claiming Stand Your Ground for stabbing her male roommate to death after she said he held her down and tried to strangle her. By the following year, 2019, Battle would win her self-defense claim. Ramona held on to hope that Brittany could win her Stand Your Ground claim the same way.

Even if Brittany somehow lost her Stand Your Ground hearing, she told her mother she was determined to go to trial. She said she would risk a life sentence in part for her children, who had heard about the shooting at school. "I want them to know that Mommy's not a murderer, that Mommy defended herself, and that you should always defend yourself," she said.

But at Brittany's first pretrial hearing, she saw how difficult claiming self-defense as a woman in Jackson County would be. When Eric Woodall, the chief investigator who'd interviewed her, was asked about Brittany's injuries, he appeared not to take them seriously. Although the rape kit had counted thirty-three, he said: "Honestly, I mean, I would have thought there would be more."

• • •

April in Stevenson was sun-drenched and mild, a brief respite of lovely days before the hot, sticky months that lay ahead. Brittany was released from the Jackson County Jail late that month after Ramona finally found two people willing to put up their properties as bond. Brittany's lawyer, Mick, filed a motion to dismiss the case using the Stand Your Ground defense, as Brittany had requested. The hearing was scheduled for the summer.

As news spread of Todd's death and Brittany's arrest, Stevenson and wider Jackson County began gossiping about what really happened that night. Rumors flew that Brittany had been watching porn with Todd before the rape, that Ramona had been at the shooting, and that the killing was a drug deal gone wrong. People said that Brittany was a meth-head, a whore, or a crazy bitch out for revenge. Ramona was beside herself trying to respond to all the innuendo online. "Seeing people run their mouths without even knowing what happened is pitiful," she wrote in the comments of one news report posted to Facebook. "Both families are hurting . . . Do you really think you're helping anything?"

Some wondered, like Jeff did, if the rape had just been rough, drug-fueled sex. Chris, Brittany's brother, could not believe the suggestion. "All these people out here saying, 'Oh they were dating, and it was just rough sex,'" he said. "No. I'm pretty sure we all know what rough sex is. I wouldn't wish being raped on my worst enemy."

Since the shooting, Chris mostly stayed at home, sleeping all day and working night shifts cleaning restaurants or playing video games until dawn—anything to keep his mind off that night. It was too painful to go out and keep hearing what people were saying about him and Brittany.

Not long after Brittany got out of jail, she met with a local rape victim advocate named Sandra Goodman. Sandra had come across Brittany and Ramona a couple of years earlier outside the Jackson County Court-house when Brittany was struggling with addiction. At the time, despite Brittany's substance use, Sandra found her to be sprightly and funny, a young woman full of fire and shine. The Brittany she met after jail was a "nervous wreck," Sandra said, which she attributed to the rape and shooting, and also to Brittany being abruptly taken off her anxiety medicine in jail. In Sandra's line of work, which included regular meetings with local rape victims, some of whom she knew before their assault, it was common to see animated women turn uncertain or erratic afterward. In her eyes, these were rational reactions to profoundly irrational, traumatic events.

Sandra, who grew up in Georgia, was vice president of the Healing Bridge, a nonprofit in LaFayette, Georgia, that provided free services to victims of sexual assault. (The group is now defunct.) The nonprofit regularly took clients from Jackson County, where Brittany lived, because resources there were few. Sandra was a firecracker of a woman, with platinum-blond hair, bright blue eyes, and a fondness for cherry-red lipstick. She drove a big black SUV and lived in a big house on Sand Mountain. As a rape victim advocate, Sandra helped women, and sometimes men, who were assaulted in the area get connected with talk therapy, financial support, transportation to court hearings, and other resources.

Sandra saw rape as an epidemic in Jackson County and said that authorities often "don't acknowledge it" or pursue arrests, despite rape having been outlawed in the region since before Alabama became a state. She believed that most people accused of sexual assault in the county had never been charged or even questioned. "A lot of times they take a woman's statement, and that's where it stops," she said of local police. "They just turn their head, and no one gets punished. It's the victims that get punished in this system."

In all her years as an advocate, Sandra said she'd never seen a case that so plainly showed how the criminal justice system treated a rape victim as Brittany's. She believed that the police never should have arrested her, and that it was ludicrous for her to be indicted for murder. With all the documentation of Todd's violence that night—the bite marks, the petechiae from strangulation, her deep purple bruises, and more—it was obvious to Sandra that the case should be dismissed as self-defense.

Instead, Brittany would have a Stand Your Ground hearing and potentially go to trial, which Sandra knew from experience would be doubly traumatizing because Brittany would have to repeatedly relive the event in the lead up to and during the trial. So Sandra got to work, taking

Brittany to therapy at the Healing Bridge and meeting with her regularly to talk. After Brittany went to several sessions, Sandra said, "Slowly, you could see her coming back to life."

Around this time, Brittany's husband showed up to attend one of Brittany's pretrial hearings. He stopped at Ramona's house beforehand, carrying a self-help book under his arm about how to be a better husband. Wearing a baseball hat and jeans, he spoke quietly in his baritone voice from Ramona's recliner. He recounted how, after learning that Todd had raped Brittany, he'd kicked through a table at work. He was acquainted with Todd because he had once lived in a mobile home park near him and heard about his many brawls around town. "I told her the last person you need to be around is Todd Smith," he said. He thought Brittany never should have picked up Todd at the park that night. "She's got a hand in it [what happened], and it's stupidity," he said. "But nobody asks to be raped."

After the pretrial hearing, Brittany and her husband reminisced at the house about beautiful times with their children before they'd both lost custody. He credited Brittany for helping him "straighten up" and get off pills. For a period, life had been good together. "It was wonderful, I couldn't ask for a better wife or mother," he said. He told her he hoped they could get back together as a couple and see the kids more often. He said he was sober and had gotten his anger in check.

Brittany wanted to believe what he was saying. She remembered when they lived as a family in a red clapboard house, where they'd made a handwritten cookbook of recipes together, and at Christmastime decorated a Charlie Brown tree. But she also knew not to trust it. After that hearing, Brittany told him they should stay separated and asked him not to show up to her court dates again.

As Brittany awaited her Stand Your Ground hearing in October, she tried to keep her mind off the case. She visited her children at her uncle's house, where they buried her in hugs and bragged about the art they made while she was gone. Though they'd heard about the shooting, Brittany did not tell them she had been in jail, saying only that she was "away." After visits with her kids, she holed up at her mother Ramona's house. The red-brick house with white columns she'd loved was no longer hers. She said that after the shooting, her landlord gave her just a few days to leave.

The rest of that spring 2018, Brittany left the house mostly just to go out for runs. She ran track in high school, and northeastern Alabama was lush and green that time of year. One day in May, Brittany was running at a local park when a man on a motorcycle stopped and parked beside her. He did not speak, just watched her as she circled the track. His gaze unnerved her so she quit her run early. When the man showed up a second time a few weeks later, following her to the MAPCO gas station where she'd stopped the night of the shooting, Brittany confronted him and asked who he was. He was muscular and rode shirtless, mirrored sunglasses obscuring his eyes. Brittany had never seen him around town before. According to Brittany, he said that he was a cousin of Todd's, who was shot by a "white nigger." "He was just letting me know that he knew" about the shooting, Brittany said, "and to let me know who he was." (Jeff said he did not know the relative.) When Brittany got home, she told Ramona about it, who told her to "keep your ass at home where I can protect you."

After that, Brittany stopped leaving her mother's house altogether, unless she was going to see her children. She was afraid that the man on the motorcycle or some other member of Todd's family would hurt her. She was still having nightmares about Todd and his pit bulls. The Healing Bridge therapy sessions were helping, but most days she just wanted to curl into a ball and sleep. Ramona, who missed her fierce, funny daughter—even addiction hadn't stolen her humor—tried to coax Brittany out of the house to do errands. Brittany agreed to one trip to Walmart, but in the store she saw someone she thought was a relative of Todd's. Breathing heavily, she ducked to the ground beneath the rows of clothing. Ramona didn't ask her to leave the house again after that.

At night, as Brittany and Ramona lay side by side in Ramona's wide bed, which they'd slept in together ever since the shooting, Brittany panicked whenever floodlights passed. "Lay low, Mom," she said, "so that if they shoot through the windows, it won't hit us." Ramona told her daughter that she was being dramatic. She knew about PTSD, but thought Brittany's fears were overblown. But Ramona didn't know that another relative of Todd's had begun plotting to hurt Brittany.

Soon, more women in Jackson County heard about Brittany's case, mostly by word of mouth, since her side of the story had received no coverage in local media. Many were upset and outraged, feeling as if the woman awaiting trial could have been them. Kayla Pearson, a neighbor of Ramona's in the public housing complex, and a single mother of four high-spirited children, knew what it was like to face a violent man on drugs. She said she'd split from her husband of fourteen years after he began using meth and attacked her. "He stomped my head in until I passed out," she said. "I think meth just makes you really don't care. It makes you a completely different person." Another local mother, Nicole Green, told Ramona outside the courthouse that a group of men in Jackson County had sexually assaulted her as a child. She said that her ex-husband had also once held her hostage at gunpoint. Both times, she felt authorities blamed her instead of pursuing the men who'd hurt her. "Instead of being treated like the victim, it was more like my fault," Green said. "They said if I did anything to him, I would have been the one going to jail." She shook her head in disgust. "What was I supposed to do," she asked, "let him beat me and end up dead?"

A couple years before Brittany was arrested in Stevenson, in the nearby town of Fackler, Alabama, in 2016, the body of a woman named Stacy Sullivan was found near the railroad tracks. A year later, law enforcement said that her death remained unsolved because of a long delay in receiving the forensic report. Later, they told me the problem was an overall lack of evidence. When a second woman, Samantha Frison, was discovered dead in 2018, police at first said that she'd been stabbed, then told local news that a car had hit her. The two deaths made the women of Jackson County even more certain that something was off within their community.

The Violence Policy Center, a gun-crime prevention group, analyzes state-by-state FBI homicide data annually to determine where women are most at risk. Throughout the 2000s, Alabama was one of the states with the highest rate of women being murdered by men, until it essentially stopped sending homicide data to the FBI in 2010. "The [number of] women getting killed or almost getting killed is going up because they aren't doing anything about it," Nicole Green said, "because they don't want to waste their time." Ramona, whose outlook had become bleaker since Brittany was indicted for murder, saw it more starkly. "They hate women around here," she said.

But Chuck Phillips, the Jackson County sheriff, did not think domestic and sexual violence was especially common in his county, at least no more than anywhere else. Phillips was a blunt force of a man with ruddy skin and a gray and white goatee. He often sat with his arms crossed, his skepticism baked in after years on the job. He believed this about the county even though the number of aggravated assaults in Jackson County was double the state average per capita, according to Alabama Law Enforcement Agency data. His office also categorized some domestic violence complaints, such as if a man slapped a woman, as "harassment" instead of assault.

Phillips maintained that his county's statistics were not outrageous, and that the violence tracked with the local drug problem. "People get high, they get stupid," he said. He attributed increases in violence to new, more potent strains of meth coming to Alabama from across the U.S.-Mexico border. While people used to manufacture meth on Sand Mountain from items they bought at the grocery store, he said they were now buying purer meth imported from Mexico. Studies show substance abuse is a significant contributing cause of domestic violence, though it is not the only factor.

Phillips added that it was hard to know who was at fault when he or his deputies responded to a domestic violence call, so they often followed an ad hoc process in making arrests. "You pick one of them and say, 'Okay, well, you're going to jail,'" Phillips said. "Usually, it's whoever's got the most bruises." Even after the officer picked a perpetrator, the other person would usually protest, the sheriff said. And even if he made an arrest, the victim generally didn't press charges, a common problem with domestic abuse. Meanwhile, repeat offenders like

Todd Smith rarely went to prison because Alabama's prisons were over-crowded, and they also rarely got help in the form of counseling or long-term drug treatment. As a result, the same people kept cycling in and out of Phillips's jail, and they became part of another unfixable problem in his county—one that distressed many Jackson County residents but that they seemed forced to accept.

Jeff held it together at Todd's funeral until he saw his twenty-three-year-old daughter, who had considered Todd a second father, "about to climb into the casket." Jeff finally lost it and cried. For all his flaws, Todd had been his best friend, a ride-or-die friend, a brother to him, and like a father to his children.

The more Jeff thought about Brittany, the angrier he became. He thought about the party where he was sure he'd seen Brittany. He thought about the suppressed grief of Rojo, Todd's father, with whom he had been living since Todd's death. He thought about how Todd acted on Xanax, and how Brittany had a prescription. On Facebook, Jeff wrote around that time: "My gosh I live with my uncle . . . and the bitch fed him Xanax all weekend long . . . [she] was running around butt naked at our house that weekend. I got up to piss and it looked like national geographic in the house. I seen it with my own damn eyes what the whor did!!!"

Jeff later deleted the post. But the more he thought about it, the more he wanted revenge. His many tattoos included the word "outlaw," written in fancy script, full caps, and a depiction of the Joker, whom Jeff thought perfectly represented life on meth. "Steal, kill, it's a real dark lifestyle," he said. On his Facebook page, Jeff posted Joker memes that represented how he felt: *Why should I apologize for the monster I have become?* one read. *No one ever apologized for making me this way.* He had never before ordered someone killed, but this time he did not care about the consequences. Someone had to pay for Todd's death, Jeff said, and that person was Brittany. "When you make that phone call . . . there's no turning back," a friend told him.

Still, Jeff picked up the phone.

HYSTERIA

Ancient physicians and philosophers have called this disease hysteria, from the name of the uterus, that organ given by nature to women, so that they might conceive. I have examined many hysterical women, some stuporous, others with anxiety attacks. The disease manifests itself with different symptoms, but always refers to the uterus.

—Claudius Galen, second century A.D. physician and philosopher, in his work *In Hippocratis Librum De Humoribus*

After a long, sweltering summer, so hot Ramona never turned off the A/C, Brittany went to court for a pretrial hearing in October 2018. A week later, the circuit court was finally due to hear her Stand Your Ground claim. But when Brittany arrived at the Jackson County Courthouse in Scottsboro, she found her hearing rescheduled. She said she had rarely heard from her lawyer James Mick in the past few months, despite frequent efforts to reach him. Fed up, she wrote him a frustrated email: "You told me to be there today, so I was . . . Was it rescheduled by you? I left a message for you to contact me . . . NEVER HEARD FROM YOU . . . If you are too busy for my case don't beat around the bush. I need someone with MY best interest in mind."

Her hearing was canceled because Mick had requested the court have Brittany evaluated by a state psychologist, which she said Mick never told her. The evaluation would assess her competency to stand trial and her mental state at the time of the shooting. He told the psychologist that Brittany needed evaluation because her behavior was "erratic." Mick also filed a motion to pursue a plea of not guilty by reason of insanity. It is unclear if Mick intended to use the insanity defense to clear Brittany—a defense that is rare and hard to win—because, she and her mother said, he did not share his reasoning with them.* Perhaps he thought claiming insanity would be more successful than Stand Your Ground.

Lawyers around the world have been using some version of the insanity defense for battered women for over a century. But perhaps the most famous, successful use of the defense came in the 1970s, when a Michigan woman, Francine Hughes, who had endured more than a decade of severe abuse, went on trial for setting fire to her live-in former husband's bed and killing him. As chronicled in the 1984 film *The Burning Bed*, starring Farrah Fawcett, Hughes was cleared of the crime after her lawyer successfully argued that she went temporarily insane from the horrors of the abuse.

The case marked a turning point for the movement for battered women's rights, with more police departments and social service agencies aggressively working to prevent domestic abuse. It also made early use of a theory and defense called "battered-woman syndrome." Developed by psychologist Lenore Walker, the defense held that women who face severe abuse develop psychological symptoms akin to extreme PTSD. By email, Walker wrote me that "often the facts show that at the time of the killing, in the woman's mind it is not just fear from that incident, but fragments of other abuse incidents that heightens their fear of deadly force or harm from the abusers." Battered-woman syndrome helped courts connect the dots between a woman's experiences with abuse and why she reacted the way she did.

But advocates later took issue with battered-woman syndrome because of the way they said it pathologized women, as if they had a disease or disorder. By the mid-1990s, U.S. health agencies were in agreement, stating that the use of the word "syndrome" was no longer appropriate for abused women. Lawyers started to use the defense less. Mary Anne

---

* Mick declined to comment on Brittany's case.

Franks, the University of Miami School of Law professor, is among its more recent critics. In her 2014 paper on Stand Your Ground, Franks asserted that while self-defense laws argue that a person's use of force was justified, battered-woman syndrome suggests a woman has "acted wrongly but is so defective in some significant sense that she cannot be held accountable." She told me that even when the battered-woman syndrome defense was not used in women's self-defense cases, they are still "treated pathologically, treated as if there is something wrong with their brains."

In December 2018, Brittany met with the state psychologist her lawyer, Mick, had requested, nearly a year after killing Todd. They met at Mick's office, a dun-colored, shingle-style house across from the Jackson County Courthouse. Brittany arrived feeling anxious and near tears that Mick had ordered an evaluation that she said was without her consent. Ramona accompanied her daughter to the office and was upset to see the psychologist was male. To lighten the mood, she joked to Brittany that he looked just like Otis Campbell, the portly, disheveled town drunk from *The Andy Griffith Show*. Brittany and the psychologist were ushered into Mick's conference room, with a fake bouquet on the table and a miniature replica of Lady Justice hanging on the wall. Ramona was asked to wait outside.

Brittany said she and the psychologist talked for several hours, during which time he asked her in detail about her mental and social history, plus the assault and shooting. The interview went poorly from the start, with Brittany unwrapping nearly a dozen mini Snickers bars she'd taken from Mick's receptionist's desk to eat, which the psychologist described in his report as "compulsive eating." Brittany later said she hadn't eaten anything that day and was hungry. Many days, Brittany and Ramona subsisted on a meal or two from McDonald's or Burger King with a Mello Yello because of a lack of money. And ever since the shooting, Brittany could not find a job in town, so they were all scraping by on Chris's minimum-wage job and Ramona's government benefits.

The psychologist also wrote that Brittany cried so much at the interview's start that he had to get her tissues. (At first, the psychologist told me he did not remember Brittany and, later, that her account of their interview was inaccurate.) He noted in his report that she was hard to interview because she was "frequently crying," "acting panicked," and "asking questions about her future." She was also "hostile," he wrote. Brittany told me that was because the psychologist laughed at her when she described Todd mimicking her voice after the rape. *We're friends,* she'd said to him, and Todd had mocked her an octave higher: *We're friennnds.* "Anyone would have been pissed off at someone laughing at them," she said, adding that she'd "cursed out" the psychologist for doing so.

In his report, the psychologist wrote that Brittany was suffering from paranoid thoughts and had trouble differentiating fantasy from reality, in part because she believed Todd Smith's family might hurt her. "His family has a hit out on me," Brittany told him, something she'd heard around town. The psychologist diagnosed Brittany as potentially delusional and showing symptoms of a psychotic disorder, which he said could be exacerbated or caused by substance abuse. It is possible that Brittany had relapsed at the time of the interview, though she maintained she was clean. Either way, the psychologist wrote that if she were to get outpatient or inpatient mental health treatment, or possibly substance abuse counseling, it could happen at Bryce Hospital—a state hospital for the seriously mentally ill.

On the road between Jackson County, Alabama, where Brittany resided, and Marion County, Tennessee, where Jeff and Todd grew up, roadkill is often strewn across the asphalt: a crushed armadillo, opossum, or deer, and occasionally a dead turtle or puppy. The roadkill is a discordant sight amid the tangle of lush forest surrounding it, but residents barely notice it, saying death has long haunted the area. A popular ghost story in the county was the tale of how colonial settlers had attacked the village of an indigenous leader there centuries ago, killing his people in the face of their fierce resistance. People believed they now lived and walked above the buried corpses, and as a result, many said the region was cursed.

In the month right after the shooting, Jeff Poe had privately messaged

Brittany on Facebook, asking her to meet him in person. Brittany declined, but Jeff kept at her. "I just wanna ask you one question[,] just me and you. Nobody else," he wrote. "You owe me that much."

Jeff had picked up the phone. But in the end, after months of resentment and rage, he said, he decided not to put a hit out on Brittany. Killing Brittany would not bring Todd back from the dead, not his wild laugh or stocky walk. He realized that both families were hurting. "I didn't want the blood on my hands because I'm not a killer," he said. Instead, he messaged Brittany again on Facebook in late 2018, writing, "I just want to tell you that I forgive you for doing what you did."

Brittany replied soon after. "I am sorry for you and your family's loss. From my heart, I am."

"I'm sure Todd did some fucked up shit to you," Jeff wrote back. "I'm sorry."

He posted another Joker meme on his Facebook page: *You see my smile, Not my pain.*

After the interview with the court psychologist at Mick's office, Brittany penned a handwritten letter to Jackson County Circuit Judge Jenifer C. Holt, who was hearing her case, to ask for a new attorney. She wrote that she had problems getting in contact with Mick, that she had not "been adequately represented or treated like a client by him," and that she had "fired him twice, but he refuses." Brittany never gave the judge the letter, deciding she would say something in person. But that February 2019, when a hearing was held to determine whether Brittany was competent to stand trial, she saw she had bigger problems. In a well-pressed suit and shined shoes, Jackson County District Attorney Jason Pierce argued that, given the psychologist's report, "The most appropriate and perhaps the only placement for Ms. Smith would be at the Bryce Hospital."

Formerly known as the Alabama State Hospital for the Insane, Bryce houses hundreds of patients the courts have committed for mental disorders. Pierce leaned into the idea that Brittany was potentially psychotic and delusional, telling the court that her shooting of Todd may have resulted from "one of [her] delusions." Brittany could not believe what she was hearing. She had passed a drug test the day before, but Pierce argued that Brittany could have faked it, because falsified drug tests to avoid punishment were an ongoing problem in the county.

Pierce went on to say that, in the interim, Brittany should immediately be put in jail for the safety of herself and others.* In his oversized suit and halting voice, Brittany's lawyer, Mick, interjected. Mick told the court that Brittany had done nothing wrong since being out on bail, and had passed all her drug tests. He reminded the judge that there were photographs of her many injuries from Todd, "of bruising from her neck all the way down to her toes." "By incarcerating her, we're treating her as a defendant," he said. "And I believe she has been a victim in this particular case." As Brittany listened to Mick talk, she felt her lawyer was finally speaking up for her.

Caroline Light, who authored the book *Stand Your Ground*, said that in the courtroom drama, female defendants in self-defense cases are often viewed in one of two frames. "A woman capable of violence needs to be pathologized: Is she angry or is she crazy?" she told me. While Brittany's case dragged on, two more women in Alabama attempted self-defense claims, and both were forced into one of the two frames. Deven Grey, a young black mother, fatally shot her white partner in Calera, Alabama, in December 2017. Police arrested her with a bleeding ear and facial fractures, and Grey said her partner had shot at her, beaten, dragged, and pistol-whipped her that night. A year later, when Deven had her Stand Your Ground hearing, prosecutors argued that she didn't fire the gun to defend herself but because she was jealous—angry—over another woman. Then, in 2019, Linda Doyle, an older white woman in Alabama, was found with multiple stab wounds in the vagina after she shot and killed a husband she said was abusive. Prosecutors argued Doyle was so unhinged she must have stabbed herself to stage the murder, but her attorney steadfastly maintained it was self-defense. Doyle was sentenced to ninety-nine years. Her lawyer is appealing. Light, who directs Harvard

---

* Pierce declined to comment on the case.

University's undergraduate studies program on women, gender, and sexuality, said that a court "often sees black defendants as angry, and white defendants as crazy or hysterical."

Brittany felt she was being pushed toward "crazy." Armed with the psychologist's report, Judge Holt, a powerful and longtime circuit judge on the cusp of retirement, declared that Brittany was not competent to stand trial and needed institutionalization at Bryce. "Ma'am," Brittany ventured after Holt's verdict, "when we were talking, we were talking about what happened in jail, my mental break in jail, I'm—I'm being treated, you know, now. And I have been able to walk and see my kids and be—you know, be a human being again. And I've not harmed anyone. And I'm—well, I thought I was doing well," she said, faltering.

"That's the order of the court," Holt replied with finality. Brittany asked if she could do outpatient therapy instead, so she could continue to see her children. Holt said there was no other place Brittany could receive "psychotic medications," as well as detox from any potential drugs she was on, even though Bryce is primarily a psychiatric hospital. Holt also ordered Brittany into immediate custody in the Jackson County Jail until a bed freed up at Bryce, which was located several hours away in Tuscaloosa. "Is there a way we could expedite that?" Mick asked, meaning her time at Bryce, where patients sometimes get stuck far beyond their intended time. Holt said she didn't think the delays were so lengthy for women and that Brittany would likely be at Bryce for just ninety days.

Ramona, who was in the courtroom, counted ninety days from February in her head. "That's all her kids' birthdays," she cried out. Annoyed, Holt ordered Ramona to leave her courtroom for being a disruption. As Ramona was escorted out, Brittany called out to her mother: "Tell them Mama didn't do anything wrong, don't tell them—" "That's enough," said Holt. "You don't tell them that I'm in jail," Brittany went on. "I won't," Ramona promised. "Tell them that I love them and that I'm sick, okay?" Brittany said. "And that I'm getting well."

Then Brittany was put in handcuffs and led away. Brittany would be at Bryce for far longer than ninety days.

• • •

After Brittany was taken into custody, Ramona fired off a furious letter to Mick. "Are you trying to get my daughter to PLEA to some sort of insanity plea??" she wrote. "That's RIDICULOUS when you have EVERYTHING you need to WIN her Stand Your Ground hearing. BRITTANY IS NOT CRAZY . . . If my daughter ends up in a friggin' mental hospital, or worse, PRISON, you'd better believe me when I say that I'm fixing to show my ass worse than I already have . . . THANKS, HER CRAZY ASS MOTHER."

Mick did not reply and told me that Ramona was not his client.

Sandra Goodman, the victim advocate who had worked with Brittany at Healing Bridge, was appalled to hear that Brittany was being sent to Bryce. Sandra believed there was no reason Brittany should be sent to the hospital, "none at all," and that "she has PTSD from the rape and the judicial system."

With Brittany in jail and Bryce on the horizon, Ramona decided she had to draw more media attention to her daughter's case. After connecting with a local activist named Sherrie Saunders, who was outraged by the story, Ramona was invited by Saunders to appear on her podcast, *United Voices,* which aired for free online. "This story is an extremely sad story," Saunders told listeners in an episode that aired in February 2019, just days after Brittany's competency hearing. "It's gonna make some of you folks angry. I hope it's going to make you angry enough to help this person, Brittany." Saunders then turned over the mic to a caller who identified herself as Paige Parker—Todd Smith's ex-wife.

Paige began speaking in her thick Southern drawl, enunciating each word to ensure she was well-heard: "I was held captive numerous times by Todd and beat over the years from Todd." She and Todd had married in the early 2000s, when Paige was in her early twenties, and she told Saunders the abuse started two weeks after they wed, then steadily escalated from there. More than once, she said, Todd broke her ribs, jaw, and nose, and bit her on the face. Paige described emotional, physical, and sexual abuse. Arrest records show Todd was charged with domestic violence five times during their marriage and spent time in and out of jail. Jasper, Tennessee, police chief Billy Mason, whose department had arrested Todd several times, told me: "That's the deal with court that a police officer can't stand, because nobody stays in jail as long as they need to." It is unclear if Todd was ever sent to anger management, therapy, or addiction treatment.

Paige told Saunders that the story that reminded her most of Brittany's was when "I was duct-taped and tied to a chair." "I had been held captive by him for days, beaten, raped, sodomized, everything Brittany had went through and—and more," she went on. "I was bleeding from my eyes, broken nose, ribs, black eyes." Paige added that she once stabbed Todd to defend herself, and arrest records show Parker was arrested once for domestic violence during their marriage. When I asked a local police officer about Paige and Todd, he blamed the violence on her, saying of Paige: "She's a handful" and "fights like a man."

In 2003, Paige filed for divorce from Todd, which appeared to only worsen the violence, which is often the case with abusers. She got an order of protection against him the following year. "Everything Brittany is saying is true," she finished on the podcast, saying she was sharing her story to explain why people should believe Brittany. "He is the thing of nightmares."

After Saunders interviewed Ramona, she finished by calling Brittany a heroine. The podcast spread far and wide in Jackson County, and was later turned to by local and national media.

Several weeks after it aired, on a frigid cold day in March 2019, Sandra, Ramona, and several other local women decided to hold a protest outside the Jackson County Courthouse. Among the women who showed up was Paige Parker, Todd's ex-wife, who was rail-thin with bright hazel eyes, a long brunette bob, and a tattoo that read: *Survive*. After the podcast interview, she had connected with Ramona and wanted to do more to help Brittany. All the women held hand-drawn signs, reading "Stand Your Ground," "Justice 4 Brittany," and "Jailed 4 Protecting Yourself Is Wrong." Paige's said "Rape Victim Held in Jail." The women stood for hours in the chill outside of the imposing court building, with its tall white Roman columns and a big clock tower at the top. When passing women heard what they were protesting, some shared their personal stories of violence. Women said they had been abused or raped and that Jackson County officials had done little for them. "We heard all these horrific stories that day," Sandra said. "The good ol' boys club," added Ramona.

Many of the women who stopped to talk were especially distraught to hear that Brittany was being sent to Bryce. It confirmed their worst fears that they could not fight back, no matter how much violence they faced, and that instead they would be treated as crazy. The day after the women's protest outside the courthouse, Brittany was shuttled from jail to Bryce Hospital in Tuscaloosa, some three or more hours away from home.

Women in Alabama have long fared poorly in self-defense cases, though that outcome is highly dependent on several factors. Sometimes, that loss is aided by a prosecutor who relied on myths about abuse: that a woman's claim is invalid because she didn't end a relationship with an abuser (why did Brittany invite Todd to her house even if she knew he was bad news?), didn't call the police about the violence (as Brittany didn't), or allowed the abuser into her home (as Brittany did).

Perhaps equally crucial in determining the outcomes women face is the media coverage or public attention the cases receive. No one covered the developments of Deven Grey's case as it happened, and so the prosecutor was able to argue, unchallenged in the public eye, that she'd shot her partner out of jealousy instead of after years of severe abuse; Grey lost her Stand Your Ground claim. When I examined local reporting on women who killed alleged abusers over the last several decades, many of the women were described as "cold-blooded murderers," "evil," and "heartless," with no mention of their history of abuse, which was often easily available in their court files.

When the media does report on prior abuse, women see different results. Jacqueline Dixon, a thirty-eight-year-old woman from Selma, Alabama, was charged with murder for shooting an abusive husband in July 2018 from whom she had previously gotten an order of protection.

Her case garnered national attention—Dixon's mugshot, which showed her crying with her eyes closed, was reprinted numerous times—and ultimately a grand jury declined to indict her. Brittany clung to the outcome of Jacqueline Dixon's case, while Ramona worked to get her daughter's case national coverage.

In April 2019, Brittany's story did. A short feature on her case was published in *The Appeal,* an online criminal justice website with a national readership, with the headline "Alabama Woman Faces Life Sentence for Killing Man Who Allegedly Raped Her." A few sites aggregated the story, and I read it. The story said that Brittany, after shooting her alleged rapist, had been sent to a psychiatric hospital after experiencing a nervous breakdown in jail. It quoted her mother, Ramona, saying that her daughter wasn't insane, she just hadn't been properly treated for her PTSD after Todd's attack. I called Ramona, who spoke to me for hours that evening, and invited me down to Alabama to come see everything for myself, and also to go to Bryce to meet Brittany.

On our first car ride from Stevenson to Tuscaloosa that June, Ramona chain-smoked through a cracked passenger window and gulped down a Mello Yello. She told me she was mentally preparing what to tell Brittany on the visit. The ninety-day window her daughter should have been at Bryce had come and gone, and it was still unclear when she would get out. Mick's office had told Ramona that there was a backlog among patients who needed to see a psychologist for release, as Mick had predicted would happen, but Ramona did not see that as a reason to keep her. She clutched a plastic bag holding homemade cherry and blueberry cobblers, Brittany's favorite, to sneak in since no outside food was allowed. She and I followed the forested highway for nearly two hundred miles, a trip that usually took gas money she'd saved up for weeks. Finally, the road opened up to the winding, tree-lined campus of the University of Alabama. There, past a warning sign in red capital letters, stood a grand, white-columned entrance: Bryce Hospital.

When Bryce opened in 1861, it was praised as a reformist mental institution, but the quality of care deteriorated as the hospital grew. In 1970, patients filed a class-action lawsuit against the state of Alabama over lack of care and mistreatment, which led to the federal minimum standards of care for the mentally ill. Bryce was overhauled at that time but by 2019, when we visited its new building, many patients complained to me about neglect or abuse.*

The stories Brittany had already told Ramona over the phone about her all-female ward were distressing and sometimes absurd. Brittany said her roommate told her she was institutionalized after skinning her sister's arm and shoulder and eating them. Another patient regularly lay on the floor and played dead, reminding Brittany of Todd lying dead on her kitchen floor. A third patient ate batteries and the rings of the shower curtain. "What in the holy hell have they got you in there with?" Ramona had asked on the phone. "Cannibals," Brittany replied drily, and they both cackled.

That afternoon, Ramona and I were let into the hospital cafeteria, which was high-ceilinged and sterile, with big round tables and a row of soda and candy machines. Brittany emerged after a few minutes, greeting us with a tired smile. She wore a gray, long-sleeved T-shirt, red Chaco sandals, and jeans, and a nurse accompanied her to supervise our conversation from another table. Brittany protested her mom's cobbler, saying she had already gained too much weight at the hospital. But after a moment, she relaxed, eating furtive bites beneath the table, and told us about the latest incidents at Bryce: that one of the male nurses beat women, that the staff liked to instigate fights among patients, and that, after she refused to pick up another roommate's feces, the same male nurse had pushed her against the wall and twisted her arm behind her back, and later taunted her and asked her to flash him, a story corroborated by another patient.†

Ramona already knew that Bryce was stressful because Brittany had been sending home pages of a diary she kept. "May 16: injured elbow . . . sexually assaulted in my sleep," she wrote in her looping script, about

---

* The Alabama Department of Mental Health declined to comment.

† Bryce's patient advocate did not return calls; it later emerged that the advocate had been arrested for possession of child pornography and did not work there anymore. He pleaded not guilty.

waking up to a roommate touching her. "June: My shoulder hurts so damn bad today." "June 5: Donna hit 17-year-old Jaleria." Then came neater, more deliberate handwriting: "I'm in my feelings today . . . I haven't seen my kids in months. I bet they look different. I bet they're a little taller. I never knew how painful motherhood could be." Brittany also sent Ramona less somber entries, describing the humor of day-to-day life at Bryce: "Steph . . . wiped her nose with my hand one day . . ." and its surprises: "I woke up this morning with a small Heath bar in bed with me :) That made my day."

As Brittany spoke to us in the cafeteria, she tried not to get upset. "I've seen so much in here. There isn't another person who can keep their composure like me," she said, and began to cry. Ramona shushed her and rubbed her back. Brittany told her mother that if they were going to treat her "like a caged animal," she was going to start acting like one. Ramona urged her not to do anything that would keep her longer at Bryce. Brittany promised she wouldn't but said it was hard not to lose her cool. "I found myself in here, but now I'm losing myself," she told me.

Before the thirty-minute visit was up, Ramona approached the nurse in scrubs who'd watched the conversation, and asked her if she thought Brittany should be at Bryce. The nurse replied that she thought Brittany had been "at the wrong place at the wrong time," and that she was focused on getting her out of Bryce. Ramona nodded. She found the sentiment equal parts reassuring and alarming.

Another nurse, Tamichael Mallisham, had been at Bryce for almost a year when Brittany arrived that March. Mallisham was one of the patients' favorites. I called her up to see if she thought Brittany deserved to be at Bryce. Mallisham told me that when she met the "new girl," Brittany seemed scared but not to have any issues grievous enough to warrant being at the hospital. As Mallisham got to know Brittany more, she said she became more convinced she did not belong. Most of the patients at Bryce had severe mental disorders and could not function in the outside world. They had mania, were self-harmers, or were violent. "What Brittany had going on was a whole lot of depression because of what happened to her," Mallisham told me. "The situation, not being able to be with her kids, anxiety of all the stuff that she had been through, and not knowing what was going to happen." She felt that Brittany had acted and responded the way anyone would have in her situation, and in fact had handled it better than most.

Brittany had an infectious humor that made a lot of the patients want to be around her, but at night she often cried in the ward, and Mallisham tried to comfort her. Like Ramona, she warned Brittany not to act out in any way that would cause her to stay longer at Bryce. "Do what you gotta do to get out of here," Mallisham told her. "Do it to see your babies." Brittany calmed down whenever they spoke, which she said was not the case with her other patients.

When I spoke to Mallisham, she told me that she had been raped and had a daughter as a result, an experience she thought made her a better nurse because she could empathize with her patients. Every woman she met at Bryce had faced some form of physical, sexual, verbal, or mental abuse in their life before being institutionalized, she said. I suggested that was a remarkable fact. "No, what's remarkable is that men can do this to females, and they label us as crazy," she said.

As Ramona and I drove home from that visit to Bryce, Ramona seemed more fired up than before. She was determined to get Brittany out of Bryce, acquire better legal representation, and get her daughter's trial moved out of Jackson County, where she felt that Judge Holt, and any potential jury, would be prejudiced against her for being a poor woman and a former drug user. The reduction in Brittany's bond, to $100,000, was still higher than needed, which local news reported was because of her history with the court.

If the trial wasn't moved out of Jackson County, Ramona told me she would make sure everyone in town knew the whole story—that it would be impossible to hide what her daughter had been through. "I guess I'm a thorn in your all's rose," she said as we pulled into Stevenson.

In June in Alabama, the trees bend from the weight of the heat. Mosquitoes land and cluster, leaving red welts on arms and annoyance in their wake. Dogs roam free or strain on leads, children shriek as they chase each other, and teenagers get high in the woods, pushing the limits of when to come home. The roads smell of rain.

One evening a few days after we visited Bryce, Ramona invited a group of women over to her backyard in the public housing complex to brainstorm how to fight for Brittany. The women sat on the scratchy grass or in lawn chairs, sharing lasagna, cocktail shrimp, and baked chicken. Ramona had made a cake. Sandra, the rape victim advocate, was there, along with Todd's ex-wife, Paige, and Paige's mother, Anita Parker. So was Sherrie Saunders, the online radio host and activist, who had now put out two episodes on Brittany's story. The women barely knew each other, but the conversation was constant. It did not matter that Sandra was a rich woman with Dior eyeglasses and a sprawling house up on the mountain, while Saunders was a working-class lesbian mom with a tendency to speak crassly. It did not matter that, after her divorce from Todd, Paige had become a tattooed free-spirit whose favorite activity was identifying mushrooms in the forest, while Ramona was life-weary and a homebody who stayed sane by taking long baths and watching Netflix in bed.

All of them had been through similar violence. Sandra, who grew up just across the border in Georgia, told them her father had raped her there for years. When the sheriff was finally called to her house when she was a teenager, he "told my parents to whoop me for lying," she said. At eighteen, Sandra left home and never saw her father again, and went to therapy "to take back my power." Saunders, the radio host, said her father in Alabama had raped her, too, and was never punished because he'd been a sheriff's deputy. "I'm getting back for my father, for my eight-year-old kid, for what happened to me in Jackson County back in 1981," Saunders said, to nods of affirmation all around. "I'm getting my justice, and I'm doing it through Brittany." Paige's mother, Anita, who had made chirpy conversation earlier, her iced wine clanking in a tumbler, narrowed her eyes. She said she was disgusted by how women were treated in the region, "that you're supposed to keep your mouth shut if you're a woman because you don't deserve anything better." She talked about how it was the culture of the South to keep everything hidden, especially domestic abuse.

Anita told me she remembered being at a baseball game when Paige was eight, and how Todd's aunt had joked about the prospect of the two getting married when they were older. Even back then, Anita hadn't found the joke funny. She knew what went on at Todd's house. When Todd and Paige later married in the early 2000s, Anita refused to attend the wedding in protest, because of all the brawls Todd had gotten into around town. She couldn't understand why Paige, who she saw as smart, funny, and personable, would choose him. But she also knew Todd had been the most popular boy in high school with the coolest sports car, and there was no stopping her daughter.

Not long after their wedding, Todd and Paige moved to a mobile home on Monteagle Mountain in southern Tennessee. The plateau was accessible only by one of the most perilous roads in the country, and Anita would later see it as an effort to isolate her daughter. At the time, she had not thought much of it. She did notice that she and Paige no longer spoke every day, which she chalked up to her daughter moving on to a different stage of life. But whenever Anita called Paige and asked her how she was doing, Paige often changed the subject. Her daughter seemed increasingly anxious and withdrawn. One day, Anita realized Paige hadn't called in a while and wasn't answering the phone. Worried, Anita drove up to see her without an invitation.

The mobile home looked peaceful atop the plateau, yet she could not shake the feeling that something was off. According to Anita's account, she knocked on every window and, at first, could not see or hear any movement inside. But she knew Paige was there and Todd was not, because the car was gone and Todd did not let Paige use it, which had always seemed strange to her. Anita banged on the back door. She thought she could faintly hear the sound of a TV. Finally, she caught a glimpse of Paige, sitting on the couch "like in a trance," she said. "And of course, he had beat her up. Her forehead was like out to here." Anita motioned a half hand's width from her forehead. "He bit her, he did all these sadistic . . ." She trailed off. "I mean it took a few minutes of [me] banging and screaming to get Paige to snap out of it," and open the door. "But once she saw me, she said, 'Let's go, Momma, let's go.'" As they left, Anita noticed that the phone cords had been ripped out of the walls.

All these years later, Anita still chided herself for not earlier recognizing the signs of abuse. Perhaps Anita knew what was going on but had not wanted to accept it. After she brought Paige home, Anita said, her daughter filed for divorce, and Todd responded by threatening to kill her. Anita vowed to never let Todd near her daughter again. But Paige soon got work at a nearby restaurant and told her mother that, one day after work, she was meeting Todd at a fast-food joint to get her belongings. When Anita woke up in the middle of the night and Paige hadn't come home, she panicked. Paige told Saunders on the podcast what had happened next: Todd badly beat her, then duct-taped her to a chair and put her in the Tennessee River to drown, until a friend found and saved her.

With Paige missing, Anita sprang into action. "I had a plan, and I didn't tell anyone, not even my husband, because when you plan something like that, it's not a good idea to tell anyone," she told me, her voice dropping conspiratorially low. Anita waited for her husband to go to bed, which he did early, and drove over to her sister's house. She was certain Todd was going to kill Paige, "so I gathered the items [from my sister's] that I needed for my plan to no longer let him hurt her or anyone else."

As Anita drove up the mountain, her sister called Anita's husband to tell him that his wife had made an unusual visit to her house. Anita had almost reached the interstate on her way to Monteagle Mountain when a car flew up behind her. It was her husband, urging her to go back home. But Anita was insistent. They argued and finally decided to drive up to Todd's mobile home together. Paige was sitting, beaten, by the far wall when they walked in. Anita said she picked up a baseball bat and beat Todd with it. Then her husband pistol-whipped Todd with his gun and fired a shot beside Todd's head before breaking the bat over Todd's leg. "But that was nothing," Anita said, compared to the second beating she gave Todd with the shards of the bat, while thinking: *God, that is minimal compared to what you have done to my daughter.*

No police records exist of the 2004 incident. But according to Anita, Todd's injuries were so severe he was taken by helicopter to a hospital, and the local police, perhaps seeing that both sides were at fault—that a kind of frontier justice had taken care of the punishment—told them all to go home. As Nisbett and Cohen explained in *Culture of Honor*, the South was a low-population frontier for a long time, which led its citizens to "create their own system of order," which involved the "rule of retaliation: if you cross me, I will punish you." This appeared true for both men and for women.

When Anita got the phone call years later that Todd was dead, she said she should have felt relief, but all she felt was numb. She cautioned her daughter against getting too wrapped up in Brittany's case, which could be retraumatizing for her. After Paige was interviewed on the podcast, Anita said her daughter began looking sickly and pale. She accompanied Paige to Ramona's barbeque for support but hoped it would be the last involvement her daughter had.

As the party broke up, the women said their goodbyes. "Be careful on your drive home," Anita told Paige, before Ramona walked them all outside.

Just be careful.

After nearly seven months at Bryce Hospital, Brittany was finally released in September 2019. She was taken back to the Jackson County Jail and assigned a bond of $6,000, which Ramona pawned the titles of the family's two old cars and her mother's wedding ring to pay.

Ramona picked up Brittany from jail on a blindingly sunny day, and they went over to Brittany's uncle's house to see the children. As Brittany walked in, her eight-year-old son, the aspiring paleontologist, ran up and told her about all the dinosaurs he'd seen in *Jurassic World 2*. "I even saw the roaring dinosaur!" he said, as Brittany's ten-year-old boy, who was quiet and sensitive, entered the room. When he saw Brittany, he leapt into her arms, causing them both to fall back onto the couch. He held his arms tightly around his mother's neck and did not let go. Brittany closed her eyes, drew him close, and kissed him on the head, until both of them began to cry.

"Here, Mommy," her eight-year-old interjected, holding one of his plastic dinosaurs. Brittany only nodded and held her oldest child tighter.

• • •

Brittany's Stand Your Ground hearing was finally scheduled to take place in January 2020, about two years after the rape and shooting, after the court decided last minute to get Brittany a second court-appointed attorney. Ron Smith, a well-respected attorney from Huntsville, Alabama, joked that he was the "clean-up guy" to bring Brittany's case home, after it had dragged on for nearly two years. He was broad-shouldered, nerdish, and affable, known to be a straight shooter. Brittany felt better with him on her case.

Ahead of Brittany's self-defense hearing, the Jackson County District Attorney's Office made Brittany a last-minute offer. In a letter, the office wrote that, in consultation with Todd's family, they were offering her a plea deal of twenty-five years in prison if she pled guilty to manslaughter. Brittany laughed at the letter, then angrily dismissed it. "I'm not pleading guilty to anything," she told me, especially not with her children watching. "Because I'm innocent, and I will go to jail an innocent woman before I plead out to anything I did not do."

STATE OF ALABAMA V. BRITTANY SMITH

In the seventeenth-century painting "Judith Slaying Holofernes," Judith slits the neck of the general Holofernes because, according to the Bible, he was going to destroy her hometown and her people. In some translations, Holofernes also had been about to come after her with his "uncontrollable desire."

The artist, Artemisia Gentileschi, was herself raped by her mentor and responded by going after him with a knife. At Artemisia's trial in Rome, she was vehement that the rape happened, and that she had reason to fight back, court records show. "E vero, e vero, e vero," she said as they twisted cords around her finger in court to test her honesty. "It is true, it is true, it is true."

The morning of Brittany's Stand Your Ground hearing, January 14, 2020, Ramona set multiple alarms on her phone: a rooster's crow, a police siren, frogs croaking, and the deafening blare of an air-raid horn. She had not been sleeping well, nor had Brittany, so she was afraid they would not wake up in time for court. Ramona dreamt of her parents that night, one hovering over each shoulder. Brittany, who woke up groggily in her mother's side room, also dreamt of her grandmother. MawMaw was laughing in the dream, which Brittany saw as a positive sign.

In recent weeks, Brittany had been gathering geodes from around the Tennessee Valley and chiseling them open to find the crystals that lay inside. It was a meditative practice, something to do instead of falling prey to meth, which old friends had been offering her and which once again seemed tempting. As Brittany got up in her pajamas, her dirty blond hair tangled and eyes swollen from sleep, she selected a few stones from her bedside to bring to the courtroom for luck. Rocks from the earth, hard and solid, would make her feel sturdy on the stand.

When Brittany's mother came to check she was awake—court was in just a couple of hours—Brittany asked her mother what to wear. "Dress to the nines, baby. If you're going out, go out in style," Ramona said. "I'm not going out," Brittany replied, making a face. "I know, baby. I know."

Brittany settled on blue jeans, a flowered shirt, and a loose sweater. She applied light makeup and tied her hair in a single side braid, "like Katniss," the rebellious protagonist of the *Hunger Games*. Katniss foraged in the woods, overcame her painful childhood, and was a protector. "You look gorgeous, honey," Ramona told her daughter. But Brittany didn't want to look gorgeous. "I wanna look . . ." She didn't know how she was supposed to appear. Pretty, but not too pretty. Brave, but also demure. Clean-cut, that much was clear. Her lawyer, Mick, had advised her to cover her tattoos, which she would try to do, even though she found it silly. Her long sleeves would cover much of her ink: four elements to represent her four children; text that read *You are my Sunshine*, because she loved to sing it to her kids at night; and *que será, será*, written on her arm in script, meaning "What will be will be." She got the last tattoo after Baby Will died. She could not do much to cover the pink punk tiara on her neck.

On the car ride to Scottsboro for court, Brittany rolled down her window, lit a cigarette, and blasted a Tupac song about running from the police. Then she switched to a Baptist pop anthem, whose words she belted out the windows. She needed her favorite songs to give her the cocksure strength she'd require in the courtroom. As she and Ramona pulled up to the courthouse, she nodded. She was ready to take the stand.

Courtroom two of the Jackson County Courthouse in Scottsboro has wooden pews, a raised wooden dais for the judge, and large wood windows that were cracked to let in some air. Gold-framed photos of the court's former justices, all white men, hung on the walls. Brittany's lawyer, James Mick, sat on the defense side of the courtroom alongside Brittany's new lead attorney, Ron Smith.

Smith, who lived in the much bigger city of Huntsville, an hour from Stevenson, told me he believed her story was credible and that her shooting of Todd was clear self-defense. "It is extremely consistent with what you would expect a police officer to do if they walked into a situation and somebody was being choked out," he said, because many police forces considered a chokehold deadly force. For days before the hearing, Smith stayed up late finding former case law to support Brittany's self-defense argument, despite the scant funds he was getting to defend her. He was sure they had the law on their side, and that he and Mick just had to convince the judge to see it the same way.

On the other side of the courtroom sat District Attorney Jason Pierce, who was prosecuting the case for the state, and who had previously said Brittany belonged at Bryce because she may have shot Todd out of a "delusion." Pierce wore a royal blue suit and his glossy brown hair combed to one side. He scanned the room and smirked to himself. At a Stand Your Ground hearing, the burden was not on the state but on the defense to prove that Brittany's killing of Todd was justified. Pierce's job was far easier—to make Brittany look guilty. Eric Woodall, the Jackson County investigator who had questioned Brittany when she first confessed to the shooting, the day after it happened, sat beside District Attorney Pierce, ready to help prove the state's case against her.

The pews creaked under the weight of the attendees. Several local and national reporters, including myself, had arrived, and some flipped through notebooks and scribbled text. I had been following Brittany's case for about nine months at this point, and published a lengthy article in the *New Yorker* about her. Local reporters who had written briefs on the case were now following it closely after the increased national attention. In a middle aisle, Brittany's supporters sat scrunched together, including several female friends, some of Ramona's neighbors, Sandra Goodman, Sherrie Saunders, and a few women that nobody knew. Todd's cousin Jeff found a seat off to one side with his nineteen-year-old daughter. Brittany sat up front with her lawyers and averted her eyes as

Jeff entered the room. She hoped the security guards had walked him through a body scanner.

Several other members of Todd's family sat near Jeff but spoke to no one and kept their eyes cast to the ground. Amanda Reed, Todd's ex-girlfriend and the mother of his child, was not in attendance but wrote to me later via Facebook that she wanted people to know Todd was a "good man" and "didn't deserve what happened to him."[*] In a back pew, Sheriff Chuck Phillips and his deputy sat with their arms crossed.

A few people were conspicuously absent from the courtroom. One was Paige Parker, Todd's ex-wife, who could have provided crucial testimony for the defense about Todd's propensity for violence. In recent weeks, Paige had heard through the grapevine that Brittany was a former meth user. After hearing that, along with her mother Anita's concern over her having to relive Todd's abuse, she decided she didn't want to be associated with the case. Another absence—perhaps more acutely felt—was Chris McCallie, Brittany's brother. Chris was a key figure in the case, given that he'd brought his revolver to the scene, and said he was being choked out by Todd when Brittany fired it. But Chris had his own pending charges—for lying to the police about who was the shooter and wiping down the gun—and his attorney for those charges advised him to plead the fifth and not speak. Also, he had a mild learning disability, and Brittany's lawyers worried he could possibly get confused on the stand. So he wasn't at the Stand Your Ground hearing. Chris later told me that, if he had testified, he would have made one point clear: "It was either him or us."

Dawn Hendricks, a private investigator who Smith had hired to help on Brittany's case, sat in an adjoining room preparing witnesses for the defense. Hendricks was a former police officer who had left the force to become an investigator for defense attorneys because she saw that the defense side often needed more help. "I'm for the underdog. I think I've always been for the underdog," she said. Hendricks had short spiky hair, wore tight pastel-colored polos, and carried a mug that read: "Why y'all

---

[*] Todd's aunt, who had custody of his daughter, did not want to comment.

tryin' to test the Jesus in me?" She felt optimistic about what the judge would hear from their witnesses.

But Hendricks also worried about the prosecutor, Pierce. She knew that prosecutors often tried to cast doubt on a female defendant's credibility and that Brittany's drug use, even if unmentioned, would hang heavily over the hearing. After all, Jackson County was small enough that everyone knew everyone's business, and people harshly judged the meth addicts in the county. She believed the fact that Brittany had lost custody of her children would also hurt her. "For a woman to lose their children, you know, you're done," said Hendricks. "You're no good in society anymore." And she thought that Brittany's initial lie about who was the shooter would make her seem dishonest to the prosecutor, who would continuously bring it up.

Still, the principle of self-defense was deeply ingrained in Alabama, whose state motto is: *We Dare Defend Our Rights*. Those words are even emblazoned on the state crest. So Hendricks thought that if they could overcome the gender bias and prove Brittany had been endangered, they had a good shot at winning the Stand Your Ground hearing.

The crowd hushed as Judge Jenifer Holt took her seat at the courtroom's dais. Holt peered over her glasses. She was close to retirement. If she denied Brittany's Stand Your Ground request, she would likely preside over Brittany's murder trial in the coming months, as one of her final cases. It was 1:40 p.m., already ten minutes past starting time. "This is CC-18-323, the State versus Brittany Joyce Smith," she said imperiously. "Are the parties ready?" Pierce, Mick, and Smith affirmed that they were. Brittany inhaled sharply and nodded from her seat.

The first witness to take the stand at the Stand Your Ground hearing was Jeanine Suermann, the sexual assault nurse examiner who had performed Brittany's rape kit exam. The courtroom quieted. Suermann, in her tidy ponytail and neat skirt, described her qualifications to the court. At Crisis Services of North Alabama, she'd performed 112 sexual assault cases, plus 85 other cases that included domestic violence. She was also an emergency room and forensic nurse. Suermann testified that Brittany came to the center early that morning and told the nurse she'd been raped and fought back, that she "scratched him everywhere I could."

Suermann went on to describe the thirty-three injuries she found on Brittany. She spoke in a light, almost bouncy voice, as if not to weigh down the court with the gruesome details. As Suermann spoke about abrasions that were "consistent with a bite mark," a bruise in the shape of a handprint, and findings that indicated strangulation, many people leaned forward from their pews. Suermann also repeatedly mentioned the petechiae—the red, raised patches that can indicate the use of extreme pressure—that dotted Brittany's hairline and neck. As she spoke, photographs of Brittany's injuries were projected on a screen for the court to see. Brittany looked straight ahead or at her feet as the pictures clicked by, willing herself not to cry.

"Your conclusion?" Mick asked. "I feel like she was strangled," Suermann said. "I feel like she's got a lot of contusions and bruises. So I think she was probably hit multiple times and probably held down." Suermann said the injuries were extensive and added that the incident might have left Brittany with PTSD that would impact her for years. Mick asked Suermann if she could say with certainty that Brittany had been sexually assaulted, which was not necessary for Brittany to claim self-defense but would help her credibility. Given that there wasn't a definitive sperm sample, Suermann said she could not. Judge Holt pursed her lips at this. Suermann added that most sexual assault cases had no DNA evidence, so this did not mean much.

For the cross-examination of Suermann, prosecutor Pierce handed things over to his assistant DA, a woman, who listed several reasons not to believe Brittany. She pointed out that Brittany had marked "unsure" on the first page of her rape kit exam about what exactly Todd had done to her, did not urinate for a drug test after the exam, and told Suermann she did not want the rape kit sent to DHR, the agency that took away her children.

Still, Ron Smith felt hopeful after the conclusion of Suermann's two-and-a-half-hour testimony. Brittany's story "was corroborated by her injuries," he said. He thought it was clear to anyone who listened that Todd had been a severe threat. Many in the courtroom appeared shaken by what Suermann described, including Jeff. He left the hearing midway through her testimony with tears in his eyes. "I couldn't take it no more," he said. "It put me in a sick state of mind listening to all that today."

To Brittany, he wrote on Facebook, a year after he had nearly ordered her killed: "I'm sorry from the bottom of my heart."

Two more witnesses—MAPCO cashier Paige Painter and Kayla Pearson, a close friend and neighbor of Ramona's—both called by the defense, testified after the nurse in support of Brittany's story of assault, though Pierce sought to poke holes in their testimony any way he could.

After Painter's testimony about Brittany as a regular and her experience that January night, Kayla Pearson took the stand, wearing a sober expression as she testified that Brittany had been in rough shape when she drove her to the hospital the day after the assault. "I knocked on the door, told Ramona I was there, and then [Brittany] come out," Pearson said. "Then I actually had to pull my car further up to the steps—Brittany was having a hard time getting down the steps to walk to the car. So I pulled my car up further, and she was kind of hunched over. She had two fingers buddy-taped together." Pearson took a deep breath and continued. "At that point, I really didn't see too much, it was dark, and it had been snowing, it was really cold. But she got in the car, and she kept saying that her—like her throat had hurt. And she kept trying to hold her throat, [saying] that when she talked and stuff, it was hurting her. She looked like she had been through a lot."

The testimonies of the nurse, cashier, and neighbor made it indisputable that Brittany had been brutally assaulted. So the assistant DA and Pierce pressed the women instead about whether Brittany really had been raped. Pierce affected a smarmy tone—first wheedling, then insincere, it seemed—as he sought to cast doubt on Brittany's story. Had she specifically said that Todd raped her? *Yes*, Painter, the cashier, said: "I know for a fact she said that to me." But was she sure? Pierce suggested that perhaps she was confused or had only heard that story from Brittany later. Both the cashier and neighbor insisted that Brittany said she'd been raped at the time. Still, Pierce implied, the rape might have been a figment of Brittany's wild imagination—or even a bald-faced lie.

The prosecutor was just getting started.

In criminal court, it has long been debated whether a person's history of misdeeds should be brought up if they are involved in a different crime. Some believe learning about a person's past helps better understand them, while others argue it only prejudices a judge and jury. "Prior bad acts," as they are called, can sometimes be introduced to show a person's character, so long as it is not considered overly prejudicial. Brittany's defense attorneys and the prosecutor sparred during several witness testimonies over whether Todd's prior bad acts could be included.

Pierce did not want the court to hear of Todd's some eighty arrests, half a dozen of which were on domestic violence charges against multiple women, including Todd's ex-wife, Paige Parker. It could only help Brittany's case to hear that Todd had allegedly tied up his ex-wife and raped and sodomized her, and beaten his own father so severely that he kicked Todd out of his home. Brittany's attorneys knew this and had brought in several witnesses to try to establish Todd's penchant for violence. Judge Holt said she would decide on whether Todd's past could be taken into consideration after hearing from some of the witnesses.

One witness who tried to talk about Todd's history was a strawberry blond, freckle-faced woman who had worked as a dispatcher for the Stevenson Police Department. She testified that, in 2009, Todd was brought into the station, came into her office, shoved her against a desk, and tried to rip off her shirt. "If someone hadn't of come in," she said, "I have a feeling it would have gotten pretty bad." She added that Todd was removed from her office at the station but threatened that he'd be back, then afterward periodically stalked the building.

Another witness, a man who grew up with Todd, began telling the court of bruises he'd seen on women that he believed Todd had abused. Pierce objected to the use of this evidence as hearsay, and at the end of his questioning, asked the man what his necklace represented. The man wore a pentagram around his neck, a symbol significant to Wiccans. "I'm into witchcraft," the man said, then paused in confusion at the question. "No further questions," said Pierce, who had told the judge that old, secondhand testimony of Todd's history should not be allowed to continue. The man interjected: "I'm not sure how that has anything to do with my religion."

Ignoring the exchange, Judge Holt agreed with Pierce's argument. Brittany's attorneys visibly deflated. No other witnesses would address Todd's violent past—his arrests, his fights, or his prior domestic violence. For better or worse, Todd and Brittany's interactions would be considered in the vacuum of that night.

Sometimes, a history of abuse isn't presented in a case at all. In 2012, Tracey Grissom, a mother of two, shot her ex-husband, Hunter, in Tuscaloosa, Alabama. Grissom's defense attorney argued Hunter had been abusive ever since Grissom filed for divorce. But eyewitnesses testified that Grissom began shooting Hunter that day without provocation, and the prosecutor argued she'd wanted his life insurance. At Grissom's jury trial, the judge did not allow jurors to hear evidence of her abuse. Her lawyer, Warren Freeman, told me by phone that a friend had taken photographs of Grissom's injuries, which were as extensive as Brittany's, or worse. He sighed heavily as he said the jury never got to see those pictures. When Grissom learned she'd been sentenced to twenty-five years in prison for murder, she wailed in the courtroom: "It's not fair . . . I didn't do anything wrong! All I did was protect myself." Later, a juror said that if she had heard the details of Grissom's abuse, she would have voted to acquit.

When Brittany finally took the stand that January afternoon, a local reporter remembered later, "You could've heard a pin drop in that room." Brittany stared into the middle distance as she raised her hand, then looked at the judge as she swore on the Bible to tell the truth, the whole truth, and nothing but the truth. After she sat down, she took a deep breath, and draped her Katniss braid over one shoulder. "[I'm from] Kimball, Tennessee," she began, and said she was living in Stevenson, Alabama, on January 16, 2018, the morning the shooting happened. "That was my home—my house that I was trying to make a home," she said. Internally, Brittany reminded herself of advice a lawyer friend gave her that week: *Look at the judge when you speak. Keep your answers short and to the point. Don't cry too much.*

As her attorney Ron Smith questioned her, Brittany described meeting Todd to buy the puppy, Todd's call to pick him up from the park in the snow, and talking with him afterward in her living room at home. "I was trying to give him some advice," she testified. "So he gets upset and tells me that I think I'm better than he is. And he—he just kind of went crazy." She described the assault in detail, her voice wavering only a little. "He strangled me until I was unconscious, and I woke up naked and in my own urine . . . He finished having sex with me, he was raping me." She paused on the stand. "And then he got up, and he acted like absolutely nothing was wrong."

When it came time to describe the shooting to the courtroom, Brittany was clear on the key details: she had asked Todd to leave, he threatened to kill her and her brother Chris, and he was choking Chris when she shot the gun. "Were you afraid of Todd?" her lawyer Ron Smith asked her. "Yes," Brittany said. "Were you afraid he would hurt you?" "He did hurt me."

Smith tried his best to preempt questions from the prosecutor that could cast doubt on Brittany's story. He asked Brittany why she would not take the opportunity at MAPCO to tell a police officer, who had apparently been inside the store when she came in. Brittany said she was worried that Todd could see her through the store's glass windows and that she did not trust the police. Smith asked why she would lie at first and say that Chris was the shooter. "I had just been through a traumatic experience, and it came out of my mouth," she said. She had other explanations—the prospect of her kids coming home, the sexism in Jackson County her mom always complained of—but this answer was the simplest and perhaps the truest. She had just been attacked and killed someone, and she'd been terrified of what came next. Smith reminded the court that Brittany went into the police station of her own accord the following day to tell the truth.

Finally, Smith tried to head off questions from Pierce about the rape itself. Smith knew that court cases were not only about the law, they were also about emotion and credibility. He assumed that the prosecutor would continue to try to discredit Brittany's story of sexual assault and that it could influence Judge Holt's Stand Your Ground decision. If Brittany had lied about a couple things, then a judge was more likely to think she was guilty. On the 911 call, Brittany told the operator in a strained voice that Todd had "tried" to rape her—not that he'd been successful, though she also told officers who arrived that night that "he choked me" and "he raped me."

"All right," Smith said to Brittany in a gentle voice. "Now, when you called nine-one-one, do you remember telling them that he had tried to rape you?" She told him she didn't remember the call that well. Smith asked if perhaps she was embarrassed or ashamed for being raped and didn't want to tell the whole world about it. "No, sir. I did not want to tell everybody about it," Brittany said, looking down at her feet. The first time she'd been raped, in her twenties, she had told almost no one, except the nurse for the rape kit exam that went nowhere. "Yes, it's embarrassing," she said, then gazed out at the audience in their pews, as if to say that she was not ashamed anymore.

In the 1970s, decades before Brittany took the stand, two women killed their rapists in high-profile cases in the United States. Inez Garcia, a curly-haired woman of Cuban and Puerto Rican descent, was charged for shooting and killing a man she said had helped rape her in an alley in Soledad, California. Like Brittany, at first Garcia said that the men had attempted to rape her. Later, she said they had raped her, but that she'd felt ashamed to tell the whole story. Garcia was convicted of murder in 1974 and served two years but won on appeal. Marge Piercy, a progressive activist and poet, wrote a poem called "For Inez Garcia" around that time. "The man's body is a weapon, and the woman's / a target," Piercy wrote. "We are trained to give way . . . Speak to the rapist nicely. . . . Kiss the knife."

Also in 1974, a black woman imprisoned in North Carolina named Joan Little killed a white correctional officer who she said had tried to rape her, stabbing him eleven times with an ice pick. Little had grown up in a shantytown, struggling to survive as she cared for nine siblings. Her first criminal charge came at nineteen or twenty. Little, who had a round afro like Angela Davis's—and Davis was a fierce supporter—was charged with first-degree murder and sentenced to death. Around the time of her trial, Little wrote a poem called "I Am Somebody!" in which she wrote that she "killed a white" in self-defense, the jury didn't care, and people were saying she deserved the electric chair. She would do anything to prove her innocence, she added, because "I may be considered the lowest / on earth; but I am somebody!" With the help of the Black Panther Party, who picketed outside the courthouse, Little was ultimately acquitted— likely the first woman to successfully argue in the United States that deadly force was required to defend herself against sexual assault.

In the weeks before Brittany's Stand Your Ground hearing, Ramona told Brittany that she worried about how the judge and Jackson County saw them. "I know they consider me a little nobody in Stevenson," she said, as her daughter put on makeup in the bathroom before her last pretrial hearing. "Because they don't respect females. They don't respect you."

"I don't know what you're talking about," Brittany interrupted, putting down her mascara and turning to face her mother. "I'm somebody."

When it was Pierce's turn to cross-examine Brittany, he languidly walked back and forth before her on the stand. "Good evening," he said, affecting a tone of false politeness, and then asked, "What's sodomy?" Several people gasped at Pierce's first question. Brittany calmly gazed back at him. "It is where someone rapes you in your anus," she said. Pierce asked if she had claimed to be sodomized, and Brittany acknowledged that she had, to online radio host Sherrie Saunders, in a Facebook Live they'd done in addition to the podcasts. The rape kit exam had shown a rash on her anus, and it had been difficult to walk after the assault, as her mother's neighbor, Kayla Pearson, had just testified. Brittany told Pierce that, given the rape kit exam's findings, she thought Todd must have raped her anally while she was passed out. But after listening to the sexual assault nurse examiner's testimony, Brittany understood there was no hard evidence that this happened. To Brittany, though, this wasn't proof it didn't happen. When Pierce asked if she hadn't been truthful, Brittany bristled. "We really don't know if I was or I wasn't," she said with barely disguised contempt.

Pierce was not dissuaded. "Did you know if you had been raped?" he said. "Yes, sir," she said. "Why would you lie about not being raped?" Brittany said she didn't remember the 911 call very well, explaining that she had just been through a "traumatic experience," and later saying: "I have been through some things." The prosecutor again pointed to the moment in the call where Brittany used the word "tried," and, when the operator followed up to ask if she'd been raped, Brittany said no. "But I don't remember the nine-one-one call. I don't remember a lot," Brittany told him. The prosecutor shook his head, as if this was absurd.

As the afternoon wore on, the sun dipping beneath the thicket of Alabama forest out past the courthouse, the prosecutor's interrogation of Brittany only grew more intense. They went back and forth, until finally Pierce told Brittany: "It seems like you have selective memory," implying that she chose what to say she remembered.

It is well-known in the world of victim advocacy that many women don't immediately come forward to say they've been raped. This can happen because of self-blame, not recognizing it as rape, shock, or stigma, which Brittany's defense attorney Smith alluded to when he questioned her. Adde Waggoner, a sexual assault prevention educator at Crisis Services of North Alabama, where Brittany got her exam, could have explained this reality to the court had the defense called her as a witness. "It is [often] too traumatic for [a rape victim] to recognize that what happened to them is rape. They've been in that protective mindset of trying to survive." Waggoner acknowledged that people sometimes make false rape allegations but noted that a person was more likely to be struck by lightning than have a false rape allegation lodged against them.

But Pierce needed to make Brittany look like a liar—and it had already been established that she had lied about who the shooter was—so he carried on. "Are you a truth teller?" he asked. "Yes," Brittany replied. "But you've already lied twice to nine-one-one."

Karla Fischer, a lawyer and psychologist who has testified in more than two hundred cases in which a woman killed an abuser, said prosecutors questioned the credibility of a woman in every case in which she appeared. "There's this idea that if you lie about one thing, then you'll lie about everything. And if you're a liar, you're a murderer," Fischer told me when I presented her with the fact pattern of Brittany's case. She found that train of thinking absurd: "There is a difference between trying to cover up your crime versus not being able to acknowledge it at the moment."

Pierce's cross-examination of Brittany also fixated on why Brittany had called her mother instead of the police, arguing that the decision made no sense. "So somehow you believed your mother would be in a better position to handle violent, angry Todd than a police officer?" he asked, incredulous. Brittany said she didn't believe either would have been well-equipped to handle Todd. "I just feel safe with my mom," she said.

Ramona did not fit any clichéd vision of a soft, nurturing mother. She was broad-shouldered, a brash talker, and fierce when angry. She had confronted Brittany's ex-husband multiple times when he got abusive over the years, and intimidated or beaten him into stopping. She did not find it strange that Brittany called her that night to handle Todd, but neither side had asked her to testify. Brittany reiterated to Pierce that she did not trust the police, and also said that Todd threatened that if she involved the police, he would kill her.

Over the many months I covered Brittany's case, I checked in often with AL.com reporter Ashley Remkus, who was born and grew up in Alabama and had covered crime in the state for years. After the Stand Your Ground hearing, I asked Remkus if she thought Brittany's explanation about not going to the cops made sense. "It's not uncommon, in this part of Alabama, that people would not contact the police because of mistrust in law enforcement, mistrust in authority generally, and [in not] taking women seriously," she said. Several women in the courtroom felt similarly about the police and whispered about it with each other in the pews around me. Paige Painter, the MAPCO clerk, told me that when her father and mother fought when she was a child, her mother was always the one who went to jail. Kayla Pearson, Ramona's neighbor, said the police had not done anything after her ex-husband "stomped my head in" after he got on meth. Sandra Goodman, the rape victim advocate, and

Sherrie Saunders, the podcast host, blamed police officers for not arresting their fathers when they reported sexual abuse as children. It seemed that only the prosecutor, Pierce—and perhaps Judge Holt, too—found it unbelievable that Brittany would not turn to the police for help.

In *Justifiable Homicide*, Cynthia Gillespie wrote that the prosecutor wields two weapons in cases where women kill their abusers: casting doubt on a woman's credibility, and making it seem as if the woman was unreasonable to believe she was in danger. Pierce concluded his interrogation that day by doing both. He reminded Judge Holt that Brittany had lied about the shooter and possibly about being raped. Then he questioned Brittany about how Todd had not had a weapon on him that evening, suggesting the threat was not as grave as she'd believed it to be. "His hands," Brittany interjected. "And his penis. And his mouth . . . I saw several weapons." Her voice rose in defiance. "The thirty-three wounds on my body?"

Holt chided Brittany, saying Pierce got to direct the questioning. "Yes, ma'am," Brittany said, though she was glad she had pushed back. Holt told Brittany she could step down from the stand. It was nearly seven p.m., and the hearing would continue the next day. As the first day of court adjourned, few had any idea whether Brittany would win her Stand Your Ground claim and walk free, or lose and face trial—and potentially life in prison.

Over the past several decades, the incarceration of women in the U.S. has grown at nearly double the rate of men. The Bureau of Prisons estimated that 230,000 women and girls were behind bars as of 2019. By 2020, that number had dropped to about 150,000, due to many incarcerated people being released during the COVID-19 pandemic, though that decline was not expected to continue. Almost two million people remain imprisoned in total in the U.S., more than in any other country. No national data is available on how many women who are, or have been, imprisoned for violent crimes claimed to have been acting in self-defense. For years, this missing number has frustrated women's rights advocates.

One significant study, by the Department of Justice in 2004, surveyed sixty women at a maximum-security prison in the southeast U.S. It found that nearly half of the women said their crime was in self-defense or retaliation after abuse. "The women acted in response to being pushed, slapped, punched, beaten, choked, raped, or threatened with a weapon," the study's author wrote. No group has ever completed an equivalent nationwide study.

In early 2019, freelance journalist Justine van der Leun, frustrated about this lack of data, decided to conduct research on her own beyond just one prison. She sent out 5,098 surveys to incarcerated women across twenty-two states. In a 2020 piece jointly published in *The Appeal* and *The New Republic*, she discussed her findings: at least 30 percent of women serving time for murder or manslaughter said they'd been protecting themselves or someone else from physical or sexual violence, from "men who had broken their ribs, backs, knees, skulls."

Still, this was not a national number. Journalist Rachel Louise Snyder, the author of *No Visible Bruises: What We Don't Know About Domestic Violence Can Kill Us*, suspected that the share of women imprisoned for self-defense was much higher. In collaboration with Stanford University, Snyder is conducting a national census on women incarcerated for killing their abusers, which will take years to complete.

Rachel White-Domain, who heads the Women & Survivors Project at the Illinois Prison Project, which fights to free those who have fought back against violence, estimates that, since the creation of prisons in the United States, tens of thousands of women have been criminalized for defending themselves. She described her clients' experiences this way: "Some have been in constant positions of terror and violence, where it's unsafe to walk to school, where they could be shot, where there is sexual abuse or domestic abuse happening in the home their entire life, where they were homeless as minors or teenagers, or where they form a relationship with the exchange of sex just to live." Eventually, they fought back against these conditions, she said. "Everyone in prison is a survivor."

The "abuse-to-prison pipeline" is today a much-studied phenomenon. A 2010 study on a female Illinois prison population found that, before arriving in prison, an incredible 98 percent of women said they had experienced physical violence, 85 percent had been stalked or emotionally abused, and 75 percent had been sexually abused. A quarter of respondents also said they had experienced trauma symptoms since childhood. A 2006 California prison study on the effects of childhood trauma cited similar numbers, with its authors, two researchers at the University of California, suggesting that "the trauma that results from such abuse is a key contributor . . . to criminality among women."

Karla Fischer, the psychologist and lawyer, sees it differently. She believes it is not that trauma leads to criminality, but that women with a history of abuse may respond more intensely to abuse inflicted upon them. "It's not overreacting," she said. "It's knowing that people will hurt you, that they will follow through on their threats, that certain things done to your body are painful. I think people with a history of violence may be more accurate with their perceptions of what people are capable of."

Fischer said that Brittany's experiences of abuse would have informed how she perceived Todd's violence in the moment. She thought that Brittany's lawyers should have hired a domestic violence expert to testify at Brittany's Stand Your Ground hearing, which could have informed and even influenced Judge Holt's decision. Ron Smith, who was added to the case in September 2019, just four months before the Stand Your Ground hearing, did not have much time to hire experts who could discuss its impacts or present an assessment of Brittany's PTSD, and also thought it was better to save them for trial.

If anyone had asked Brittany in court, she would have had a lot to say about the impact of trauma on her actions that night—she might have talked about being sexually abused as a child by someone she knew well, or her memory of watching her father fight her mother and calling 911 at age four. Though Brittany had mentioned it to a police officer the night she shot Todd, she might have explained more about being raped in her twenties, and how nothing happened when she reported it to law enforcement. And she might have said that several men she dated in Jackson County had turned abusive, as had her husband, culminating with when he threw her off the porch while she was pregnant.

Many studies show that abuse begets experiencing more abuse, and that a person who witnesses or experiences abuse as a child is more likely to face violence later in life. Some experts suggest women are at risk of revictimization because of low self-esteem or because violent behavior has been normalized for them as a way that people address conflict, though if women receive mental health support, they are more likely to recover from abuse-related trauma. Brittany only sporadically had access to counseling over the years—it was not something she could usually afford.

Without anyone to explain the impact of abuse and trauma on Brittany, she would have to try and convey it to the judge on her own.

Before entering the Scottsboro, Alabama, courthouse for the second day of her Stand Your Ground hearing, Brittany read aloud from a book of daily wisdom based on Bible verses. "You are surrounded by a sea of problems," the entry read. "The future is a phantom seeking to spook you." She swore to herself not to be spooked—not by the prosecutor, any of the witnesses, or the judge. She told herself she would keep speaking confidently and not cry.

The courtroom was as packed as it had been the day before. Brittany again braided her hair to one side like Katniss. Pierce wore what appeared to be the same blue suit. The defense had called two forensic experts, and the prosecution was putting two police officers on the stand. Photographs were projected early on in the day showing Brittany's kitchen (where Todd and Chris fought, with beer bottles overflowing in the trash), her bedroom (her bed a tangled mess after the assault), and her hands (which were bruised and cut). A photo was also shown of Todd Smith lying dead on the floor.

In the absence of an expert on domestic or sexual abuse to testify about its effects, Brittany, who was back on the stand, tried to explain the reality of trauma on her own. "It was also explained to me at Bryce that, you know, PTSD—" she began, before Pierce objected that the comment was offhand. It would be one of the only mentions of Brittany's time at Bryce Hospital, as if her seven-month stay at a psychiatric hospital hadn't meant much. Pierce focused far more on her texts from the night of the shooting, especially one exchange between Brittany and her mother:

BRITTANY: "Mom, Todd has tried to kill me literally. Don't act like anything is wrong. Call MAPCO and ask for Paige . . . He will kill me if he knows."

RAMONA: "Okay. Where is your brother?"

BRITTANY: "I'm fine. He is leaving . . . Don't come over here, please."

RAMONA: "If you would quit this bullshit your kids would be home in no time."

Don't come over here, please. There it was in print, Pierce suggested. Brittany had told her number one protector, her mother, not to come over. Wasn't that suspicious? And also: *If you would quit this bullshit your kids would be home in no time.* Ramona, who was never called as a witness, told me that by "bullshit" she meant Brittany was hanging out with addicts again—often a prelude to a relapse, or indicative that she had already backslid. *If you want to get bit by a shark, jump in an ocean full of them,* her father had said.

After lingering on the exchange for a while—texts that made Brittany look like a woman who had brought this upon herself—along with other texts from the night, Pierce said he had no further questions.

Karen Hart Valencia, a senior forensic scientist in the toxicology section of the Alabama Department of Forensic Sciences, blinked with seeming uncertainty as she got up on the witness stand. Her job was to receive evidence from coroners and police and write reports, and she was only occasionally called to testify in court. But it made sense that she'd been called for this case. Although Todd had been just over the legal limit for alcohol and taken only a therapeutic dose of Xanax, his level of methamphetamine was four times what police officers or toxicologists like her typically saw in a DUI case.

Valencia testified that there was no safe level of meth but that the amount Todd had taken was considered a "very high amount." Ron Smith, Brittany's defense attorney, tried to get Valencia to illustrate just how dangerous that would make Todd. "Would methamphetamine cause somebody to be more aggressive?" "Yes," she said. "Combative?" he went on. "Yes." "Are they able to go days without sleep?" "Correct, yes." Smith, who generally did not rely on emotion, allowed a little drama to seep into his line of questioning. Emphasizing how much meth Todd took that night was essential to show he'd been a serious threat.

"Have you seen hypothetical situations," Smith then asked the forensic scientist, "or read reports, or are familiar with situations where somebody has struggled with law enforcement and they're being tased, fighting, and they just keep fighting and they're not feeling anything?" He asked if that was consistent with a person using meth. "Yes," Valencia replied. "Several officers tased the person, restrained them, and—and it takes several to—to bring them down?" "Yes." Valencia nodded, then summed up Smith's argument for him: "Somebody who's doing methamphetamine would be more likely to get in a fight and . . . and keep fighting."

It was a visceral picture: Todd, extremely high on meth, aggressive, combative, wired, and able to fight like the Terminator. It was consistent with how Brittany described his behavior that night, especially the testimony that when she shot him, it at first didn't seem as if he was hit. "All right," Smith said, satisfied. "That's all I have."

The other forensic witness, Angela Fletcher, was also a scientist at the Alabama Department of Forensic Sciences. She spoke blandly, with little modulation to her voice, perhaps to avoid any appearance of bias. She was called to testify about the DNA at the scene, which notably did not include Todd's semen. She was also there to explain why the department initially said Brittany's fingernails did not show Todd's—or anyone's—DNA beneath them. This made little sense if Brittany had "scratched him everywhere I could," as Brittany had testified. Just days before the Stand Your Ground hearing, the department sent a letter to the court saying they'd made a mistake and debris was found under Brittany's nails after all. Fletcher said they noticed the error in an internal review. A local blogger whispered to me that this oversight was no surprise, given that the Alabama Department of Forensic Sciences had suffered from backlogs, closed labs, and numerous errors in recent years, which he and other local media had reported on. He said it begged the question of what else the department had missed in Brittany's case. Fletcher offered that they could retest the debris, but not until Brittany's Stand Your Ground hearing was over.

As Fletcher finished, Brittany felt her mistrust of the judicial process deepen. She thought that if examiners made an error with the DNA under her fingernails, they could have missed Todd's semen, too.

The prosecution rested its case by bringing in two witnesses of their own: Eric Woodall, the lead investigator who had questioned Brittany, a thin man with a weasel-like face, and the investigator who worked beneath him on the case, who had interviewed Chris. Both men testified that they did not see any marks on Chris's neck that night to suggest Todd choked him, though it seemed an oversight that no one had taken any close-up photographs of Chris or his neck that night to document any injuries. They displayed just one blurry photo. Woodall also testified that he had not seen any urine on Brittany's sheets, contradicting her testimony and statements to the nurse that she peed on herself when Todd strangled her.

Pierce closed with what he likely hoped was a triumphant parting shot. He asked Woodall about a pivotal moment in Brittany's interview with him, when she described how, at one point, Todd and Chris fell to the floor. "So [Todd] was actually on the ground [when Brittany shot him]?" Pierce asked. It wasn't entirely clear that she did, but if Brittany had shot Todd while he was lying on the ground, it would be difficult for her to claim self-defense. Self-defense law had narrow guidelines, and someone lying down was not generally considered an imminent threat.

Judge Holt mostly stayed quiet as the parade of witnesses took the stand, and spoke up to respond to objections. Now she told the attorneys they could make their closing arguments, their last chance to convince her of whether Brittany should face trial or go free.

"We believe we have met the burden of proof" that Brittany was standing her ground, Ron Smith said, resuming his professorial tone. To him, the justice system should not be about persuasion or narratives but sticking to the letter of the law. He maintained that the law was on Brittany's side. "She was justified in her actions," he went on. "She believed Todd . . . was going to cause serious bodily injury to herself or her brother."

Smith then introduced what he hoped would be an indisputable legal argument, one he'd come up with only that week. According to Alabama law, any person who stayed in a home after being asked to leave was considered a burglar, which meant that Todd burglarized Brittany. Even if Judge Holt doubted Brittany was raped, Smith hoped that she could accept a more well-trodden self-defense argument, and a more masculine one—that Brittany was justified in protecting her home.

"[Todd] was told to leave. He did not leave. He unlawfully remained after instructed," Smith said, noting that Stand Your Ground applies to a burglary. Smith rattled off several cases in which defendants were exonerated for killing those who burglarized their home. He shuffled his papers as he looked for case names, seeming lost before again gaining momentum. "Once you start struggling with the owner of the property or the tenant of the property . . . there is an implicit revocation of your permission to be there. So we'd argue that that's what happened in this case," he said. Brittany "was justified in her actions."

Pierce grinned at Smith's last-ditch attempt. The prosecutor closed by arguing that Brittany's brother, Chris, was the initial aggressor for introducing a gun, not Todd. He again questioned Brittany's judgment of the seriousness of the threat. "Alabama law establishes that hands and fists do not qualify as deadly weapons," Pierce said, though Smith interrupted him to point out that Alabama case law was not settled on that. Either way, victim advocates might consider Pierce's argument a sexist one, because men more often use hands and fists in domestic violence homicides, while women who defend themselves often resort to knives or guns.

Finally, Pierce once again questioned Brittany's trustworthiness. "The other issues that the State would note would be the . . . the lack of credibility" of Brittany, he said, "and a complete and utter lack of injuries to Christopher McCallie despite the claims that he was having the hell beat out of him at the time she fired the shots."

Holt thanked both lawyers. She said she'd allow the fingernail clippings to be tested for DNA, consider the evidence, and make her decision. The crowd got up from their pews and shuffled out of the courthouse into the blinding midafternoon sunshine, no one quite certain of the impending outcome.

After the hearing, a young woman who was an old friend of Brittany's stood, looking distraught, outside the Jackson County Courthouse. When I approached her, she told me she was shaken by seeing what Brittany went through on the stand, and not just because they'd been friends as kids. It hit closer to home, the woman said, because she had an ex-boyfriend who had turned abusive, once putting her head under a tire while his friend revved the engine. He also held a phone line around her neck, threatened her with a knife, and "cold-cocked me in the face," she said. She'd considered defending herself at the time but was worried that she would be the one arrested. Now, she was glad she hadn't. "What would happen if I'd shot him?" she asked, shaking her ponytail. She asked me not to publish her name because she was still afraid the man would come after her.

At home in Stevenson that afternoon, Brittany was frustrated and worried that the judge did not seem to believe her. "They don't do anything around here for rape victims. That's why nobody tells," she told me. Ramona was infuriated and posted on Facebook: "We all know that the Stand Your Ground Law was not created for women." But Dawn Hendricks, the investigator for the defense, cautioned them not to make any hasty conclusions. To her, the witnesses made clear that Brittany had been in danger and was defending herself against Todd. After all, self-defense was woven into the fabric of the state. *We Dare Defend Our Rights. If you cross me, I will punish you.* Hendricks thought Judge Holt might announce the outcome the following morning and told them to reserve judgment until then. But the judge did not decide the following morning, the morning after, or the morning after that.

PROTECTION

They say that Neptune, lord of the seas, violated [Medusa] in the temple of Minerva . . . So that it might not go unpunished, [Minerva] changed the Gorgon's hair to foul snakes. And now, to terrify her enemies, numbing them with fear, the goddess wears the snakes, that she created, as a breastplate.

—Ovid's *Metamorphoses*, published in 8 A.D., translated in 2004 by Anthony S. Kline

Weeks passed before Judge Jenifer Holt ruled on Brittany's Stand Your Ground claim. The case had increasingly drawn media attention, both local and national, and comments of support for Brittany poured in on Facebook: "I have fought these same type[s] of people . . . my heart goes out to [her] because I know that fear and desperat[ion] way to[o] well," one woman wrote. "I've been raped, I know the dangers and the scars," added another. "If we can't defend ourselves when being harmed in such a cruel way, why do we have rules, laws and constitutions [?]" . . . "I'm a domestic violence survivor and the police never helped me either. This is wrong on so many levels. I pray she gets justice soon!" . . . "I admire the lady for doing what she did!"

Brittany was amazed at how many people were reaching out to her from "different backgrounds, races, and sexualities," to tell her they'd been abused and the police hadn't responded. Ramona closely followed the reaction online. It was January 2020, about two years since Todd's shooting, and that winter Ramona slept under four blankets at night, one a weighted blanket to calm her. She kept thinking about how people in the county viewed them as "little nobodies," as she described it—but little nobodies who now had supporters all over the world. "When you get a ton of little nobodies together, especially pissed-off women . . ." Ramona said, "they become somebody big. We are somebody, we have a voice, [and] we're fixin' to use it."

Even Jeff decided that he wanted Brittany to win her Stand Your Ground claim. "Probably feels funny for me saying that," he said, considering that he was Todd's cousin and had wanted her dead. But he didn't want to see her go to prison, not after hearing the testimony of the nurse examiner. Paige Painter, the MAPCO cashier, felt even more strongly that Brittany should win her claim. She said that if Brittany were found guilty and sent to prison, she'd lose all trust in the criminal justice system and the local people who ran it.

Despite the groundswell of support and media attention, Ramona worried that Judge Holt did not seem convinced by the testimony presented at the hearing. Ramona obsessed over inconsistencies she'd noticed: *Did the sexual assault nurse use Toluidine blue [a solution used to detect genital and perianal injuries] when she evaluated Brittany? Had the detective grabbed the right bedsheets? What more did the police know about Todd that they weren't telling? How could they have missed the DNA under her fingernails? If they had missed that, what else had they overlooked?*

Ramona grew more pessimistic as the weeks passed, while Brittany tried to think positively. She kept telling herself that it would work out. *They're not going to break me*, Brittany told herself, and repeated self-help mantras she watched on YouTube in the mornings. That winter, Brittany made her children a colorful poster in cursive lettering that read "You are my sunshine" to remind them of the song she used to sing them to sleep. At night, to keep herself from worrying, she sat in her mother's side room and chiseled away at her rocks, working to find the glitter of the crystals beneath.

As Brittany, Ramona, and Chris awaited the judge's ruling, the cracks at home began to show. The whole public housing project got bedbugs, but the weather was too cold and its residents too poor to throw out the plagued mattresses and blankets. Chris had lost his gig cleaning restaurants at night. Their apartment, which had just one bathroom and two small bedrooms, was too cramped for three adults, so Chris slept on the couch in the living room. Chris and Brittany began to bicker, and Brittany and Ramona fought, too. The house easily got messy, since Ramona could not stay on her feet long enough, and Chris and Brittany rarely cleaned it. The longer they were all at home, the more Ramona felt like they were "rats in a cage."

One day, Brittany suggested they all get out of the house and visit a local waterfall and take a hike. Everyone was excited on the ride over, but once they arrived, Ramona could barely reach the bottom of the falls because of pain in her sciatic nerve, and Chris heaved from too many cigarettes. Only Brittany had the energy to run down and dive into the freezing water pooling around the falls, then climb atop the giant rocks beside them.

Not long after the bedbugs, Chris and Brittany were driving home from the store when they got into a bad fight. Later, neither could say how the dispute started, though it was most likely over Jeff, Todd's cousin. Jeff had started coming by the house in the weeks after the hearing, and he and Brittany had struck up an unlikely friendship, with Todd's death serving as a strange but powerful link between them. Ramona and Chris distrusted Jeff, considering he had wanted to kill Brittany, but Brittany insisted it was healing to be around him. One night, she and Jeff gave each other matching DIY tattoos, symbolic representations of a verse from the Book of Corinthians in the King James Bible: "Therefore if any man be in Christ, he is a new creation: old things are passed away, all things are become new." They both wanted desperately to be reborn.

In recent weeks, Brittany and Chris had also been fighting about who was responsible for Todd's death. Brittany sometimes blamed Chris for showing up at her house with his gun and firing it first. "Well, I knew where I was aiming," he replied.

One of these conflicts—neither could remember which—came to a breaking point in the car one afternoon in February. Brittany threw her iced coffee at Chris, and Chris punched her in the mouth. Brittany began bleeding from her gums. She called the police to report the assault, which angered Ramona. The family had enough problems, and if Brittany pressed charges, she knew both her children might soon be in jail. Brittany could not believe her mother's reaction.

"Is it okay for him to hit me and make me bleed? So it's okay?" Brittany asked in a mutinous voice, as the two of them waited on the front porch for the cops to arrive. Chris had retreated into the house. "This is a family," Ramona told her, as if to remind her that family problems should be solved at home. "No, it's not," said Brittany, meaning not a functional one. "Not when I'm bleeding like this, and my head's busted up, no." Ramona asked if she wanted to see her brother go to jail. "No, but I don't want him thinking it's okay to abuse women for no fucking reason." Brittany spat out her words. "He's not going to," Ramona said.

"He just did."

The minutes ticked by, and no police officers arrived. Brittany began to cry. "Momma what was I supposed to do?" she asked plaintively. "Let him keep beating me?" Ramona, fed up, told Brittany to be quiet. Later, Ramona could not explain exactly what she was thinking that afternoon, which bled into evening. Perhaps she'd felt that Brittany was at fault for starting the fight, or that too much drama followed her daughter. Perhaps she was just exhausted from trying to keep both her children from behind bars.

In the movie *The Burning Bed*, when the daughter tells her mother about her husband's abuse, her mother replies, "If you make a hard bed, you have to lay in it."

That February 2020, Judge Holt finally issued her ruling: a nineteen-page document denying Brittany's Stand Your Ground request. "The defendant did not credibly demonstrate that she reasonably believed it was necessary for her to use deadly force in this situation," the judge wrote, and spent pages explaining her decision. I called AL.com reporter Ashley Remkus to ask what she thought of Holt's ruling. "Well, she basically said Brittany was a liar," Remkus told me, adding that she'd never seen a judge go out of her way in a lengthy ruling that way. But Remkus also thought it made sense with the huge spotlight on the judge from all the media coverage. Many of her readers were upset with Holt and people were calling for her firing, so she said perhaps the judge was trying to defend her reputation.* My story in the *New Yorker* had argued that women with persuasive self-defense claims were being criminalized and treated as murderers, and many of the other stories on Brittany that followed had the same take. But to Holt, Brittany's self-defense claim was not persuasive.

In her ruling, Holt wrote that Brittany had provided "inconsistent accounts of the events surrounding Todd's death," given that at first she lied about who the shooter was. She argued that Brittany had "many opportunities to seek protection from Todd if she was afraid he was going to kill or harm her," even though Brittany had testified that she didn't trust the police. And, although Brittany had proof she was physically assaulted, which was enough for a self-defense claim, Holt made clear that she doubted that Brittany was raped. The judge argued that the physical evidence was inconsistent with a sexual assault, despite the nurse's testimony that a lack of DNA was common in a rape case. Many judges are not trauma-informed, meaning that their rulings on domestic and sexual abuse cases often rely on their personal perceptions instead of the realities of violence. Holt appeared to be no different.

Brittany was asleep when the ruling came in. She had been oversleeping ever since the Stand Your Ground hearing. Ramona was incensed over the verdict but didn't wake Brittany to tell her. She wanted her daughter to stay blithely unaware for as long as she could. Ramona believed this never would have happened if Brittany was a white man. She still thought that if Chris had shot the gun, he never would have been arrested. Online, Ramona watched thousands of angry comments pour in in response to the ruling.

When Brittany finally woke up, she tried not to lose her composure. She said she was prepared for a no, but then began crying. "She saw the pictures of me; he almost beat me to death, he did rape me, and he tried to kill my brother," she said. "So how can she say this?" According to a

---

* Judge Holt declined to comment on the case beyond her ruling.

2020 *Arizona Law Review* report called "Retraumatized in Court," some 60 percent of surveyed lawyers said their clients were retraumatized by the "behavior, statements or actions of court personnel."

Dawn Hendricks, the investigator for Brittany's defense, was upset but not shocked by the outcome, given her law enforcement experience in Alabama. Still, she had hoped for better. "Typically, in the South, in Stand Your Ground, it's men standing up and protecting their life, liberty, property, and all of this that we've always heard," Hendricks said. "Men get praise for that, standing up and protecting themselves. Where, if a woman does that, or a minority, it's viewed a lot different." Her voice took on a frustrated resignation. "You say it's okay for women to defend themselves, but when they do, be ready for what society has for you." Hendricks did not think that self-defense laws needed to change, but instead, society's perception of what a woman should be—that a woman shouldn't ever be violent.

Karla Fischer, the domestic violence expert who testifies in cases of women who kill abusers, believed the problem was more systemic. Prosecutors and judges are mostly elected, and few want to be perceived as soft on violent crime. Holt seemed to have positioned herself as a law-and-order judge, telling the *Jackson County Sentinel* just before retirement that a case in which she put a man on death row was the "most important case I presided over." Holt also told the paper that she "always felt comfortable with my decisions" over the course of her twenty-four-year career, something I found unnerving given the weighty impact of the decisions judges make, and how drastically our perspectives on criminal justice as a nation have changed over the years. Holt maintained a Twitter account with a photo of herself in her judge's robes, but mostly tweeted her opinions about Alabama football.

Multiple Jackson County residents told me they felt Holt had ruled against Brittany because Brittany was a meth addict who'd appeared in court on petty drug crimes before. They said judges and prosecutors saw addicts in the county in a certain light: *Addicts committed crimes. Addicts lied.* Fischer said that women like Brittany, who are both a criminal defendant and a victim of abuse, "get stuck" in the defendant category by those same prosecutors and judges, because the criminal legal system does not allow a person to be both. Outside of Jackson County, readers fixated on the fact that a female judge had denied Brittany's claim, saying that she must have internalized misogyny.

Judges at rape trials, both male and female, have continuously shown that they are well behind the times. At a California trial in 2008, Superior Court Judge Derek Johnson said that if a woman did not want to have sex, "the body shuts down . . . the victim in this case, although she wasn't necessarily willing, she didn't put up a fight." In Canada in 2014, Alberta Federal Court Judge Robin Camp asked a rape victim, "Why couldn't you just keep your knees together?" Two years later in New Jersey, state Superior Court Judge John Russo asked a woman who had been raped if she knew how to fend off a sexual assault. "[Did you] close your legs?" he asked. "Call the police? Did you do any of those things?" Like Brittany, the woman had not called law enforcement until later on.

At Brittany's trial, she'd face a panel of jurors from Jackson County—before the same Judge Holt.

While Brittany prepared for trial, women from around the country reached out to her by social media, email, letter, and phone. Amy Herrera, who was charged with murder in 2012 for shooting and killing a husband she said was abusive, wrote Brittany from Albuquerque, New Mexico. "To Brittany: You seem like a very strong woman, and that will serve you well in whatever comes next," she wrote me by email, to pass on to Brittany. "But I also know that strength doesn't mean you don't have those moments . . . I know what it's like to think about the injustice of having barely survived your abuser just to be threatened with having that same life taken away by being imprisoned." Herrera had claimed self-defense and fought a five-year legal battle. She said she was very sorry Brittany would have to go through a trial, but that she was "so worth the battle."

Herrera was ultimately acquitted in 2017. She told me this was, in part, because she could afford a private attorney, who found every legal issue and loophole. She knew Brittany did not have the same luxury.

Debi Zuver, a California woman who was incarcerated for some fifteen years for shooting and killing her abusive boyfriend in the year 2000, also asked me to send Brittany a message around the same time. Zuver had only recently been released from prison, and her voice was soft, fragile, and measured on the phone. She lived in a small apartment in San Francisco, and it had been a challenging year and a half of freedom. "I'm still learning how to navigate this world, safe boundaries, who to trust, red flags, warnings, and all the things I thought I knew," she said. When she read about Brittany's case, she felt the shock of recognition. Like Brittany, she had difficulty fully remembering the night of the shooting. To her, it was "in bits and pieces like a broken movie," which did not help Zuver at her trial. She said when she was up for parole, she was diagnosed with mental health issues—she also believed wrongly—and narrowly avoided being sent to a state-run hospital, as Brittany had been.

"Be precisely who you are, always speak your truth, and be fearless," Zuver told me in a message for Brittany, "because at the end of the day, we are the only ones who know who we are." After all she'd been through, Zuver said she believed she was made of a steel equivalent to *The Sword in the Stone*—"That beautiful, perfect steel that only a certain few can extract."

Sometimes, Zuver said, she could not believe that she was not still in her twenties, dating a man who beat her, with her world about to collapse. She was older now, and she was free; she had a job at a restaurant, an apartment, a driver's license, and a car. It would be a long process for Brittany to get to that point, but she believed Brittany would. "Tell her we are all phoenixes, and we were born to burn," Zuver said finally, "and then we rise, and we make our own."

Both Amy Herrera and Debi Zuver no longer used those first names. They'd adopted new ones, perhaps because too much of their information was online, or their old names no longer fit them. They were different women now—women transformed.

Alabama, New Mexico, and California are not unique in criminalizing women who kill abusive men. It happens in every state in the U.S., and to every kind of woman, though it happens to vulnerable women the most. Many have heard the name Cyntoia Brown, who killed a man who bought her for sex as a teen and spent fifteen years in prison until Tennessee's governor famously granted her clemency in 2019. Far fewer have heard of Alisha Walker, a sex worker who stabbed a client in Chicago after he came at her with a knife because, she said, she wanted him to wear a condom, and he didn't. Walker spent five years behind bars.

It is overwhelming how many women in the U.S. who have claimed self-defense have served so much time. The names and stories could go on like an endless scroll. CeCe McDonald, a black trans woman who stabbed a man she said assaulted her and her friends on the streets of Minneapolis, was charged with murder, then second-degree manslaughter, and took a plea deal of forty-one months. Willie Mae Harris, who is blind, was serving a life sentence in Arkansas for shooting and killing a husband she said was abusive before she got a commutation after thirty-four years. Tewkunzi Green, a mother from Illinois, served thirteen years for stabbing to death a boyfriend she said had abused her; her mother had also killed an alleged abuser. At an advocacy event after she was freed, Green said, "It hurts your soul to have to defend your life because someone is beating on you, and you asked someone to just leave you alone."

Men are also criminalized for fighting back, though far less often. David Garlock and his brother killed a man who he said sexually abused them for years as children, starting when Garlock was eleven. They were sentenced to twenty-five years. "Should my brother and I be punished?" Garlock told me by phone, years after his release. "Yes. Is twenty-five years excessive? Yes. We were trying to escape; he had tried to kill us numerous times . . . The system wants to only view you as a victim or an offender."

Many of the stories were of women who were imperfect victims in the eyes of the court, like Brittany. Take Colville tribal member Maddesyn George, who shot and killed a man she said had raped her, just like Brittany, and afterward stole his gun and his methamphetamine. George pled guilty to manslaughter, for a sentence of six and a half years. "The big dilemma in criminalized self-defense," Rachel White-Domain of the

Women & Survivors Project told me, "is: Are we saying this [action] is not criminal? Or not worthy of prosecution? Or something we can mitigate? Or a crime, but the person doesn't deserve as much punishment?"

Outside of the United States, the answers to these questions are just as mixed. Often, women are absolved if enough people speak up on their behalf. British woman Sally Challen, who beat her husband to death with a hammer after decades of coercive control, was sentenced to life in prison for murder until a public outcry saw her conviction overturned in 2019, and she was freed. In South Africa, a woman who became known in the national media as "Lion Mama" was charged in 2017 with murder for stabbing to death one of three men who were in the middle of raping her daughter (she wounded the other two), until collective outrage led her charges to be dropped. Yakiri Rubio, who slashed her rapist's throat in Mexico after he abducted her, was charged with murder and imprisoned until, in 2014, her case drew international coverage and her action was instead deemed "excess of legitimate self-defense."

There are many more stories—too many to count. Some women don't make it through at all. In 2011 in Saudi Arabia, an Indonesian housekeeper named Tuti Tursilawati was sentenced to death for killing her abusive employer, who she said was sexually and physically abusing her. Tursilawati was beheaded in 2018.

Others rot away in prison, even if they are heroines in the public eye. In Turkey, Nevin Yildirim remains behind bars serving a life sentence for cutting off the head of a man who she said repeatedly raped and then impregnated her; afterward, she threw his head in a sack in the village square and declared: "Here is the head of the one who stained my honor." When she was sentenced to life in 2015, women appeared throughout central Istanbul carrying sheets with Yildirim's face, and banners that read: *Nevin's voice is our voice.*

After learning of the judge's ruling, Brittany's defense attorneys immediately began preparing a response. In March 2020, Ron Smith filed a "writ of mandamus"—an action similar to an appeal, but in this case for Stand Your Ground claims—to the Court of Criminal Appeals of

Alabama. It was a long-shot request to the court to order Judge Holt to reverse her decision.

If Brittany lost that, her lawyers would make the same appeal to the Alabama Supreme Court. Smith argued in his request that Holt "made findings of fact that are not supported by the record" and that the majority of the evidence indicated the shooting was in self-defense. "Brittany shot and killed a man who was in the process of attacking her brother," Smith wrote. "This was the same man who had strangled, beaten, and raped her only hours earlier."

Around the same time, Brittany received word that the fingernail clippings had been tested. Todd's DNA had been found in the newly discovered debris underneath her fingernails after all, supporting her testimony that she had scratched and clawed at Todd while he assaulted her. But it was too late for her Stand Your Ground claim, and the prosecution argued this should hardly matter.

As months passed, waiting for the appeals court to decide, Ramona, Chris, and Brittany tried to resume their old life in Stevenson. COVID-19 had swept the country and the world, but Jackson County largely ignored the pandemic that spring, with few people wearing masks. The three of them preferred to stay home anyway. They fought less now that the appeal process was in motion, each of them hanging on to that modicum of hope. Ramona sat outside in the warming weather and gossiped with her neighbors, who often migrated to her porch, and who had hung up a sign that read "Front Porch Therapy: Free."

Since the shooting, Chris had developed a habit of sleeping all day. He played video games at night, often in the realm of horror or survival. He particularly liked *Left 4 Dead 2*, a survival first-person shooter game that was cathartic to him for its faraway violence. Fighting hordes of zombies helped him process what happened with Todd and stop screaming in his sleep. Both of Chris's charges still loomed: one for tampering with evidence, because he'd wiped down the gun after Brittany shot it, and another for falsely stating he was the shooter. He assumed his charges would get handled after Brittany's trial concluded. One afternoon, Chris left the house to get a tattoo of Optimus Prime, the hero Autobot from *Transformers*. "Everyone likes the evil Transformer because it's more fun, but I wanted the good one," Chris told me, as a reminder of who he was or hoped to be.

Brittany saw her children as much as she could. Her older daughter, blond-haired and rosy-cheeked, drove a pink plastic car across Brittany's uncle's yard as Brittany ran alongside her, screeching along in excitement. The two boys told her all about the other kids and their classes at school. Her baby girl showed her mom her dance moves to the latest pop songs, her wild black curls bouncing. One afternoon, Brittany visited the cemetery where her lost baby, Will, was buried and ran so hard and long afterward that she felt she could not breathe.

After these visits, Brittany went hunting for more rocks, fossils, and arrowheads to avoid relapsing on the drugs that were all over Stevenson. Cherokee, Chickasaw, and Creek people had collectively lived in the Tennessee Valley for thousands of years before European Americans forced many of them West—MawMaw had been half Cherokee—so arrowheads were not impossible to find. Brittany stayed up late at night sorting them. After the trial was over, if she went free, she planned to open a New Age–style store that sold healing crystals and gemstones, Tibetan prayer gongs, books on numerology and chakras, and more. Several women at Bryce had introduced her to this world, which brought her solace in addition to the Christian faith she'd grown up with. She said she wanted to help others the same way.

That month, an old friend of Brittany's came by Ramona's house and offered Brittany meth, and Brittany considered it. Meth could make her forget about the rape, Todd's face after the shooting, and his body lying dead on the floor. Meth could take her to a place where the trial was no longer on the horizon, and all she could feel was confidence. Instead, she told her friend to throw it out the window. She had relapsed before and would again, but she was free for that one day. Instead of doing drugs, she went to the river with Michael, a new man she was dating with round glasses and a quiet way about him. He was a carpenter whom Brittany had met when she asked him to engrave a hammer for her dad, Ricky, as a gift for Father's Day. Brittany liked Michael's woodwork and his kindly smile, and they soon began hanging out.

It was peaceful at the river, with the gurgling water and worn-down stones on the sandy shore. Brittany took off her shoes and put her feet in the water as Michael wandered nearby and butterflies fluttered over-head. She thought of her most recent visit with her children, when her older son told her about a dream "where the whole world got covered in dust, and the children saved the world from all the bad things." She kept thinking: *How did he get so smart?*

By August 2020, Brittany had lost both her appeals. She said James Mick, her original lawyer, who was still on the case, suggested again that she take a plea deal for manslaughter to avoid trial. Brittany was again incensed by the idea. A few years prior, a Jackson County woman named Tammy Keel had killed her husband by shooting him, burning his body, running him over, dragging him behind her vehicle, and setting the car on fire. Keel pled guilty to manslaughter after saying her husband had threatened her with a rock. Brittany did not think their cases were re-motely comparable. She told Mick she'd never take a guilty plea.

Meanwhile Brittany's lead lawyer, Ron Smith, began preparing for Brittany's trial. This time, he found a local therapist specializing in PTSD, whose testimony could explain why Brittany acted the way she did. Brittany took a lengthy test at the therapist's office with many an-swer bubbles to fill in. She was afraid to honestly answer questions such as "I think someone's after me," as she had with the state psychologist who sent her to Bryce, because she saw where that had gotten her before.

Then, in September 2020, Brittany failed a drug test. She had been mandated to take them throughout the long wait for trial and had not tested positive once. Now, she tested positive for methamphetamine and alcohol. She claimed she had not taken anything, and Ramona backed her story, because the drug testing company that administered the tests was known for giving people false positives. But some of her old drug friends had started coming around, the stress was enormous, and it was likely she had begun using again. Her history of trauma and addiction, combined with her learned distrust of the police, judicial, and health systems, had steamrolled over the smart, confident, and frank girl who lay beneath, leaving an uncertain and not always candid woman in its place. When Brittany made a mistake, her first impulse was often to guard and obscure, but she always seemed to own up to the truth in the end. "It's so hard to resist drugs around here," she told me later. "You'd do drugs, too, if you lived here and dealt with everything."

Other members of Brittany's family were upset and disappointed at the news. The uncle who cared for Brittany's children was perhaps the most frustrated that she couldn't get clean, get her life together, and reliably show up for her kids. Brittany's dad, Ricky, felt the same way. "If she would just straighten up they would allow her to see the kids and spend more time with her," he said. With Brittany's failed drug test, Ramona knew the fight to keep her out of jail would only be tougher.

Despite Brittany's positive drug test, Judge Holt ruled that she could stay out of jail until trial. But Brittany had already begun to unravel. On the car ride home from the hearing, Brittany flinched when her boyfriend, Michael, tried to put his hand on her leg. "Don't touch me, please," she said with force. "All right," he said, and withdrew his hand to his lap. Later, she told me she'd flinched because of a recent camping trip with Michael where he'd gotten drunk, they fought, and he wrapped his arms around her throat and strangled her. Even with his gentle demeanor, Michael had turned out, once again, like the other men in Jackson County who roughed up women.

Ramona was enraged for Brittany. "Michael said he choked Brittany because he was drunk and high," Ramona said drily. "But when I'm drunk and high, I don't do that."

A few weeks later, Brittany and Michael got into another fight. This time, according to Brittany, Michael poured a beer over her head, threatened to do more, and left the trailer. After he was gone, Brittany lit two matches and dropped them on the mattresses in the house. Ramona, who was just pulling up to the trailer, saw flames licking through the window. She ran inside the trailer, called the fire department, and stomped out much of the fire. Her daughter stood in the kitchen, unmoving.

"I don't know if she come apart or was pissed," Ramona said. But she knew her daughter was in serious trouble now. "I fought like hell to keep Brittany out of jail. I told her she was gonna end up in jail if she kept staying with him. I begged her when he choked her: 'Do not go back over there.'"

When the fire department and police officers showed up later, Brittany did not lie to them. She told them exactly what she'd done. It was estimated that there was minor damage to the trailer, and Brittany was arrested for arson in the second degree, which is defined as setting a fire to an empty building. Later, Brittany had trouble explaining why she did it. "I don't know," she said. "He had just poured beer all over me. I know I wasn't trying to burn the house down, though."

Brittany and Ramona often blamed every problem they had on the corruption and sexism in Jackson County and the criminal justice system. Sometimes the system was at fault, but sometimes Brittany was. Brittany had never been a perfect victim for trial. The criminal justice system likes to put people in the courtroom drama in binaries: victims are good, and perpetrators evil. But these categories are deeply misleading. Studies have shown that many incarcerated women are dealing with some kind of complex trauma, and that many are also struggling with addiction.

Norwegian sociologist and criminologist Nils Christie developed the notion of the "ideal victim" in 1986 to describe a "person or a category of individuals who—when hit by crime—most readily are given the complete and legitimate status of being a victim." According to Christie, the ideal victim should be weak, doing something respectable, in a place they couldn't be blamed for being, and hurt by a big and bad, unknown offender. History shows us that the ideal victim is also often white and middle or upper class.

Brittany had already failed these definitions on several counts because she was poor, a former drug user who'd lost custody of her children, knew Todd and drank with him that night, and was not weak, meek, or passive but defiant in court. Now, having shown her capacity for reactive behavior, Brittany's status as victim was further eroded.

Lily Kay Ross, who did her PhD research on victim and survivor labels in gender-based violence cases, wrote in a thread on Twitter that there are two ways victims must behave to get sympathy: by taking responsibility for themselves and working heroically to overcome adversity, or by becoming Christ-like victims, who are weak and meek and passively turn the other cheek. Brittany did the opposite. After Michael strangled her, as other men had before, she sought to burn their relationship to the ground.

Of the 230,000 women the Federal Bureau of Prisons counts as currently incarcerated, roughly a quarter are in for violent offenses. It is not only unclear how many women have been imprisoned for killing their abusers, but also how many cases have walked the line between self-defense and reprisal. A 2008 analysis of dozens of studies, conducted by researchers at the University of South Carolina and Yale, found that men were often driven to be violent because of a desire for control, while women were more likely than men to be motivated by self-defense and fear. Their analysis also found that some women were motivated by retribution, in response to either physical or emotional hurt. One of the studies suggested that women acted in retaliation about half the time.

When presented with Brittany's arson, Rachel White-Domain of the Women & Survivors Project said it did not surprise her. She said that those who are living in constant conditions of violence have to claim their space and safety, even if that means setting a mattress on fire. White-Domain noted that judges, prosecutors, and attorneys, "people on the other side of the looking glass, just don't live those kinds of lives."

After the arson, Brittany knew she faced the real possibility of life in prison for shooting and killing Todd, which could now be viewed as the first of two retaliatory actions she'd taken against men who abused her. She had always said she'd never take a plea deal, but now that she was back in jail for arson, the possibility of a life spent at Julia Tutwiler Prison loomed large before her. Tutwiler was one of the most troubled female prisons in the U.S. In 2015, a Department of Justice investigation found that women incarcerated at Tutwiler Prison were being sexually harassed, raped, and impregnated by guards, then punished if they reported the abuse. It wasn't a stretch for Brittany to fear she could be assaulted there, although prison conditions had apparently improved since the investigation. If Brittany took a plea deal, she might avoid prison altogether.

According to Karla Fischer, the domestic violence expert, most women who kill their abusers take plea deals in the end (as do the majority of criminal defendants). Fischer estimated that 80 percent of the women's cases she handled ended in pleas. Overall, about half of the women whose cases she appeared for were ultimately convicted of a lesser offense, while the other half received higher charges than they'd initially faced. Fischer said that in all her years appearing as an expert, she had only seen one woman acquitted at trial.

The Jackson County District Attorney's Office had originally given Brittany a plea deal offer of twenty-five years for manslaughter. Now, according to her lawyer Ron Smith, they said Brittany could plead guilty to murder and arson and serve some seven months in jail, after factoring in her time served, or take manslaughter with a longer sentence. It made no sense that a murder conviction would put Brittany away for far less time than what they offered for manslaughter, but Ramona's neighbor, Kayla, thought she understood why. "They just wanted to get her for murder," she said, meaning the judge and prosecutor in Jackson County.

Brittany read over the details of the pleas in jail and considered her options. If she pled guilty to murder, she could be out of jail by May and see her babies. Women following her case around the world would be disappointed, but Brittany felt it was no longer about proving herself. Nearly three years in, it was about survival.

Brittany took a guilty plea in October 2021. Ramona sobbed when she found out. Brittany was in isolation in jail when she signed the papers, so Ramona could not call her daughter to talk her out of it. "I just wanted to say to her, 'Brittany don't do it, baby, don't do it, this is self-defense,'" Ramona said. "But she's tired, we're all tired," she sobbed. "We wanna fight but damn, we're so fucking tired."

Brittany's lead lawyer, Ron Smith, impressed on her that the murder conviction would always be on her record—that it would follow her every time she tried to get a job, housing, or custody of her children. Brittany told him that it was worth it to see her children sooner. She knew she would not receive less time at trial, not with Holt as her judge, who had written a nineteen-page order questioning her credibility, and not with Jason Pierce as her prosecutor, who was determined to make her look like a liar. And certainly not after her arson following Michael's abuse. "Well, I know that I did it for my kids," she said from jail after taking the plea. "They'll feel better knowing that it's over with. You know, like, I made a decision, so my mom's okay, my brother's [okay], everybody's okay . . . My kids are okay. And I'll be okay. Mentally, I'm just trying to stay sane back here."

But in the weeks that followed, in the quiet nights in the women's unit that followed the noisy, mayhem-filled days, Brittany was sometimes less confident in her decision. She had been dead set on not pleading guilty, and she felt that she'd let many people down, including herself. "It's something that I fight with every day," she said. Like Kayla Pearson, she felt that, after so much negative attention on Jackson County's handling of her case, the authorities wanted her to take the murder charge just to say that they'd been right about her all along.

As Chris had predicted, his charges were adjudicated now that his sister's case was over. The court dropped the charge of tampering with evidence, and Chris pled guilty to giving a false statement, for which he got twelve months of supervised probation. He didn't mind the sentence, given that he had barely left home since the shooting.

In the end, after all the years her case dragged on and all the money and effort to put her behind bars, Brittany would serve just seven months more in jail, and Chris twelve months of probation. The outcome felt anticlimactic to many who had followed the case. Women around the country who connected with Brittany's story seemed not to know what to make of it, though it seemed to me a perfect reflection of both the willful and arbitrary failures in America's criminal justice system. Later, Brittany's lawyer told me that he wished they had tried the case, because he thought a jury might have done the right thing. Ashley Remkus, the AL.com reporter, thought that the system in Jackson County had failed any way you looked at it. "If you think that Todd is a victim, do you consider what [Brittany] got justice?" she said. "And if you don't think he was, and you think she was the victim, then I can't imagine you think that she got justice either." No matter whose side a person was on, Remkus didn't think there was justice to be found in Brittany's case.

As Brittany served her seven months in jail, she worked hard to find herself again, and to finally process the fact that she'd taken a life, no matter how much Todd had put her through. She meditated, prayed, and wrote letters to family and friends. To avoid the dirtiness of the jail, she tied her hair back in tight braids and kept her uniform clean. When the women were let out in the jail yard, she picked clovers through the fence. She learned that clovers opened up in the day and closed at night, a fact she loved. She adopted a pet worm she called Herm after "Herman the Worm," a song she'd listened to as a kid, and fed him orange peels and cornbread. At night, Brittany could see Mars from the square window by her bed and told her mom to wish on the same star.

She and Ramona talked on the phone every day. Ramona joked to Brittany that she missed her so much she was going to get a public intoxication charge, just so she could hug her daughter in jail. Ramona always put on a happy face for Brittany when they talked. But as twinkling Christmas lights were strung up in the housing project, it grew tougher to keep up the act. All of Ramona's neighbors discussed the gifts they were getting their kids, while Ramona worried about whether she'd have enough money to put on Brittany's books in jail for calls.

In May 2021, Brittany was released from Jackson County Jail, just in time for her oldest son's graduation and to catch Alabama's spring wildflower bloom. She moved back in with Ramona, who had kept her fake Christmas tree up for months, with presents under it for Brittany to open for every holiday she'd missed, including Valentine's Day jewelry in ruby red wrapping. Anytime Ramona went to Walmart or the Dollar Store while Brittany was locked up, she picked up a cheap toy for the kids and put them in a tote for Brittany to give them when she came home. Ramona said she just wanted to "piece our little family back together."

On house arrest in the apartment, Brittany kept herself busy with a Facebook page she created called *Flawed but Fearless*, which nearly 150 local women joined. She posted inspirational videos or memes about domestic violence, starting life over again, and finding independence as a woman. Many women who joined the group said they had experienced domestic violence or sexual assault. One woman, a friend of Ramona's who lived in Jackson County, joined just weeks after she'd sent Ramona a series of gruesome photos, in which she had two black eyes, a giant knot on her forehead, bruised cheeks, and blood spattered across a gray T-shirt. The woman said her husband hit her and punched her in the face after she tried to stop him from making a suicide attempt. The husband was arrested, charged with domestic violence, and spent six months in jail, which the other women found encouraging. Sandra, Brittany's rape victim advocate, shared her own stories with abuse, while another woman talked about struggling with addiction, like Brittany. Others shared memes about not being believed.

After a while, Brittany posted about herself to the group: "For years I was lost. I wanted to fit in. I wanted people to like me, but I was this awkward girl who had a problem allowing people to get to know who I really was. I was [a] funny, goofy, shy, imaginative, beautiful soul, but I never felt good enough. So as I got older I started using drugs and drinking." Brittany wrote about getting married, having children, and how much she loved being a mom. She shared about how she got hooked on drugs and relapsed and her children were taken away. "I LOST MY HEART. Felt like I had nothing to live for anymore . . . When I finally came to my senses, I sobered up and started doing what I needed to get my babies back." Then she met Todd. "Well, I'm sure you all have heard or read about my rape and how I was charged with murder. I thought my world was over. But let me tell you something, my world is just beginning."

In May 2021, Brittany had another altercation with Michael, who she'd offered a second chance at dating after he apologized and told her he had gotten clean. She also had been informed she could not live in Ramona's public housing complex as a convicted felon, and so Michael's trailer was her next-best option. This time, Brittany filmed their fight. In the video, she says she's recording Michael because he has just threatened to kill her. He shoves a heavy kitchen island, which is covered in kitchenware and topples over. "Stop recording me and my bullshit!" he screams, and also pulls down a bookshelf behind him, which crashes to the ground. "Stop!" Brittany screams back, and the video cuts off.

Brittany called the police shortly after, who arrested Michael and charged him with "domestic violence strangulation/suffocation." She told me that Michael tried to strangle her and her mother pulled him off. Michael wrote me via Facebook to say he was innocent, and that "she held that phone pretty good for someone I beat." But he later pled guilty in Jackson County to assault in the third degree, which is generally an assault caused by someone's hands or body. Michael was ordered by the court to take anger management classes, and Brittany secured a no-contact order against Michael from the court. For once, she felt that the police had believed her.

Not long after, in July 2021, an appeals court in New York issued a landmark ruling for domestic violence survivors. It reduced a sentence by more than ten years for Nikki Addimando, a mother of two who shot and killed her boyfriend and the father of her two children, who she said had been physically and sexually abusive. Like Brittany's, her experiences had been written off by some—in this case the prosecutor—as rough sex. A new law in New York, the Domestic Violence Survivors Justice Act, allowed for reduced prison sentences for those who had experienced domestic violence like Addimando. In California, "Sin by Silence" laws allow courts to consider new evidence for women who killed an abuser and whose abuse may not have been presented at trial, and in Illinois, an amended law added abuse as a mitigating factor at sentencing. Advocates said not enough women had seen the benefits of those laws yet, but that the winds were shifting.

A year later, in July 2022, California governor Gavin Newsom pardoned Sara Kruzan, who killed her trafficker at sixteen, and that same month, the Wisconsin Supreme Court said it would allow teenager Chrystul Kizer to argue that when she killed her trafficker it was self-defense. The court went so far as to suggest that it did not matter if Kizer shot him while in imminent danger because trafficking could "trap victims in a cycle of seemingly inescapable abuse." Importantly, the criminal justice system was acknowledging that when it came to abuse, self-defense could happen on a continuum. At the same time, many states began introducing "second look" bills, where those serving long sentences in prison could be reevaluated for release; some of the bills even had a clause for domestic violence.

As for Brittany's case, no Alabama laws were changed as a result, no pardon issued. But the ongoing conversation around her case mostly revolved around the complexities of criminalized survival, which seemed to me like the legacy of her story. On social media, those discussing her case debated the issue of perfect victims ("The public wants a perfect victim and that rarely is the case"), the impacts of trauma and how difficult they could be to understand ("Rape victims do things that just do not make sense. That is what trauma does to you"), and how, though no one would ever know the exact truth of Brittany's story—whether it was self-defense or retaliation or somewhere in between—it had undoubtedly revealed something troubling in our criminal justice system ("[It's] an example of preferring to send an innocent person to jail rather than risk setting a guilty one free").

Meanwhile in Jackson County, rape victim advocate Sandra Goodman said she'd noticed that, ever since Brittany's case was adjudicated, the police were making more domestic violence arrests and the courts were handing out more abuse convictions. This was difficult to prove with the lack of good recordkeeping in the county, but, judging by the local jail roster and court records, it appeared to be true. I kept thinking that if it hadn't been for Sandra representing Brittany, Ramona's unflagging advocacy for her daughter, and local activist Sherrie Saunders and her podcast, perhaps nothing would have ever changed.

The larger changes in the country, too, didn't come out of nowhere—they are the result of organizers and advocates, including women inside prisons, who have made good trouble for years. This includes people like Karla Fischer, who, as an expert witness, tries to keep women out of prison, and people like Rachel White-Domain at the Women & Survivors Project, who works to free them. And there are so many others. Since 1987, the National Defense Center for Criminalized Survivors (formerly the National Clearinghouse for the Defense of Battered Women) out of Minnesota has assisted women charged with crimes relating to their experience of abuse, raised public awareness around the complexity of the issue, and trained members of the criminal justice system. More than thirty years after its formation, Cindene Pezzell, the legal director for the center, told me, "The very reason that [women] have to use self-defense in the first place is still not just being considered, but also used against them." However, she also believes that today there is more empathy and understanding around these cases, and why they happen.

Survived & Punished is a newer coalition of organizers, legal advocates, and impacted people fighting to free criminalized survivors, which began in 2013 in Chicago. The group had its beginnings in a grassroots campaign that advocated for the release of Marissa Alexander, the Florida mother who had faced decades in prison for firing a warning shot at her abusive husband. Today, Survived & Punished leads similar campaigns to free people from prison, particularly people of color who have defended themselves against an abuser, as well as publishes reports to try to influence and transform legislation and policy. Mariame Kaba, a co-founder of the group and one of the foremost abolitionist organizers working today, said in a 2022 interview with *Harper's Bazaar* that she noticed a certain defeatism in conversations around abolition, which she could not accept. "This does not need to be this way. No, we can do something different. We must."

Kaba and the coalition argue that incarceration—with its punitive nature and forced isolation—is not the solution for women like Brittany. The group recommends shifting resources for survivors away from imprisonment and toward public health and housing. In Brittany's case, that could have included therapy, addiction treatment, and housing for when she was released from jail, so she didn't have to return to Michael's. "While no survivor's situation is simple, criminalization further complicates ways out of abuse, harm, and trauma," Survived & Punished organizers wrote in an online toolkit in 2018. "We organize for more restorative resources and transformative options."

Restorative justice, rooted in indigenous traditions of responding to conflict, may include approaches like community service or victim-offender mediation. It may bring affected parties together to address the harm that was done and people's needs in an antihierarchical approach—especially when compared to a judge who looks down at a criminal defendant from on high. Transformative justice rests on the idea that the community should examine and address the harm's root causes. In Brittany's case, this could have included conversations between her and Todd's family to talk about the fundamental reason it happened, the damage done, and how to get to healing—akin to what Brittany and Jeff seemed to have done on their own, in the absence of encouragement from any authority.

In Stevenson, after Michael was arrested, Brittany moved back in with Ramona, hoping the public housing officials wouldn't catch her. She was excited when she got permission from her parole officer in October 2021 to visit her kids for Halloween. Halloween was big in the area, with kids and adults riding on four-wheelers in costume through town, scary clowns and zombie children positioned in front yards, and a former jail transformed every year into a cobwebbed haunted house. Brittany's oldest son planned to be a scary bunny from the movie *The Purge*, and Brittany helped him spatter on fake blood, while her younger son chose to be a burning Godzilla. Her youngest baby girl dressed up as Rapunzel, while her older daughter was Wonder Woman. "I may have a Purge and a burning Godzilla in my life," Brittany told me, laughing. "But I also have a Wonder Woman on my side."

But Halloween ended poorly after Brittany's parole officer said she had had permission to see her kids off in costume but not to trick-or-treat with them. As a result, Brittany spent forty-five days back in Jackson County Jail on a parole violation. When Brittany got out, she was undaunted and continued to make plans for her future. She signed up for advocacy and journalism classes in the spring, which she hoped would give her more credibility to speak about her experiences with domestic violence and addiction. In the meantime, she started writing a book about her life. The writing was cathartic but slow-going because she often needed breaks to breathe. Meth remained omnipresent in the county, and Brittany considered using again. It would blunt the pain of her memories and allow her the feeling of elation for a day or two. But then Ramona talked her down, telling her, *Hell, baby, you've survived worse,* and Brittany stayed clean.

That winter, Brittany got one more tattoo, which depicted the goddess Venus. She chose it because the symbol for woman came from Venus and because the goddess had indirectly caused, yet helped others survive, the violent fall of Troy—an upset of power that was never expected to happen until it did.

BOOK II
ANGOORI

VENDETTA

The first time, it had been an outpouring of rage . . .
Then, I said to myself it was justice pure and simple . . .
But I never killed without reason.

—The Bandit Queen, as quoted in her 1997 autobiography,
I, Phoolan Devi

New Year's Day, 1963. Angoori Dahariya was born, tiny and wailing, into a poor farming family in a small village in a big district, with little promise of education as a girl. It was the same story for many girls in northern India at the time. She had three brothers and five sisters, until two of her sisters passed away. Angoori was an unassuming girl who tried to blend in with her siblings, but her buckteeth often set her apart. She had a square face, broad nose, and close-set eyes, which could make her seem forbidding when she was not. The disconnect between her reality and how people saw her was evident in her name. The word "Angoori" meant "grape," which was about as ordinary as a name could get, while her last name, "Dahariya," meant "roar" like the bellow of a lion.

Angoori's family were Dalits, a word that translates to "broken" or "scattered," and which some Dalits used proudly while others rejected it. For centuries, Dalits, previously known as "untouchables," had been deemed so lowly and impure as to be excluded from the four castes in India. Several Hindu texts outline the caste system, though perhaps the most prominent to do so is the ancient and influential *Manusmriti*, or *Laws of Manu*, a Sanskrit text that argued that those from a lower caste should serve the upper castes "meekly" and without acquiring wealth. It listed a series of gruesome punishments for violators: a low-caste man who tried to teach a high-caste man his duty should drink hot oil, while a low-caste man who sat on the same seat as a high-caste man should be branded and banished.

In 1927, Dalit lawyer, economist, and social reformer Dr. B. R. Ambedkar and his associates burned a copy of the *Manusmriti*, one of many challenges Ambedkar issued to caste discrimination in the country. The Indian national constitution of 1950 banned the notion of untouchability, largely due to the work of Ambedkar, who had become India's first law minister. But when Angoori was born in the 1960s, the movement for Dalit rights—though potent—had not translated to true political power, and many Dalits continued to live lives of poverty, servitude, and exclusion. Rural Dalits largely lived under a sort of feudal system, below their high-caste landowning bosses.

Angoori's father was among them, a Dalit farmer who worked high-caste people's land, cultivating potatoes, mustard, and rice. The upper-caste landowners took most of the profit and paid him little because they were powerful and they could. Angoori's mother ground wheat and made flour from it, the powder often getting stuck in the creases of her hands. When Angoori and her sisters got old enough, they helped around the house. Her father came home late every night to their thatched hut, where the family ate a small dinner after dark. "I faced difficulty getting two square meals. That was my life then," Angoori told me later. Between fieldwork and household chores, she sometimes got time to play with her siblings or tie a red ribbon in her hair, but on many days there was little to excite her.

Still, there were signs that India was changing during this decade, and that Uttar Pradesh, the poor but populous northern state where Angoori lived, might also transform. Angoori's village was so tiny it could not be found on any map, but nearby towns were getting paved roads and electricity. In 1966, Indira Gandhi became India's first female prime minister, against the complaints of rival politicians who dubbed her a "Goongi Gudiya," or "dumb doll." Among Gandhi's achievements was investing in the so-called Green Revolution to modernize India's agricultural system. The move brought state subsidies and fertilizer to states like Uttar Pradesh to alleviate the poverty plaguing families like Angoori's.

But Angoori's village was on the fertile Indo-Gangetic plain, where the soil was rich and red, and a lack of fertilizer was not the main problem. An obsession with hierarchy—which the British had exploited during colonization—was arguably far more damaging. Even after the Green Revolution, Angoori's father continued to make little money because he was a low-caste farmer. Angoori was encouraged to drop out of school after class five, and was married off by her family at fifteen, though she was determined to get a job, any job, when she grew up. *May you be the mother of a hundred sons,* the old saying went. Girls were considered a burden on the family.

Still, a wedding meant fine clothing and good food, and so it was a source of excitement for Angoori. Her new husband, Sewa Lal, was from a district an hour away, and was common-looking but kind. He worked as a scrap dealer, going from village to village on his bicycle collecting metal, which he got in exchange for salt and sweets he made of jaggery (or unrefined cane sugar), and then sold. A man of few words, he went quietly about his work and did not like to disturb others. Angoori bore their first child at eighteen. Their second child died of a high fever when the girl was just two years old because they could not afford decent medical care. Angoori told herself it was common to lose a child as a Dalit woman, and she had to accept it and move on. She bore another daughter and two sons, all of whom she made sure went to government schools. She spent her days cooking and cleaning at home. "I was like a very ordinary woman then," she said. Sewa Lal saw it differently. To him, as a young mother, "she was afraid of everything."

To supplement her husband's income for their growing family, Angoori learned to make cardboard boxes that could hold sweets, shoes, or gold-tone bangles. As her children grew older, she sent them out to local shops to sell them after school. The boxes sold for twenty-five paise, one quarter of a rupee, and made a margin of ten paise per box (or less than a cent). Angoori obsessively made the boxes late into the night, sometimes cutting her fingers with scissors as she worked, insistent on giving her children the schooling she never had. "I used to wash my hair once every fortnight," she said of that period, because she had no time to herself. Her life might have continued on like this if she had not tried to improve her station in life, which Dalit women were not supposed to do.

In 1992, the year a Hindu right-wing mob demolished a mosque in Uttar Pradesh, setting off months of rioting between Hindus and Muslims, and taking some 2,000 lives, Angoori and her family, who were Hindu, moved out of their village in search of a better life. That same year, hundreds died in India from drinking hooch—cheap, illegally made liquor—and a major securities scam rocked the country, proving that India's newly free market suffered the same troubles as anywhere else. But Angoori's focus was on their move to Tirwa, a bustling town surrounded by farming villages, which was covered in a fine layer of dust and clogged by exhaust, yet much bigger than the tiny village where she was born. In Tirwa, her children could get a good education, and she and her husband could make decent money. She got a job as a polio worker, helping deliver the vaccine for an infectious disease that until then was paralyzing more than five hundred people daily. Over several months, she saved 7,000 rupees, or about $270 then, which she proudly collected at home.

That year, Angoori and her husband saved enough for a down payment on a small plot of land in Tirwa of about eight hundred square feet. The land belonged to a family from whom they'd been renting already—a high-caste family, which made Angoori nervous. But the family seemed kind, and all the landowners in the area were upper caste, so they had no choice. Angoori and Sewa Lal paid for the land in monthly installments. Over several months, they constructed a two-room hut of straw, stones, and bamboo pipe. They planted a small garden in the backyard with tomatoes, chili, and papaya, where their three children liked to play. From the fruits of her garden, Angoori could make chutney and curry, the sweetness and tang like hope in her children's mouths.

Angoori was proud to have her own home, but it did not always feel secure. During the house's construction, several of her upper-caste neighbors pressured her to leave, saying in barbed undertones that no one wanted a Dalit family there. Despite the passage of more recent national legislation to protect Dalits, Angoori knew most people still considered them impure, which meant they continued to get all the dirtiest jobs, including sanitation, disposal of dead animals, and scrap collection, like her husband Sewa Lal did. In his 1935 classic novel *Untouchable*, Mulk Raj Anand described how Dalits could not use wells or streams, or else high-caste people would see their water as polluted. "They think we are dirt because we clean their dirt," Anand's main character lamented. Some sixty years later, throughout the 1990s, this was still true in many places. On Angoori's land, the landowning family constructed small structures seemingly at random, and to make their lives unpleasant. Even if it was illegal to do so, there was little Angoori's family, as Dalits, could do. She understood that because the other high-caste families did not want them as neighbors, her landlord wanted them gone.

Women from rural areas, especially Dalit women, rarely, if ever, owned land in Uttar Pradesh. Still, Angoori handled the monthly payments for their land because she was making more money than her husband. Although the house was complete and the property half paid off, Angoori fretted at night, worrying their little plot of land might be snatched away at any moment.

In 1999, seven years after they moved in, the seeds of the community's displeasure bore bitter fruit. Angoori's landlord told her that the other high-caste residents had demanded he evict her because they were tired of living beside a Dalit family. He said that she had never bought the plot outright and that her paperwork was inauthentic. Angoori was bewildered. She had spent so much on the land and the house, their entire life savings. Her oldest son was fourteen and settled in his secondary school, with more education than she'd ever accessed. Finding a mettle she didn't know she had, she told her landlord in an even voice, "We're not leaving."

That summer, according to Angoori, her landlord showed up at her house with four or five men. It was high noon and sweltering hot. Temperatures sometimes hit 107 degrees Fahrenheit in Tirwa that time of year. According to Angoori, she was home with her two sons when the men forced their way into the house, beat her and the boys, and threw their belongings outside the home. Timid Angoori, who had never fought anyone, picked up a bamboo cane that she kept at home to chase away domestic animals, and hit her landlord with it as hard as she could.

"Then the landlord got a hold of my hair and threw me against the wall, and my head split open," she said later. "Blood started oozing out of my head."

Angoori was afraid the men would kill all three of them, so she frantically sent her oldest son out of the house to find help. That way at least one of them would survive. Her younger son, who was twelve, had been beaten unconscious. The men dragged Angoori and the boy out of the straw hut and told her they were never allowed back.

A Human Rights Watch report that year called out high-caste landlords in India for acting with impunity in carrying out attacks on the landless Dalit class. "The 'landlords' wanted to reassert their feudal tyranny over the poor who have started becoming more vocal," the report wrote. Sewa Lal, a submissive man, was upset but accepted the news as inevitable for a Dalit family. Angoori was so agitated she could not stop crying. For two nights afterward, the family slept on the side of the road with nothing to eat. Earlier in their marriage, when their children had cried from hunger, Angoori once crept over to a nearby farm and stole mustard seeds and leaves, frying them for her children to eat. At the time, she'd vowed her family would never suffer that way again. But after years of hard work, her children were hungry and homeless again, and she felt the urge to steal once more. She had already beaten a high-caste man and thought it didn't matter how many more petty crimes she committed.

But after a few days, her husband found a short-term rental in a different area of Tirwa, and life stabilized for the family. Still, Angoori could not calm down. It seemed impossible to rebuild their hard-won life. The area smelled of burning plastic and the dust settled over their rental apartment like soot. She filed complaints with the police and several local politicians but said they all turned her away. No one wanted to hear a Dalit woman's sob story and the police, who were mostly upper caste and male, were known for dismissing their stories. She'd also heard the landlord's brother was a prominent lawyer in the area, and his influence far outstripped hers.

Several times, Angoori walked by her old house and garden, where the papayas would soon be ready on the tree. She said her old neighbors taunted her as she passed, calling her a "goonda," or "thug," for having beaten a man. But Angoori held her head high. Something had shifted inside her the moment she'd picked up the bamboo cane. "My kids suffered, and this made me angry," she said. She was sure her landlord would have never dared attack her if she wasn't Dalit or a woman. In her fury, Angoori had an idea: she could become like Phoolan Devi—India's famed Bandit Queen.

Phoolan Devi was born poor and low-caste in 1963—the same year as Angoori, and in a village not far away. She was married off at age eleven to a man three times her age in exchange for a cow. At first, Phoolan was obedient to her husband, assuming her job as a wife was to make his meals and feed his cattle. But when he forced himself upon her with a knife, Phoolan, just a child, bit his hand and fled. In her autobiography, *I, Phoolan Devi,* she recalled his "nauseating serpent" and his smell "like a hyena." But she was not welcomed back home in her village, where people considered her a pariah. "Without a husband, I might as well be a corpse floating in the river," she wrote.

Phoolan's life changed when, as a teen, she fell in with a gang of bandits, which were common at the time in Uttar Pradesh. They hid in the region's rocky ravines and scrub forests and took aim at their targets as they pleased. Some of the bandits were hardened criminals, while others were Robin Hood–like figures, stealing from the upper-caste landowners and giving to the poor. According to most accounts, Phoolan was kidnapped by the bandits, though some say she intentionally left her old life behind. Whatever the truth, she became an active bandit, then escaped that crew and formed a new gang, of which she became the undisputed head. Under her leadership, the gang began targeting high-caste and male offenders.

In her autobiography, Phoolan recounted once parading an alleged rapist naked, on all fours, with a rope around his neck through town. At another point, she and her gang returned to beat up her former husband, whom Phoolan recounted using a neem branch crop on to "crush his serpent." "Once I . . . started making lists of all the people who had tortured me, who had abused me, and I was able to pay them back in kind, that pleased me tremendously," she told *The Atlantic* later. In still another instance, Phoolan and her gang traveled to a village called Behmai, where, six months prior, as a seventeen-year-old bandit, she had been gang-raped by several high-caste men. As vengeance, she and her gang marched dozens of the village men to the riverbank, instructed them to kneel and press their faces to the earth, and then shot twenty-two of them dead.

The morning afterward, the massacre at Behmai headlined every paper, and Phoolan Devi's exploits became notorious across the country. As a teenager, Angoori was enthralled by the wild deeds of Phoolan Devi. As an adult, Angoori watched the blockbuster film *Bandit Queen*, which chronicled how Phoolan transformed from a meek and powerless girl into a ferocious gang leader, though Phoolan herself took issue with the film because she was not consulted on it, and because of how she felt the graphic rape scenes added to her exploitation. The film opened with a quote from the *Manusmriti*, the Sanskrit text that endorsed the caste system, which read: "Animals, drums, illiterates, low castes, and women are worthy of being beaten." Angoori knew that's how her landlord saw her—as equivalent to a lowly animal. She kept replaying the scene of him and the other men beating her younger son unconscious.

Angoori decided she would get even by emulating Phoolan Devi. Not just Phoolan Devi, but the legendary bandit queen who'd come before her as well: Putli Bai, who was born into a family of prostitutes in the 1920s and became a bandit either through love or by force. Some stories say she rode on horseback through the ravines with a baby in one hand and her gun in the other. According to the 1972 eponymous movie about her, Putli Bai helped the poor and took revenge against the rich.

And Angoori wouldn't just be emulating Putli Bai and Phoolan Devi, but also the dozens of female bandits who sprang up in Phoolan's wake, many of them poor and Dalit and operating in Uttar Pradesh. One female bandit in the state, Seema Parihar, had supposedly kidnapped two hundred people, killed seventy, and looted dozens of houses during a nearly two-decade reign from the 1980s to the year 2000. Seema was not a Dalit but she grew up poor, and she told the media she wanted to be another Phoolan Devi who took revenge for the "poor and downtrodden."

Angoori saw herself following these female bandits' leads. *I'll take revenge upon my landlord and kill his entire family,* she thought, barely recognizing herself or her thoughts. *He made my children homeless. So I'll kill them all.* She ordered a knife made from a local blacksmith, which she began carrying under her sari. She did not tell anyone about her plan, not even her husband. To become a bandit, she would have to abandon her family. She planned to steal away from home at four a.m. one morning and never look back.

But on that fateful morning, Angoori slept in. She took it as a sign, realizing that if she left her family behind, her husband and sons might "pick up drinking and gambling," or even be killed, and her daughter could be molested. At the time, there were reports of Dalit girls and women in Uttar Pradesh being gang-raped or paraded naked through the streets. Angoori pictured vultures circling. "So then I thought that whatever I was thinking was wrong because it will finish my family," she said. "But I still thought: 'Whatever happened to me, I will not let happen to anyone else.'"

In their new rental apartment in Tirwa, Angoori tried to work out what to do. After their eviction, they had so little money that her two sons were selling copper crockery at the market after school. The boys wheeled their cart through the busy lanes of Tirwa, calling out in their changing voices to potential buyers. Angoori was ashamed her sons were working again while they were still young. But Dharvind, her older son, did not mind. He was proud of this new version of his mother, who was audacious and unafraid. He called her "rowdy" and "goonda," just like their neighbors had, but he said the words with awe.

Around this time, Angoori remembered a low-caste yet widely respected doctor she'd met at a Tirwa community clinic years ago. Dr. G. S. Khushwaha, a kindly, disheveled man with bushy eyebrows and an even bushier mustache, was known for giving free medicine in the area, and had not charged Angoori for medical care. She thought that perhaps he could help. She visited Khushwaha at his office in town, where he sat behind a desk piled high with packets of pills. The doctor was appalled by her eviction story and said he'd help her fight back. He gave Angoori food, medicine, and hand-me-down clothing for her children, then contacted a member of the local panchayat, or ruling committee, that governed the area. After a panchayat member called Angoori's old landlord, the landlord agreed to a compromise: he would give Angoori back the money she'd paid but she could never return to the property.

When the doctor relayed the news, Angoori was grateful to get her money back. But the doctor also noticed that she no longer seemed servile and had a new set to her jaw. The first time he'd met her at the clinic, Khushwaha remembered, "She was a [typical] housewife: very shy, very weak, and very poor." Now, she seemed different, enlivened. The doctor asked if she'd considered forming a nonprofit to fight for the rights of women and the lower castes. Angoori liked the idea but said she didn't think a peaceful response would change anything, and that she needed time to plan. Privately, she had already decided where to start. She was going to study how powerful people behaved, even if it took her years to understand them.

A few years later, in 2003, Angoori saw her chance when someone offered to have her meet with a man of royal bloodline known colloquially as Tirwa's king. His name was Deweshwar Narain Singh, and his whole family was influential in the area. The night before Angoori went to meet the king, she told her husband she was going to tell him her eviction story and ask for a job. Sewa Lal told her to leave their displacement tale alone. Now that they'd gotten their money back, there was no point in repeating the same sad story. But when Angoori met the king, she told him anyway and cried. He was moved by her tears. "If you were in politics, then no one would have ever dared to touch you and throw you out of the house," the king said, according to Angoori. "Join a party," he said. "And if you need help, the party will always step alongside you."

Angoori had always suspected as much. In India, where bribes were commonplace and contacts were the way to grease the wheels, she knew politics served as powerful protection—even for members of the lower castes. For months afterward, Angoori canvassed for several local politicians supported by the king—his wife was with the right-wing party the Bharatiya Janata Party, or BJP—and watched how they spoke. Sometimes she got to travel with Singh and his wife in his vehicle, which made her feel special, worthy, even a VIP.

As Angoori grew in stature, by her association with the king, the story of her eviction grew with her. In most versions, there were four or five men with her landlord; in others, there were more than a dozen girthy men attacking her. In some tellings, her son held back the landlord's hands while she punched him in the chest. Other times, the men arrived at her house with guns. In still others, the neighbors gathered around to watch the fight and assumed that Angoori would lose, only to realize she was pummeling the landlord nearly to death.

A few years after she began working with the king, in 2007, Angoori was in downtown Tirwa when she saw a crowd gathered around a man named Bharat Gandhi, who, despite his nerdish manner and professorial glasses, had a compelling way of orating with his hands. Speaking at the intersection near Tirwa's temple, Gandhi told the crowd about a movement he'd started to demand the government pay poor people a stipend. He said he was forming a national political party called Voters Party International to put forth the issue before India's Parliament, and the crowd cheered.

Angoori thought the idea was brilliant. Many poor and low-caste people could benefit from a universal basic income. There were several larger and more successful political parties in India: the center-left Congress Party, the right-wing BJP, and the socialist Samajwadi Party, which had large regional support. The current chief minister of Uttar Pradesh, Mayawati, was a Dalit woman who'd defied all odds in coming to power as the state's first Dalit chief minister, and whose Bahujan Samaj Party (BSP) was founded with the goal of helping the lower castes. Mayawati had recently proposed that 30 percent of state private sector jobs should be reserved for "backward" communities, including poor and Dalit people. But Angoori had never heard of Mayawati's BSP or any other party suggesting something as radical as a universal basic income. "Without thinking, I joined him on the spot," she said.

For years afterward, Angoori went from village to village to canvas for Gandhi's movement. Many of the villages did not have running water, squat toilets, or a private room for her to change her clothes. This was initially daunting to Angoori, but as she slept in jungles with snakes and beside riverbanks, she grew braver. According to Gandhi's office, Angoori raised nearly a million rupees for the party over several years (or some $13,000) and signed up more than a thousand people to the movement. The more she worked for the politician, and the farther his message spread, the more protected she felt. No one could throw her family out of their house again if she was this well-connected.

As Angoori continued to work for Gandhi, she became convinced that the problem of injustice was rooted in the patriarchy. At his rallies, Gandhi sometimes railed against the social restrictions on women, saying if poor women were paid a stipend they'd be far more empowered. As Angoori listened to him, she'd thought more about how Indian women were still expected to sweat in the kitchen over rotis and put their dreams aside, while women around the globe pursued theirs. The difference was obvious any time she turned on the television. She still felt Gandhi's stipend for helping poor women was a great idea, but she also believed that powerful men needed to be taken on more directly. "Men here are dominant, and they think that they can do anything to suppress women," she said later. "I'm not talking about all men, but a large chunk of men. If men start respecting women, then most of the problems will end."

During her time with Gandhi, she had come up with a more distinct and audacious plan, which she developed until she was ready to put it into action.

It was 2009, another year of instability in the country. People in India died in large numbers from Japanese encephalitis, a tropical cyclone, communist insurgents, serial bomb blasts by an armed separatist group, and a bus plummeting into a gorge. A third of the country remained below the poverty line. At the same time, there were signs of further social change: a law banning homosexuality was overturned, free school for children became a legal right, and the first Dalit woman was elected speaker of the house. Several years before, an act had been passed to protect women for the first time from domestic violence, building on older Indian laws that gave women equal pay, banned the practice of dowry, and prevented child marriages. But in Uttar Pradesh and elsewhere, these laws often weren't enforced.

In Tirwa, Angoori returned to Dr. Khushwaha to tell him of her new plan: she was going to form a group of women, as he'd suggested, only it would be a gang. Many of the female bandits who sprang up in Phoolan Devi's wake had become leaders of their crews—of thirty or more active gangs in the Chambal Valley in the mid-2000s, nearly half were run by women. "Women do not take to arms on their own, they are forced to do so," female bandit Seema Parihar told the *Indo-Asian News Service* in 2007. Like Phoolan Devi appeared to be, Seema was abducted by bandits as a teen; "once wounded by society, they retaliate like a tigress," she said. These women used daggers, knives, and guns to attack their targets, and many claimed never to miss. The bandit Anisa Begum, who was proficient with both guns and blades, reportedly used the motto: "Have weapon, will strike." As for Seema Parihar, she favored an AK-47 assault rifle or .303 revolver.

Angoori's gang would take on men, particularly the high caste, who did poor women wrong. Her women would brandish not guns but canes, like the cane Angoori had used against her landlord. These long bamboo canes—known as lathis—were hollow but extremely painful when wielded correctly. Some were bound with iron.

Lathis had a long history as a weapon, first used in South Asia by feudal landlords against their tenants, then wielded by British colonial rulers in the early twentieth century to brutally suppress Indian freedom fighters. In Angoori's time, lathis were primarily used as a weapon by Indian police, though people also kept them at home to defend themselves against stray dogs or intruders. Because the bamboo was dried, treated with oil, and sometimes tipped with iron or steel, a lathi was capable of wounding, disfiguring, or even killing a person.

Angoori told the doctor she envisioned recruiting dozens of lathi-wielding women, maybe hundreds, to take on abusive men. The idea wasn't far-fetched, given that in 2004 some two hundred women had lynched a serial rapist named Akku Yadav in the western state of Maharashtra, and also hacked off his penis. The women said police had laughed off their complaints of sexual violence by Yadav for more than a decade, out of a combination of sexism and incompetence. That lynching had happened organically, so Angoori was confident that with effort she could gather that many women. "If I have scores of women supporting me, no one can hurt us," she said.

It had been years since her eviction, but Angoori's outrage had never subsided. Her goal was simple: to prevent injustices like the one she'd faced. Khushwaha's bushy eyebrows raised in surprise. He was awed by her plan and did not try to stop her.

Now a sturdy woman in her forties, with hard eyes and sun-weathered skin, Angoori told her husband that she was going out to the villages again, this time alone, to recruit women for her gang, most of whom would be low-caste. With no political party behind her, she went on foot, by bus and train, and told her eviction story for the umpteenth time. In rural Uttar Pradesh, women mostly covered their faces, deferred to their husbands, and did not go to school or out after dark. So Angoori spoke to the men, telling them why she needed women to join her gang. But while the men sympathized with her story, they did not let their daughters, sisters, or wives go with Angoori. As the common Hindi phrase goes: *What happens at home, stays in the home.*

Angoori was despondent at first. But then she decided to go back to Tirwa and start in her town. She recruited a former neighbor, another low-caste woman named Ram Kali. Ram Kali was big-boned, tough, and tall, with bright blue nail polish and hot pink lipstick. She had watched Angoori's eviction firsthand. "If it can happen to you, it can also happen to me," Ram Kali said as her reason for joining. Angoori got her second member after she heard a local woman's husband beat her when he drank, and Angoori intervened and demanded he stop. She continued in this way, telling women she could help them by threatening the men who hurt them, until she had a dozen members in her gang.

Then, in August 2010, on one of the hottest weeks of the year, downtown Tirwa lost power for several days. A transformer had gone haywire, but many also believed the outage was the fault of a junior engineer who had been creating fraudulently high energy bills to enrich himself.

The gang had its first true target. Angoori called the dozen women she had recruited and told them to bring their lathis with them. With swaggering walks and their canes swinging, the women marched toward the center of Tirwa, ready for a confrontation.

STICKS AND STONES

For the men's spears were pointed and sharp, and yet drew no blood, whereas the wands the women threw inflicted wounds. And the men ran, routed by women!

—Euripides, *The Bacchae*, an ancient Greek tragedy

On a usual day in Tirwa, the roads are packed and anarchic. Brightly colored trucks sound horns at errant cars and motorcycles while rickshaw drivers weave in and out of lanes. Women ride sidesaddle on the backs of men's scooters, their dupattas whipping in the wind. Tractors and horse-drawn carts clog the roads, as do bony cows meandering across the street in search of discarded food to eat. Schoolchildren dart bicycles past street vendors' carts, which hawk greasy vada pav, sweet jalebis, bananas, chilis, cigarettes, and paan, rolled up and ready to be chewed and spit. Roasted peanuts let off smoke from sloped kadhai pans.

On the third day of the electricity blackout in August 2010, downtown Tirwa ground to a halt. With no fans or light, shopkeepers could not operate. Traffic stalled, and even the water supply seemed to have slowed to a trickle. As the air got hotter, people's torpor turned to anger, which spilled out onto the streets. Dozens of people gathered and marched to Tirwa's electricity department, where they blocked the road and burned effigies of the minister of electricity. Someone dragged out the junior engineer who had been defrauding people by overcharging them. Then Angoori and her gang of women arrived.

The women swept into town, swinging their canes and wearing saris of Angoori's favorite color: green. "Angoori Dahariya zindabad!" shouted Ram Kali, Angoori's former neighbor and first gang member, as she thrust her cane in the air. "Long live Angoori Dahariya!" the protesters chanted along with her, even though most did not know who Angoori was. Incited by the protesters' cries, Angoori pasted a red bindi, generally worn by women, on the engineer's forehead, while the other women beat him with their canes and threatened to kill him. Then Angoori ordered tall, tough Ram Kali to bring her a petticoat, the underfrock of a sari, and forced it over the engineer's waist. The women put lipstick on him and shoved Ram Kali's red wedding bangles over his wrists. According to some accounts, they also dressed up a second electricity official. The women made the men sit for hours while people passed by and clapped and laughed.

The message to the man was clear, said one gang member: "If you cannot work properly, then sit at home," just as women were forced to do. Others said the point was for him to feel ashamed. Neelam Kumar Saxena, a local crime reporter with well-oiled hair and a paan-chewing habit, covered the incident. I tracked him down years later, when I first visited Angoori in Tirwa, where nearly everyone I spoke to in town still remembered the incident. Neelam described the event to me as "an entirely new thing for Tirwa," adding that, while people were familiar with female bandits, no one had ever heard of a gang of women before. But he said that everyone found Angoori's actions justified. "That was the public anger towards this man. If the electricity department had just listened to the people's complaints, this never would have happened."

The Tirwa police arrested half a dozen people that day, Angoori and Ram Kali among them. The two women were charged with "creating a ruckus on the road," "thrashing the victim" (the engineer), and "giving a life threat to the complainant." But Angoori, who was once "afraid of everything," according to her husband, did not care about the criminal charges because she had gotten exactly what she wanted. Within twenty-four hours, the electricity returned to Tirwa, the junior engineer was reassigned to a different district, and the people's bills returned to normal. Angoori got out of jail a couple days after she paid her bond, but her case would stretch on for years. Most important, everyone in Tirwa had learned of Angoori Dahariya and her "Green Gang."

After the incident, Angoori again visited nearby villages and asked women to join her. She walked long distances to outlying settlements because she could not always afford a rickshaw or bus. This time, she also shared a new story: one of humiliating electricity officials into doing their jobs. Some men had already heard the story, so this time they let their wives, sisters, and daughters out of the house. The women, children on hips, were eager to tell Angoori their stories: of domestic violence, dowry harassment, beating by in-laws, land-grabbing, police abuse, abandonment by husbands, molestation, rape, and more. Many whispered their problems because they had never shared them before, certainly not with a stranger. Angoori listened and told them she could help. All they had to do was join the Green Gang.

Angoori's husband, Sewa Lal, said he could feel his wife changing. "Earlier, she was afraid of talking to anyone but my family and me. Now she was talking to everyone. She started working with a social cause, and she started working with lathis (canes). She held meetings by visiting different villages and told women to have strength against evils. She told me she was making a group of women and that they would fight if facing anyone who had a problem. I never stopped her. I admire her," he said.

Angoori recruited some fifty women from local villages, most of whom had never ventured beyond their town. The majority did not have a phone and could not read. Then Angoori gathered fifty more. She told them they'd take on anyone who dared hurt a woman, including violent in-laws, land-grabbing landlords, philandering husbands, bootleggers, rapists, and domestic abusers. Angoori said they would show up with lathis to intimidate offenders, and if that didn't work, they'd beat the men into submission.

In one early case, Angoori and several other Green Gang members stormed a house in Tirwa where people illegally made liquor. Many women in the area complained that their husbands got violent when they drank, so the gang caned the bootleggers until they promised to stop production. Pankaj Srivastava, a print journalist from the nearby city of Kannauj, learned of the Green Gang from this incident. It was common for police to raid the liquor mafias rampant in that part of Uttar Pradesh, but he had never heard of a gang of women taking them on. "For me, it was a new thing," he told me later. "Here, it's not common for women to even step out of the house." For Pankaj, a teetotaler who liked to visit temples before he began a day of reporting, the gang's action against the liquor mafia was heroic. He would report on Angoori's deeds for several years before he began to doubt her.

Word of the exploits of the Green Gang and the protection they offered spread. A woman from one village walked miles through fields of wheat or potatoes to tell another woman in a neighboring village, who walked several miles to tell one more. Soon, Angoori received more requests to join the gang than she could manage, mostly by low-caste women. In all the stories, one commonality was clear: the cops, courts, village councils, and politicians had failed to deliver justice.

As the Green Gang grew, Angoori developed a system to handle complaints and go after offenders. When she heard of a problem, she investigated it with several of her women. They interviewed the alleged perpetrator and victim, and anyone else with knowledge of the situation. If Angoori thought the Green Gang might have trouble getting into a house for interviews, she sometimes pretended to be a passing stranger in need of food or drink. Then, after several visits, the gang would decide who was at fault, and order an end to the offending behavior or risk the wrath of their canes. Sometimes they escalated the problem to the police, showing up at the station in large numbers to ensure the officers heard the woman's complaint. Without the gang, women said police harassed them or turned them away. The police saw Angoori as a thorn in their sides and seemed to think it was better to let her have her way. It helped that her pugnacious demeanor left no room for argument. Most times, the gang didn't deal with the police, and used the canes to get justice on their own.

Also in 2010, Angoori got a call for help from a woman in Jankhat, a village outside Tirwa. The road to Jankhat was potholed and overgrown, and the thorns of babul trees scratched any car that passed. Jankhat had some 1,200 households, and most of the adults worked in the fields. Every day the women woke up, cooked for their families, fed the animals, tended to the fields, cooked, slept, and repeated the process. There were always too many expenses and never enough money to go around. All the women in the village shared a single phone.

Basanti, a wiry woman with a protruding front tooth, called Angoori to tell her that an influential family in Jankhat was trying to seize her land. She said the family had verbally abused her and other Dalit women for years, and now they were trying to steal the ground beneath her small brick-and-mortar house, which she had upgraded from husk. Basanti's biggest fear was that her children would have to defecate out in the fields, both taking away their dignity and putting them at risk for health issues, if they took her land and home.

Angoori found the case familiar and therefore easy—so easy that she and her gang did not need to travel to Jankhat. Angoori advised Basanti to wait for the day that government officials came to register the land in the influential family's name, and be ready in the field with a few dozen women with canes. "If they try to grab the land, then beat them up," Angoori said.

Basanti did as Angoori told her. It was the height of summer in Jankhat, when the yellow flowers of the mustard plants dried up and were no longer in bloom. Basanti called some thirty-five women from the village to stand beside her with their lathis in the withered fields. When the influential family arrived with the officials, Basanti addressed them in her best imposing voice. "How dare you grab our land," she said. According to her account, the women ran at the officials with their canes, and snatched the men's measuring tapes, ropes, and bags.

In the famous Aba Women's Rebellion against taxation in Nigeria in 1929, Nigerian women similarly attacked men with canes. The rebellion began after colonial administrators announced they were going to impose special taxes on women who supplied food to urban markets. "Mobs of women passed shouting and singing about the town, 'What is the smell? Death is the smell,'" British historian Margery Perham recounted in her 1937 book *Native Administration in Nigeria*. "They beat upon the iron-trading stores with their sticks and threatened the traders . . . [The women] made threatening and obscene gestures toward the troops, called them sons of pigs, and said they knew the soldiers would not fire at them. At last, they struck at the district officer with their sticks."

In Mulk Raj Anand's 1935 novel *Untouchable*, one upper-caste character cries out: "Don't know what the world is coming to! These swine are getting more and more uppish!"

Another woman in Jankhat named Rani, who had searching eyes and wore a diamond-patterned dupatta, had also been in the field that day. She said she had been prepared for the worst—to be arrested, beaten, or killed. Somehow, she held her cane up against the influential family and government officials as if she'd used it all her life. Rani was surprised when the men immediately gave in. "Didi gave us strength," she said, referring to Angoori by the respectful term of sister. Rani added that she'd always felt officials saw "no value in a poor woman." The incident had taught her that wasn't true. "I know I am poor, but I know what my rights are," she said. Basanti said the officials, who had never seen women standing up this way, "were afraid and apologized and asked us to please return their things. They assured us that no one would ever grab our land, and they haven't."

The influential family in Jankhat remembered the incident but disputed the details. Ram Pratap, the family patriarch, said they'd never intended to take Basanti's land and that the issue was over the plot's borders. Pratap's son was in the field the day the women arrived. He remembered being terrified at the sight of so many women in green saris with canes. "I was fearful when they came because I was alone, and there were so many women," he said, and was grateful the matter had been resolved. Years later, Basanti still possessed the land she claimed, which she had filled with golden, knee-high wheat.

After the action, Basanti, Rani, and several dozen other women in Jankhat became members of the Green Gang. They wore their emerald green saris daily, and told Angoori they were no longer afraid to leave their houses at night or speak with the influential families in the village as their equals. Still, not everyone respected them. Girish Kumar, a government official who lived in Jankhat, curled his lip when asked about the Green Gang. "They are a useless gang, and don't do anything. They are illiterate women who will believe anything," he told me as he walked to his car from a local shop. "I don't know where it came from or where it will end."

Men in Tirwa who had not yet met Angoori remained confused by a gang made up of women. Police and other officials continued to see Angoori as a nuisance—one they tried to avoid. But the local women, many of them Dalits, immediately understood the group's purpose, and as the Green Gang's exploits grew, the group's membership swelled to hundreds. Within the first year, Angoori had developed a cult following among her women. When she told a story and laughed, her women laughed with her; when she cried, they cried, too. This was one of the first things I noticed when I met Angoori, surrounded by a half dozen of her women at home, all of whom emoted just as she did. "Angoori is like God, mother, and father," one woman told me. "I can even sacrifice my blood for Didi," said another. Angoori laughed easily but got angry with her women just as fast, especially if they did not attend her regular cane trainings or monthly meetings. "The aim of Green Gang is to end harassment of women and the poor. I urge you to add twenty women from your village," she told the women at meetings, leaning forward in her chair as she wagged a finger at them. "If there is some problem, by watching you in your green sari, the problem will end very soon."

Over the next year, women joined not only in Uttar Pradesh but also in the nearby states of Rajasthan, Haryana, and India's capital of New Delhi. Every joinee paid 20 rupees (about 50 cents) as a joining fee, for which they received an official membership card and a green sari. Angoori established a hierarchy, with her at the top, and every region had its own leader whom she treated as her deputies. If Angoori elevated a woman to leadership, that woman's sari had a special orange border. Anytime a woman went out for an action, Angoori paid her a day rate, usually about 100 rupees ($2). When an area did not have an active complaint to handle, Angoori kept the women busy with survey work. "Go find out the number of dowry or hooch [illegal alcohol] cases in your region," she instructed. Despite the fact that India outlawed the dowry system in 1961, thousands of women die every year in India from murders or suicides related to harassment over dowry. The Green Gang women noted down anyone who had illegally demanded payment from a bride's parents.

Angoori started keeping a register in which she wrote down every case, and a binder of growing news clippings chronicling the gang's deeds: "Women make a man wear a petticoat and bindi," "Green Gang up in arms against illicit liquor," "Green Gang will stop the harassment of women," "Green Gang creates a ruckus," and "The Green Gang will teach criminals a lesson." She cultivated a persona to match her position, carrying a fake Guess purse, wearing gold-rimmed glasses, and adorning herself in heavy gold jewelry. None of it was expensive, but it all looked as if it could be. She'd gained weight and her eyes looked deeper set. When she walked through the stone-covered lanes of Tirwa, she walked bare-foot, a habit of village women. Speaking forcefully, Angoori gesticulated with her hands, as she'd once watched the idealistic politician Bharat Gandhi do. People said her temper was something to be feared. She told me she got her way "by hook or by crook"—by any means at her disposal. Her self-mythologizing was part of her success. Even the police and other officials began to see her as more than a nuisance and shrink from her appearances in the station halls.

By the end of 2010, Angoori had rented an office in downtown Tirwa, near the central market in town but situated down a quiet lane for privacy, where she could receive people with complaints. By this time, both her sons were working, one as a lawyer and another in an optical shop, which allowed her to afford it. The office was adjacent to a temple to Santoshi Ma, a goddess venerated in Uttar Pradesh, who wields a sword and trident and whose name means "the mother of satisfaction."

By this time Angoori had established regular cane training, once every month or so, for all the new gang members to learn and the other gang members to practice. She bought every woman their own lathi from the local market for 40 rupees (or less than $1). At the training they faced off against one another with their canes for hours, and also talked through other techniques for going after targets: grabbing a person's collar, pulling their hair, or hitting them with their chappals, or leather sandals.

The most common complaint Angoori received was of domestic

violence, which Dalit activist Thenmozhi Soundararajan wrote in *The Trauma of Caste* could be related to anger borne out of the trauma of centuries of the caste system. Many other complaints Angoori received concerned marital issues between husbands and wives. "The Green Gang is best for cases related to family affairs," said Neelam, the crime reporter with well-oiled hair, because while police were motivated to solve more severe crimes, "with domestic affairs, they often take bribes and don't do anything."

Police officer Amod Kumar Singh, who would later head the Tirwa police station, told me that 90 percent of emergency calls Tirwa police received for help were related to domestic abuse. He blamed the violence on alcoholism, lack of education, and unemployment in the region. Despite what the media reported, Singh said it wasn't true that police were inattentive to women's complaints. He said his officers were often busy handling the region's most violent crimes, which he described as the by-product of "the demographics, the lack of education, unemployment, and political rivalries." The police were also underpaid and overworked, yet he said they had established a room at Tirwa station for female victims and a rule that police could never call women to the station after dark. Singh added that women sometimes lodged fake rape cases but that, if the case was genuine, the police did everything they could.

Roop Rekha Verma, a women's rights activist in Lucknow, a major city two hours from Tirwa, laughed aloud at the notion that the police were doing all they could. "I don't have words to describe how bad the police are" in Uttar Pradesh, she told me from her spare office in 2018, especially in investigating domestic and sexual violence cases. "Corruption is one problem. But the bigger problem is gender bias. The pre-investigating conclusion [among police] is that a woman has come to 'break the family,' or that women are coming with small complaints."

Everyone in Tirwa also knew the stories of women getting raped by the police, and of men being beaten to death in police custody.

Valentine's Day, 1981. The sky was clear, an unassuming blue. Behmai, like many remote villages in that rugged northern stretch of India, sits in a barren ravine, so there was no place for cover and no one to call for help. Phoolan Devi and her bandits arrived in the village acting on a tip. An informant told her that the two men who'd gang-raped her—"They fell on me like wolves," Phoolan Devi wrote—and killed her lover were hiding there.

At first, according to an account in *The Atlantic*, the upper-caste villagers paid the gang little attention because they were dressed like the police. The group's leader appeared to be a deputy superintendent, dressed in a khaki coat with three silver stars, blue jeans, and zippered boots. As the group got closer, the villagers saw it was actually a teenage girl with short hair and bright lipstick, who carried a submachine gun and wore bands of ammunition across her chest.

Then the girl began to speak: "Listen! . . . I know that Lala Ram and Sri Ram are hiding in this village. If you don't hand them over to me, I will stick my gun into your butts and tear them apart!" Phoolan Devi's bandits then searched and ransacked the village, but Lala Ram and Sri Ram, the men who'd allegedly raped the girl, were nowhere to be found. The villagers said they did not know where they were—that in fact they'd never seen them. "You are lying!" Phoolan Devi cried, and told the villagers she'd teach them to tell the truth. It was then that her gang marched every young man from Behmai to a river embankment and shot them dead.

The Atlantic account said that before Phoolan Devi's lover died, he had told her of an old village ballad: "If you are going to kill, kill twenty, not just one. For if you kill twenty, your fame will spread; if you kill only one, they will hang you as a murderess." Though Angoori never killed anyone, she subscribed to the same theory: the brasher the better, so that police and other powerful men would fear her.

One day in 2010, in the village of Narangpur outside Tirwa, the husband of a young woman named Sapna was taken by the police. She had never trusted the cops, but rarely had occasion to deal with them.

Sapna was a petite woman who wore pink lipstick and saris of purple and gold. She was married to a man who farmed upper-caste people's land. They had one child together and lived a quiet life in the small village where children slept on cots and chickens ran free in yards. After Sapna's husband's tractor was stolen, he reported the theft, and was accused by the upper-caste family he worked for of stealing it himself. Her husband was taken to jail, where police allegedly beat him. Sapna said that when she went to the station to see him, the officers mockingly gave her a bar of soap and told her to go home, wash herself, put on makeup, and return. By the time she got back, her husband was dead. The police said he died by hanging himself from the iron bar of a ventilator, but Sapna was convinced the officers had beaten him to death. Her fears heightened when she demanded the body, and the police did not give it back.

In her grief, Sapna called Angoori for help. Sapna and the other villagers had already blockaded the road to the police station in protest, but still she was not given her husband's body. Angoori showed up in Narangpur enraged. The more actions the Green Gang did, the more she loathed the police. It was said that after Angoori once slapped an inspector, he transferred stations rather than see her again, though no one could say where this occurred.

It made Angoori even angrier that an upper-caste family was at the root of this particular problem. Angoori gathered the villagers of Narangpur to march to the nearby police station a second time. Then, Angoori set it on fire. She and the townspeople also set alight seven police motorcycles, until several police officers—unaccustomed to this level of rage from so many villagers, perhaps aware they'd made an error this time—finally emerged carrying Sapna's husband's body.

Back in Narangpur, Angoori met with Sapna and the other villagers. They had taught the police a lesson and recovered the body, but Sapna was no better off. It would be difficult for her to financially support a child on her own. Another Narangpur woman named Ram Murti, who others in the village praised because she "walked and talked like a man," told Angoori they must do more. "If they [the police] will not respect me, I will become like Phoolan Devi, and I will . . ." said Ram Murti, and mimicked firing a gun. Angoori listened to the woman's bravado and nodded. Here in Narangpur, too, the influence of the

Bandit Queen was strong. But intimidating the police would not help Sapna any more.

Soon after, a local politician named Akhilesh Yadav scheduled a visit to Narangpur to apologize to Sapna for her husband's death, which had been all over the media due to the Green Gang's actions, and Angoori spotted an opportunity. Angoori only occasionally dipped into politics these days, helping Bharat Gandhi's party when they needed her to knock on doors, but she still knew how to make a politician respond. Plus, Yadav was a member of Parliament from the socialist Samajwadi Party, a regional party with an ironclad presence in Uttar Pradesh, and famous for its support of the lower castes. Yadav's father was the founder of the party, and Angoori thought it would be helpful for the gang if they knew her name.

When Akhilesh Yadav arrived, dozens of Green Gang members were there to greet him. Angoori wore a bandana tied around her forehead, just like Phoolan Devi had, but hers was forest green. The other women in the gang carried a suitcase of shoes, which they threatened to string around Yadav's neck to shame him in front of the assembled news media. "We'll garland you with footwear and beat you with stones," threatened Angoori, if he didn't compensate Sapna for her loss. Throwing dirty shoes was a sign of disrespect, so Ram Murti opened the suitcase to show Yadav it was full of footwear and they meant what they said.

A local newspaper captured the image and ran it in large size. Yadav gave Sapna 75,000 rupees, or more than $1,600. He would become the chief minister of Uttar Pradesh and one of the most powerful politicians in the country just two years later, in 2012, something Angoori would later exploit. When I asked Yadav about the incident, he seemed embarrassed but tried to laugh it off, saying, "Poor people sometimes do these things."

Since running the Green Gang, Angoori only occasionally canvassed for Bharat Gandhi, who remained a fringe candidate. But in 2012, she stopped working for him altogether, which she said was because she had become busy with her gang and was convinced his utopian vision did not persuade people. Gandhi and his office, however, told me a very different and arresting tale.

According to Gandhi's chief of staff, Naveen Kumar, in a 2012 by-election, they planned to run two candidates against the Samajwadi Party candidate—which happened to be Akhilesh Yadav's wife, Dimple—for the open lower Parliament seat in the district of Kannauj, where Angoori lived. But to squash the competition, Kumar said, the bigger Samajwadi Party had their rival candidates kidnapped and held at gunpoint until the deadline to file their nominations had passed.

Despite the Samajwadi Party's professed commitment to equality as a socialist party, they were accused of corruption just as regularly as any other political party. (Even the Dalit chief minister, Mayawati, ultimately saw her reign tainted by corruption allegations, and Angoori herself decided Mayawati was a fraud.) Ultimately, Yadav's wife, Dimple, won the Kannauj district seat—unopposed after Gandhi's candidates dropped out. As for Yadav, he ran for and won the position of chief minister of Uttar Pradesh that same year. "Akhilesh Yadav murdered democracy," Gandhi's chief of staff Kumar told me.

According to him, Angoori witnessed the kidnapping of his party's candidates but refused to talk to the police about it, after Samajwadi Party leaders pressured her and paid her off. Soon after, she quit Gandhi's idealistic movement and became a supporter of the Samajwadi Party. This entailed occasionally gathering a hundred or so of her women for rallies in support of their latest policy or candidate. Bharat Gandhi was apoplectic over the situation, telling me years later that Angoori was a "very bad woman" who had "backstabbed" him when she got the chance.

The chief of staff, Kumar, was also upset. He said that when he first met Angoori he deeply admired her because it seemed "she was not afraid to die." But the incident showed him that Angoori could be cowed and corrupted like anyone else. A Samajwadi Party spokesperson called Kumar's allegations baseless, saying that Angoori had been "falsely implicated in this police case" and also calling her the party's "very dedicated cadre"—which seemed to me an indirect way of saying she had done exactly what they asked of her.

Whatever happened, Angoori left Bharat Gandhi's movement

behind in 2012 and became a staunch Samajwadi Party supporter. She was savvy and knew that as her gang of mostly Dalit women grew, she'd need the largest source of local political power on her side. She declined to talk to me more about the incident, but said she had just begun building her gang back then and did not understand how Bharat Gandhi could blame her.

The year prior, in 2011, the National Commission for Women in India named Uttar Pradesh the worst state in the country for violent crimes against women, only the latest group to make this pronouncement. The headlines about the state that year were bleak: "Indian woman gang-raped and set alight in Uttar Pradesh," "14-year-old girl . . . stabbed in the eye as she fought off two men who attempted to rape her," "Girl's body . . . found hanging from a tree," "Girl killed in police station was gang-raped," and so on.

India as a whole continued to struggle to provide women equal rights. In 2012, gender experts named India the worst place to be a woman among the G20 industrialized nations, falling just behind repressive Saudi Arabia. A *Guardian* report that year cited evidence for the label: India's ongoing issues with child marriage (nearly half of women in India were married before eighteen, according to the International Center for Research on Women), continued dowry disputes (the number of dowry violations was on the rise, national crime numbers showed), and domestic violence against women (in a UNICEF study, more than half of all young Indian male and female respondents said they thought a man beating his wife was justified). But women's rights advocates also cautioned that more women were reporting violence than before—even if many complaints were dismissed—so it was difficult to know if the problem was getting better or worse.

That same year, India saw perhaps its most gruesome case of gender-based violence. In December 2012, Jyoti Singh Pandey, a twenty-three-year-old physiotherapy intern with a soft smile and dreams of becoming a doctor, was beaten, gang-raped, and tortured while riding home with a male friend on a New Delhi bus. They had just watched *Life of Pi* in a theater and boarded the bus home past eight or nine p.m. Six men on board the bus taunted the couple for being out so late, then beat Pandey's friend unconscious before dragging Pandey to the back of the bus to abuse and rape her. She fought back and bit her attackers but was overpowered. Doctors later said the men inserted an iron rod inside her during the assault, and that her abdomen and genitals were severely damaged. In the most disturbing image from the case, one of the accused reported seeing a ropelike object, likely Pandey's intestines, pulled out during the rape. The word "rape" comes from fourteenth-century Anglo-French, and was often used in the phrase "rape and renne," meaning "seize and plunder." After the men finished with Pandey, they threw her and her friend off the moving bus.

Pandey underwent five surgeries but died less than two weeks later. After her death, thousands of women in India took to the streets to demand stronger protections for women. They began calling her Nirbhaya, meaning "the fearless one." In response, India's Parliament passed the Criminal Law (Amendment) Act of 2013, which added new offenses to the definition of rape, and ensured that those convicted of rape could receive heftier sentences. Four of the men who attacked Pandey were found guilty of rape and murder and sentenced to death; one, a minor, was sentenced to three years in a reform facility. In a documentary on the Nirbhaya case, *India's Daughter*, one of the men defended himself for the rape by saying "It takes two hands to clap," and that she needed punishment for being out late at night as a woman.

Angoori had never faced sexual violence from a man herself, but she was incensed listening to local women's stories. Later, in response to public disapproval over Pandey's and other attacks, the Uttar Pradesh police sought to improve its responses to women by launching a phone line for people to call in and report incidents of sexual and domestic violence. The phone line was said to be the brainchild of the state's chief minister, Akhilesh Yadav, but people gave credit to Navniet Sekera, an inspector general in the Uttar Pradesh police, for its execution. By phone, Sekera told me that in a survey of 10,000 women across India, his office found that women who'd been assaulted said they knew their attacker 95 percent of the time. "So, we realized that the best solution is to make our girls speak up," Sekera said. "They generally don't because they've been trained not to." To combat this problem, they hired female officers to answer calls and promised women their identities would be kept anonymous from their community.

Angoori thought the phone line was smart in theory, but she knew many local women wouldn't use it. When the Green Gang received a complaint of sexual assault or incest, it usually came via a third party because the woman was often too traumatized to talk, much less willing to risk reporting it to the police. Even with promises of anonymity, a woman could easily be identified and retaliated against in her village. Angoori felt that confronting violence—men sometimes beat their wives, stabbed them, lit them on fire, threw acid on their bodies, raped them, or hung them from trees—with more violence was simply more effective.

In 2015, after the Green Gang had been active for five years, Angoori got what she would later describe as the "biggest case of my life." By this time the gang had grown from several hundred to over a thousand. She read an article about a gang rape in Kachpura, a village more than twenty miles from Tirwa. The piece said that a Dalit teenage girl was sleeping on a terrace at home when two men raped her. Several days later, the girl killed herself from the shame of the incident by swallowing rat poison, a common form of suicide in India. No one had been arrested for the crime. Over the last year, there had been a rash of molestations, rapes, and murders in the village—all seemingly without consequence. Angoori knew she had to get to Kachpura. Her husband was afraid for his wife for once, telling her that the culprits were likely high-caste, and with the sensitivity of a rape case, "anything can happen to you in a village of dominant people." But Angoori went anyway, gathering a dozen Green Gang members who she told to expect to stay in the village for a while.

When Angoori got to Kachpura, three days after the crime, she found the girl's mother, who was physically disabled, continuously crying. The woman witnessed the rape but had been unable to intervene because of her disability. Neither she nor the girl's father, who was blind, seemed capable of telling Angoori exactly what happened. Nor could anyone in the village. "No one could say anything to me out of fear," said Angoori, because they were Dalit and the consequences could be deadly. But she believed that people wanted her to stay in Kachpura and uncover the truth, "because it was a village where such cases were very common, and [police cases] were not being registered."

Angoori spent the next eight days in Kachpura, getting to know all the powerful people in town. The Green Gang members conducted interview after interview and learned that the girl had cried for help but no one had come to her rescue. They were told that the men who'd raped the girl were married, though no one would say the culprits' names. Many villagers reiterated that the rapes were an ongoing problem in Kachpura. Finally, Angoori secured a meeting with the village headman, whom she browbeat to do something to help the victim's family or face her wrath. After her threats, the headman promised to give the mother some land and a hand pump to use for water. It's possible the headman listened because Angoori had the Samajwadi Party's support.

But Angoori remained displeased. Whoever was responsible for the gang rape of the girl remained at large. Police told Angoori they could not do anything because the mother was the sole witness to the crime and would not talk. From interviews the Green Gang women had done, they'd learned that some of the influential people in town planned to take the mother to the police station and persuade her to say her daughter had never been raped.

Then Angoori had an idea. She would kidnap the mother before the powerful people got to her and convince her to give a statement to the police about her daughter's rape. Though Angoori had already been arrested for the incident with the electricity officials, she knew kidnapping the mother was crossing a line she and her gang had never crossed before. Plus, the electricity case was still ongoing in court—the charges that ultimately stuck for Angoori were assaulting a government officer on duty and hampering government work—and it was expected to go to trial. But Angoori had made her decision. When she told the other women, they weren't sold on the plan. "Even my gang members were afraid of kidnapping a woman," Angoori said. "They were afraid of getting an FIR [a police case]."

But Angoori was insistent. She and the Green Gang members pushed the woman into a car and drove her to a barn in another village some fifteen miles away. In the barn, Angoori coaxed and guilted the mother, saying, "What kind of mother are you if you are not speaking up for the justice of your daughter?" She also gave the woman false promises, saying that if she talked to the police, she'd get a pension of 1,000 rupees (or about $15) every month until she died. She knew the woman was poor and that this sum would make a big difference in her life. According to Angoori, the mother asked for two additional water hand pumps and five bighas of land (a unit of land in South Asia that differs from place to place), "and then I'll tell the truth," she said.

Although Angoori was not flush with cash, she was perceived as influential enough to make resources appear, especially something as trivial to her politician friends as a couple hand pumps and a small piece of land. Angoori agreed to the mother's demand without thinking.

She took the mother to the police station, where the woman gave her statement naming the culprits. As everyone had expected, they were two influential men in the village. Angoori threatened the police, telling them to make arrests immediately, or they'd feel the wrath of her gang. Afterward, back in Kachpura, the mother asked Angoori for the items she'd promised. But Angoori pushed her out of her car. "Go, now the police know the truth, they'll take action. I am going," she said. Angoori didn't like it when she felt that people she helped became greedy. Police soon arrested both men that the mother had named as responsible for the girl's rape, almost certainly because of Angoori, and Angoori did not worry about it anymore.

The 1968 Hindi novel *Raag Darbari*, which is set in Uttar Pradesh, satirizes nearly every village institution: police, panchayats, politicians, and the courts. In the villages Angoori visited, police handled many crimes poorly, panchayats gave medieval rulings on disputes, politicians made laws that did not help people, and the courts made very belated judgments. *Raag Darbari* reveals the corruption, dishonesty, and incompetence of all of them, and shows how hopeless an individual's fight for justice can feel. The novel's author, Shrilal Shukla, was a former bureau-crat for the state, and he held particular disdain for India's courts, which have been backlogged for decades. "The theory of reincarnation was invented in the civil courts so that neither plaintiff nor defendant might die regretting that his case had been unfinished," Shukla wrote. The novel was published half a century ago, but little had changed as of 2013, according to *Bloomberg Businessweek,* which estimated that some 31 mil-lion court cases remained open and unresolved in the country that year. "If the nation's judges attacked their backlog nonstop—with no breaks for eating or sleeping—and closed 100 cases every hour, it would take more than 35 years to catch up," the site wrote.

The backlog affected every plaintiff, especially low-caste women, for whom it was still uncommon to even file. But Priyanshi Rajput did just that, lodging a case in 2009 against her husband after just a year of marriage. In 2015, six years after she filed the case, her case remained unresolved, which is where Angoori came in.

Priyanshi, a quiet, studious woman, had married a man of her moth-er's choosing. Her family was made up of poor farmers, so her mother chose a man with a stable government job. To the ceremony, Priyanshi wore a red silk sari, heavy gold jewelry, and a garland of marigolds around her neck. Priyanshi's new husband, Arvind Kumar, had a thin mustache and wore his hair parted off to one side. In photos from the day, Arvind stands unsmiling over Priyanshi, holding a box of sweets. Priyanshi sits on a couch looking lost, her eyes vacant. She does not look up at him because a bride is expected to be demure. Priyanshi was feeling a tangle of emotions because she was about to say goodbye to her parents and move into Arvind's parents' home.

According to Priyanshi, the problems in their marriage started within just a few months. Even though the two families had agreed on a dowry, she said that her in-laws accused her parents of paying too low a sum. They now demanded a vehicle plus two lakh rupees, or more than $3,000. Pri-yanshi's parents could not afford that amount, so her mother mortgaged their farm and begin selling off small items, including groundnuts, rice, and gram flour. When Arvind's family demanded more and Priyanshi's mother could not pay it, Priyanshi said her in-laws began beating her.

A medical examiner found bruises on her body and a damaged eardrum. She said the men in the family also made unwanted advances. "His father and brother-in-law wanted to hold my hand," she told me, a euphemism that meant they'd attempted to sleep with her.

Priyanshi remembered how the beatings and other abuse intensified until August 2009, when her in-laws poured kerosene over her body. She took it as a threat that if her family did not pay the new dowry, they would set her on fire. In Hinduism, fire is cleansing, though women are also killed over dowry by drowning, poisoning, and strangulation. Women who survived dowry burnings are often left with disfiguring scars across their bodies.

After the kerosene incident, Priyanshi's parents called the police. But her mother said they had to bribe the officers and the cops did little to help. When Priyanshi's in-laws found out that her family had reported them, they threw her out of their house. Priyanshi fled home to her parents' village but knew she could not stay there because people talked about a husbandless woman. No woman had ever been divorced in their village, and she could not be the first. Her mother was distraught, asking, "How can any mother be happy when their daughter has been ousted from her husband's house?" Priyanshi had to find some way of getting Arvind to take her back, and her in-laws to stop beating her.

Priyanshi decided to take her husband to court, alleging domestic violence, harassment, and violation of dowry laws. She hoped a court would force her in-laws to allow her to return to his house safely. Her husband, Arvind Kumar, denied all charges, saying Priyanshi had instigated the problems by putting sugar in his food, even though he was diabetic.

As of 2015, Priyanshi's case dragged on, as was common in the backlogged system. The court suggested Priyanshi return to her in-laws' home before her case was resolved, but when she did, she said, they beat her so severely she was hospitalized for her injuries. After Priyanshi learned that her husband was seeing another woman, her humiliation was complete.

At a court hearing that year, Priyanshi took an official aside and complained that she'd never get justice. Six years had passed with only occasional hearings and a failed court-appointed mediation. Priyanshi said the official told her, "You won't get relief here. You need to call the Green Gang."

Priyanshi had never heard of the group before. When she began asking about it in the surrounding villages, the details seemed too fantastical to be true: the gang was made up of hundreds, possibly thousands of low-caste, lathi-wielding women, led by a woman named Angoori Dahariya, who had beady eyes and a laugh like a drain, coarse and unrestrained.

Priyanshi found herself alone on a quiet side street in Tirwa, staring up at a two-story brick house painted hot pink and the color of a lime. A banner out front showed half a dozen women in green saris, holding canes and raising their fists. Angoori's son answered the door and said Angoori was not home. Still, Priyanshi joined the gang on the spot. When Angoori called her a couple of days later, Priyanshi quietly told her about the alleged beatings, sexual advances, and her husband's affair. Angoori said she could not intervene in the court case but had other ideas. Several days later, Angoori called again to say she was dispatching members to the compound where Arvind and the other woman were staying. She insisted Priyanshi accompany them.

At first, Priyanshi's lawyer, Pradeep Singh Chauhan, an austere man who worked in a cramped office in Kannauj, was glad to hear his client had reached out to the Green Gang. He told me he saw the group as a channel between victims and the court, and a support system for women while their cases endlessly stretched on. In the Kannauj court, where Priyanshi's case was being dealt with, a judge heard four to five cases a day on average, while Chauhan estimated they each needed to hear a hundred a day to get through the backlog. Kannauj was a city famed for its perfume, which was exported all over the world—a saying went that "even the drainage in Kannauj smelled of roses." But residents said the city didn't smell as sweet as it should, and Chauhan thought justice didn't work as well as it should in Kannauj either.

Chauhan especially welcomed the Green Gang's help for clients whose problems were family violence–related. His domestic abuse case-load had steadily increased since he began criminal casework in 2001, a change he attributed to the social progress of women in the region. "A newly married girl cannot adjust with a husband anymore, and so these cases have increased," Chauhan said, meaning that more women were speaking up about the violence and even fighting back. That day at the courthouse, a man who had been cursing at a woman he seemed to know later emerged from the building holding a bleeding head, saying she'd hit him with a brick.

Chauhan hoped the Green Gang would give docile Priyanshi a voice she did not have, but he did not want the gang to wield canes against Arvind. He was a lawyer, and, despite seeing Arvind as "a real criminal," who had hurt his client in so many different ways, he believed the problem should be solved the legal way. And he did not want them to focus on Arvind's affair.

But Angoori thought Priyanshi should not have to wait so long for the courts to act. In late 2015, a group of Green Gang members marched toward the government compound where Arvind was staying with the other woman. Priyanshi, lathi in hand, stood beside Angoori, fearful but glad to finally be taking action toward her wayward husband. Inside the compound, the women found Arvind and the other woman sleeping together on a bed. *Red-handed*, Priyanshi thought. According to her, she and the other Green Gang members beat and cursed at the couple until Arvind ran away. (Arvind denied that he was beaten or ran, said the other woman was a relative, and that the Green Gang "created a lot of ruckus.")

Later, Angoori called Arvind on the phone. In her most intimidating voice, she told him they needed to treat Priyanshi with respect. She demanded that he take her back home or risk the gang's fury. According to Angoori, he sounded nervous and promised her he would. But as was increasingly true for the Green Gang's cases, solving the case would not be nearly so simple.

WE ARE BAD, AND WE CAN BE WORSE

I'm calling to tell you that, in return for your daughter's freedom, you have to give me the amount of five thousand pesos . . . As soon as you hand me the money, you get your daughter Maria back.

—Female community police force leader Nestora Salgado's threat to a man whose child she kidnapped, after he declined to give the force money for weapons to fight the drug cartels in Olinalá, Mexico, as reported by the *Yucatan Times* in 2018

It was the turn of the new year, 2016. Angoori was riding high on the gang's many accomplishments, and barely recognizable from her earlier self. Six years after starting the gang, she wore silk saris instead of cheap nylon ones, and took a hired car instead of a bus or train. The Green Gang didn't bring in much revenue from dues, which mostly went back into the gang, for the women's saris or cost of travel. But with Angoori's older son a lawyer, the whole extended family—Angoori, her husband, their three children, and their spouses and kids—were able to afford a two-story house in Tirwa. People in town also sometimes gave Angoori favors, such as a no-interest loan to fix up her house, because it was important to stay on her good side.

Angoori's daughter chastised her for not being home more with her grandchildren, but the Green Gang leader preferred to be out with her women. When Angoori was home, her two cell phones rang constantly:

a gang member asking advice, a police officer or attorney calling about a case, or a new woman or man registering a complaint. Angoori answered the same way every time: "Dahariya speaking." If anyone challenged her, she shouted into the phone: "*Hut madarchod!*" meaning: "Fuck off, motherfucker!" and hung up.

At night, Angoori relaxed at home with her favorite TV shows, one of which followed India's freedom fighters who fought the British colonizers to secure the country's independence. "I get inspired from those serials. I relate many things to myself," Angoori said. "If people like them can fight for the nation, then why can't I?"

The Green Gang leader could not help feeling her ego swell. When she traveled to the villages, the women touched her feet, greeting her like a god. She treated them like children, appearing understanding as they voiced their complaints, then growing impatient if they gave immature explanations. She often bossed them around. Her eyes could transform instantly from laughing and playful to brooding and angry. If the women ever doubted her, she forcefully reminded them how much the Green Gang had grown and how their lives had changed for the better.

Men in the villages had once made fun of the gang, calling them the "*hara dhoti wala* gang," meaning the "green underwear gang." No one dared use that moniker anymore. Not now that there were possibly thousands of members of the Green Gang. In a thick journal, Angoori had written more than a thousand women's names, accompanied by an address and small photograph, but it seemed when I visited that many members were not listed. Angoori herself could not keep track of the exact number, nor could the local journalists who tried to keep a tally. "People made fun of us, but now they give us respect," she told her women, and watched their doubts dissipate.

Angoori was the happiest when she noticed a change in a new Green Gang member. Many women, and occasionally men, approached her for the first time with their eyes cast to the ground, as shy and fearful as she once had been. But within weeks in the gang—and sometimes just days—they spoke impudently and joked about slapping cops or talking back to their husbands or in-laws. They boasted about jobs they planned to take outside the home and threatened never to cook or clean again.

Angoori felt that even though she didn't handle every case perfectly, she had transformed many women in the process. "Now they are so confident that they know how to talk to any policeman," she said. "Before, they only knew how to grow crops and bring up children."

Many local journalists held the same view. For years, they relied on her exploits to make for compelling headlines, but said Angoori's most significant accomplishment was her ability to turn girls who were as docile as cows into women headstrong as bulls. Sometimes the journalists asked Angoori to remember and recount her life as a housewife, when she made cardboard boxes day and night to afford a few roti and was afraid of her own shadow. I did the same when I interviewed her. But over time, that early period became harder for her to recall, and she had less to say about it. To Angoori, the days before the Green Gang felt very far away.

When Dr. Khushwaha saw Angoori again after years, he could hardly believe the change he saw in her. "She was on the ground, and now she's on the sky," he said, his voice swelling with pride. "There are many people you encourage who don't step forward, who don't rise. But she has. She rose, she gained confidence, and she became very bold." Angoori began visiting the doctor again in his office in Tirwa, where he continued to give medicine away for free. "You're like a piece of stone which was unpolished, and now this stone is polished," he said, in the sycophantic voice many had begun using with Angoori. "The stone could be kept in a temple, and people could start preaching it."

Angoori grinned. All the praise made her feel reckless—untouchable.

Phoolan Devi had felt that way, too, after the massacre at Behmai. She had followed her lover's advice to kill twenty-two men instead of just one, to secure fame instead of being hanged as an everyday murderess. But that advice only went so far.

After the newpaper headlines broadcast the Behmai massacre, state police began a manhunt for Phoolan Devi. The police did not know the ravines like the bandits did, so Phoolan Devi evaded capture for two years. The Bandit Queen finally gave herself up to the police in February

1983, demanding that she surrender on her own terms: that a superintendent meet her unarmed in bandit territory, her family be protected, and she serve only eight years in a VIP jail, imprisoned with her followers. According to her, all her terms were accepted.

Clothed in her khaki bandit uniform and wearing a red bandana around her head, Phoolan Devi climbed a wooden dais in the Chambal Valley before an assembled crowd of thousands. Media reports over the years had described Phoolan as a colossal woman, but it turned out she was less than five feet tall. She had a round button nose and the brown, bright eyes of a deer. She flashed the crowd a smile before she laid down her rifle beside a portrait of Durga, goddess of protection and destruction. Afterward, Phoolan Devi stood up and put her hands together in the sign of Namaste, and the crowd bellowed its support. *The Atlantic* reporter Mary Anne Weaver wrote that it felt like the Bandit Queen's story was not coming to a close, but only beginning.

Weaver was right, as female bandit after female bandit took to the ravines afterward to emulate Phoolan Devi. By 2016, Angoori's bulging folder of Green Gang coverage included the exploits of these bandits, including those of Seema Parihar, the bandit who had killed dozens and kidnapped hundreds, and Sarla Jatav, a teenage bandit who befriended her male victims in order to kidnap them and demand hefty ransoms for their release. On TV, Angoori had also learned of female bandits elsewhere in the world. In Mexico in 2013, a blond-haired woman, or maybe someone in a wig, had shot and killed two bus drivers in response to the rape of women on Ciudad Juárez buses. The woman sent a missive to newspapers calling herself an "instrument that will take revenge." The international media dubbed the woman "Diana, Hunter of Bus Drivers." Then, in Kenya in 2020, a group of women who were victims of female genital mutilation surgery began to hunt their surgeons. The women said their sisters were dying from the practice, from health issues or depression, and they had assaulted at least three people already in revenge.

Angoori also collected stories about Sampat Pal, another Uttar Pradesh woman, who formed a gang around the same time Angoori did. Pal's group was called the Gulabi Gang, or Pink Gang, and was founded in 2006, though Angoori claimed the Green Gang took no inspiration from her. The Gulabi Gang held canes and confronted abusers like Angoori, but they were a more innocent version of the Green Gang, rarely crossing the line of what Indian—or Western—society found acceptable. They did not kidnap people or set police stations on fire. They operated more like the nonprofit for women's empowerment the doctor had suggested Angoori start, but with lathis. As a result, the Gulabi Gang received global praise, widespread attention, and even a movie before ultimately fading from international headlines. Angoori respected their approach, but she wanted her gang to operate more like the bandits. Angoori had started describing herself as a vigilante.

But with this approach, Angoori knew she remained vulnerable. The police in Uttar Pradesh could arrest her, demand she stop her work, or insist she surrender, just as they did many of the female bandits in the end. After eighteen years of terror, Seema Parihar was arrested in the year 2000 on dozens of charges. Even Sarla Jatav, whose gang member (an ex-lover) spread a rumor that she died of a snakebite to avoid her capture, had been caught by police in 2005. She was waiting for a train to Mumbai, dressed in a casual pink T-shirt, Ray Bans, and jeans, when they found her.

To keep herself immune from charges, Angoori knew she had to keep the power players on her side, just as any man in her position would do. That included staying active in the Samajwadi Party, which still led the Uttar Pradesh government in 2016, as it had since 2012, when Akhilesh Yadav was elected chief minister. Whenever the party called on her to support a policy, Angoori now appeared with swarms of her Green Gang women, all of them wearing red caps, a Samajwadi Party color, as they marched through the streets and chanted slogans. In return, Angoori earned the party's support, which sometimes meant the police failed to register cases or dropped old charges against her. Someday, she thought, she might get a party title, like district president, or maybe even be elected to the state legislature.

But while Angoori had bigger ambitions through her political connections, she knew it was also crucial to solidify support at home in the villages. There was one place she hadn't done that yet, and that was with the panchayats, or village councils, which in some places held more sway than any politician, police officer, or judge.

In the summer of 2016, Angoori got her chance, when the panchayat in the village of Chandiapur issued a particularly cruel sentence for a local woman. Generally made up of five older men, panchayats dispense justice on a wide range of subjects, including conflicts within a marriage, trade disputes, or villagers who have broken cultural norms. The word "panchayat" comes from the Sanskrit words *pancha*, meaning "five," and *ayatta*, which means "depending on." Villages sometimes depend on the word of the panchayats for issues that fall outside civil and criminal courts, but they were also widely known for upholding archaic cultural norms. In Chandiapur, a poor nomadic community outside Tirwa, residents still relied on the word of its village council.

The panchayat's ruling was issued to a hardworking woman named Meena Devi, on allegations that her son had helped a local girl elope. Meena's son, Pramod, refuted the claims. According to him, after a girl in the village visited her sister for several days, a story was fabricated about the elopement because his was the only low-caste family in the area. Meena and Pramod were from the Banjara tribe, sometimes referred to as India's gypsies. "It was caste enmity," Pramod told me. Soon after, a group of men came to Meena's house and dragged her out through a grate in the roof, blackened her face with diesel oil, hung a necklace of shoes around her neck, ripped at her clothes, and made her kiss the shoes of every man there.

Meena Devi recalled the incident: "I was sobbing. They pushed me down. The pradhan [head of the panchayat] was pleading for them not to take me out and do it." The head, it seemed, had taken pity on her and thought the men were going too far. "It was because I was a woman that this happened," she said, meaning that's why they punished her instead of her son.

Pramod told me that his mother had been "mentally disturbed" ever since the panchayat's sentence. Meena nodded, saying that the incident had been an insult and a source of shame, and that a local government official had twice caught her attempting to kill herself after it happened. She said he found her trying to jump into a well, and also trying to hang herself in the fields. She wiped her eyes with her sky-blue dupatta as she spoke, as flamingos flew overhead.

If the goal of the panchayat's punishment was to shame Meena, the men had been wildly successful. Taslima Nasrin, the author of the novel *Lajja,* or *Shame,* about communal violence in 1990s Uttar Pradesh, fiercely argued against the use of religion, culture, or societal norms as a cudgel, as panchayats did. Nasrin also said: "It's foolish to confront a weapon with bare hands."

Angoori believed the same. She and the Green Gang were outraged when they heard about Meena's case. They believed men should never shame a woman or mete out punishment according to caste. Several days after they read about the case, Angoori and her gang traveled to Chandiapur with their lathis to meet Meena and Pramod and interview anyone who witnessed the incident. "Thirteen or fourteen women came wearing white caps and green saris and canes in their hands," Meena remembered. "When they came, people were scared of their large numbers. They didn't even have tea at our place. They didn't take money." Angoori and the other women took Meena to the police station, where they angrily demanded the officers make arrests of the panchayat's members. Pramod said that the police were slow to act but that Angoori continued to apply pressure and repeatedly called the local media to ensure constant coverage, something that over the years she'd learned was helpful.

Eventually, police arrested twelve men for the crime, including four members of the panchayat (the headman excluded since he'd tried to stop the punishment), plus eight other men who had participated. Pramod was grateful for Angoori's intervention, and said that other girls from the village eloped afterward because they felt the panchayat could no longer stop them. Angoori herself could not have been more pleased. The police had done as she demanded, she'd put a panchayat in its place, and she now had a village headman on her side.

Years later, Angoori learned that Meena's case was still winding its way through the courts. The twelve men had been held in custody only briefly and then released from jail. Without lasting justice, Meena remained distraught and had never let the incident go. "If I will not get justice from the courts, I will commit suicide, and God will judge them," she told me, her voice bitter and breaking. Angoori hoped Meena would get justice eventually, but it was not her problem anymore. There was too much other work to be done, and it was about to get far more complicated.

Around that time, the Green Gang got a new member who would soon rise in its ranks. Sangita Singh joined the gang after she encountered an elderly Green Gang member while she was walking down the road crying. The older woman stopped Sangita to offer her water and ask what was wrong. Sangita said that her in-laws were regularly beating her because of her skin condition called vitiligo, which in Hindi is referred to as "the white stain."* Her skin was dark and lush except for white blotches above her eyebrows, a few parts on her body, and across her hands. Sangita hid the marks well at her wedding, but after the marriage her in-laws saw the extent of it and demanded their son leave her. Sangita's husband, a handsome man with dancing green eyes, loved her and refused to end the marriage. Instead, he offered to file a complaint for her against his family at the station. Sangita was headed to the station to meet him, and while she was grateful he was filing a case, she was sure the police wouldn't do anything.

The woman in the green sari told her to call Angoori, who would spur action. In the following weeks, Angoori and her gang met with Sangita's in-laws and cajoled them into stopping the beatings. The Green Gang carried their canes but did not use them, relying instead on intimidation and persuasion. The violence soon ended, and Sangita could barely believe it. "My back was blackened, and they used to beat me with a belt. I was helpless. I couldn't do anything," she told me, her voice edged with wonder at her change in fortune. "If not for Angoori, I would be dead by now." She immediately joined the Green Gang.

* An in-law of Sangita's said the family never beat Sangita but that "in a family, such fights happen."

As Angoori handled Sangita's case, she wondered, as she often did, why abuse by in-laws was so rampant in the country. The problem was so old and common that a South Asian legend said a woman who died at the suffering of her in-laws or husbands (or some other trauma) could come back as an animated corpse known as a churail to exact revenge. Churails dwelled in trees and were seen as hideous, except when they shape-shifted into beautiful women to charm or kill men and suck their life force out of them.

After Sangita joined the Green Gang, her husband marveled at his emboldened wife. Most women in Tirwa cooked for their husbands and asked permission to go to town. But Sangita no longer made dinner daily and often seemed to have her own plans, her silver anklets jangling as she walked out the door. "Before Angoori, I only knew how to make food," she said. Now, she announced plans to become a journalist and began training at a local TV station. After seeing her transformation, Angoori appointed her as a district deputy superintendent of the gang, alongside Priyanshi, who had shown her own quiet nerve in filing a court case against her husband. At monthly Green Gang meetings, Sangita, Priyanshi, and Ram Kali, the gang's first member, sat on chairs beside Angoori, wearing their green saris with special orange borders. The other women, who were not in leadership positions, sat on mats on the floor in their plain saris. All three deputies had their roles: Ram Kali was Angoori's oldest and most trusted member, Priyanshi was a calm force and adept at organizing the women, and Sangita was enterprising, fierce, and now had media connections that would help the gang.

At the Tirwa police station in 2016, while filing a domestic violence complaint for another woman, Sangita swore at a policeman who told her he would not file her report. "You were not born of a female's womb, but of a cow's womb," she told him, tossing her dupatta over her shoulder.

There was a chant she and the other Green Gang members loved, which served to threaten cops: "Long live the Green Gang / The officer who does justice is a brother to us / The officer who gets rowdy we have a cane in our bands / The one who takes bribes we should cut his nose!" Thousands of miles away in Mexico City, a collective of anarchist women acted with the same impudence toward local cops, who had allegedly raped two teenaged girls. Calling their group the Feminas Brujas e Insurreccionalistas, they threatened police in 2019 online: "WE ARE BAD AND WE CAN BE WORSE: WE ARE YOUR WORST NIGHTMARE!"

Sangita giggled as she later recounted to me her own exchanges with cops. "Now, if I go to the police office, I get a chair," she said. "And if anyone beats me, I start beating."

Soon after Sangita joined the gang, Angoori asked for her help with a difficult case involving a girl who she was told needed discipline. The gang had had female targets before—some of the bootleggers they beat were women—but it was unusual for them to go after a girl, especially one who was not breaking the law. The girl's mother had come to Angoori for help, saying that her seventeen-year-old daughter, who had been married off at fifteen, was having an affair with another man who worked as an engineer. The girl had fallen for him while cooking and cleaning his home. The mother said her daughter hit her anytime she tried to intervene, the affair was shameful, and the engineer was an alcoholic. She asked the Green Gang to return her daughter to her rightful husband for all these reasons, but asked that they not use their canes. "Don't beat my daughter," the mother told Angoori. "Just please make her understand that 'what you're doing is wrong.'"*

For six months, Angoori and Sangita verbally pressured the girl to return to her husband, which she did a few times but never for long. The women also demanded the girl stop beating her mother, but her mother said nothing changed. Finally, the gang had enough. On a cool morning in 2016, Angoori, accompanied by Sangita, Ram Kali, and several other Green Gang members, barged into the engineer's cement-and-brick house, canes in hands. The girl's mother was out working in the fields

---

* Both the girl and the mother requested anonymity because of the attention the case drew.

and did not see them coming, and the engineer was away on work travel. Sangita knocked first, then forced her way into the house, with the other women close on her heels.

According to Sangita, the girl became agitated at their forced entrance and bit Sangita's hand. In response, Sangita struck the girl repeatedly with her cane, while Angoori used her sandals to beat her. As Ram Kali and the other women dragged the girl out of the house by her hair, several local journalists, who Angoori had tipped off to the action beforehand, began filming. "Sangita, beat her. Ram Kali, beat her," Angoori cries out in a video of the incident, which soon went viral online. "Do you care about your parents' reputation?" Angoori asks the girl. "Catch her. She is running," warns another Green Gang woman. The girl sobs and begs for help from her mother, who is not there. The women push the girl into a car, and the video abruptly cuts off.

Sangita and Angoori later bragged about the rest of the story: They drove the girl to another village and forced her to marry a third man. They reasoned that if her first husband could not keep her away from the engineer, a second husband might fix the problem. The police, however, did not agree with this approach. Nor did local or national reporters, who descended from New Delhi to castigate Angoori. "An incident of hooliganism by the Green Gang has come to light in Kannauj of Uttar Pradesh," an *India TV* journalist reported. "Green Gang members insulted the girl in the name of doing moral policing. They shamed her and thrashed her in full public view." The journalist continued, "The girl kept crying . . . but these cruel women kept on slapping her."

With the national spotlight on them, police officers returned the girl to her mother, and she was granted a divorce from the second husband. Angoori, Sangita, and Ram Kali were arrested, though all three maintained they had done nothing wrong. In her police complaint against the Green Gang, the girl accused the women of eight crimes: among them house trespass, intentional insult, voluntarily causing hurt, criminal intimidation, and assault. Angoori was jailed in Tirwa for nearly a week. Hundreds of Green Gang members descended from nearby villages to demand their leader's release, many of whom spent days sleeping outside the jail. Although the police pressed charges against Angoori, the court ultimately dismissed the case, with Angoori's son serving as her lawyer.

Years later, the girl told me she remained traumatized by the incident. "They beat me very badly. They thrashed me with canes. They banged my head against the wall." Her voice quavered as she spoke, her eyes cast to the floor. She still looked younger than her years, and was slight like a bird. Rows of laundry hung on the line. She said she never bit Sangita, who struck her with incredible force with her lathi. "And then they got me married forcefully. I don't even know the name of that guy," she told me bitterly. "It's not a crime to love someone." After she was granted a divorce from her first husband as well, the girl and the engineer got married and she gave birth to a son, even though she was still a teenager. The girl said she never recovered from the incident with Angoori and Sangita. "I am weak. I get faint," she said, staring at her feet. "I start shivering if I hear the words 'Green Gang.'"

Angoori never apologized to the girl, who she said deserved the thrashing because she had beaten her mother. "I wanted this to go as a lesson to other girls that you should value your parents," Angoori said. In collectivistic India, the family unit came first. Despite some of her more progressive beliefs on caste and gender, Angoori held a traditional view regarding family and married couples. The girl had also violated another sacred concept in the region—that of a woman's chastity. It was a story as old as the Hindu myth of Sita, who had to prove her purity to her husband, Ram, by walking over the hot coals of a fire. A woman should not leave her husband or cheat, just like a man should not leave his wife or philander. "We join families, not break them," Angoori said.

Angoori never apologized to the girl's mother either, who had pleaded with them not to beat her daughter. "It happened in the heat of the moment," after the girl had gotten aggressive, the Green Gang leader said. "I was provoked." The mother told me she wished she had never called the gang for help.

As for Sangita, she laughed when she remembered the girl's beating. Once the victim, Sangita was now the aggressor, and she did not see anything wrong with that.

• • •

The local journalists who had positively covered Angoori's exploits for years turned disapproving after the incident with the girl and engineer. Pankaj Srivastava, the journalist who frequented temples, was the most concerned. "To give justice, you have to listen to both parties. Angoori only listens to one," he told me. Pankaj had noticed this before the girl's beating, but it was plain to him now. "She acts on the complaints but doesn't find out the facts." Over the years, he felt, Angoori's investigations had become speedier and less rigorous. He still thought Angoori empowered women, but that it came at a heavy price. Neelam Kumar Saxena, the crime reporter, agreed. "She should not beat anyone or take the law into her own hands," he said, despite years of awestruck coverage of the gang. The Green Gang had made sense to Neelam when Angoori punished domestic abusers and rapists, but now that they had beaten a girl, he believed that no one person should dispense justice. Both men noticed that Angoori began using her canes less often after the girl's case went viral. "Angoori is scared since she went to jail," Pankaj said. "Because police now feel negatively about Angoori."

Angoori insisted to me that that wasn't true. "Nothing has changed for the Green Gang," she said. "Don't think I'm afraid of going to jail or the police. If someone misbehaves with me or my gang members, I'll beat again."

But Angoori's power was slipping. The media was skeptical, local police had turned against her, and even her political connections were more tenuous. The Samajwadi Party was losing its grip on Uttar Pradesh, and the following year, in 2017, it would lose the state legislative assembly to the BJP, the Hindu right-wing national party, which had strong support among the rural poor. It was a landslide win for the BJP and an embarrassing loss for the Samajwadi Party. Even women's rights activists denounced vigilante justice like Angoori's.

In 2017, a prominent Indian female politician said rapists should be skinned and paraded in public. Roop Rekha Verma, the women's rights activist in Lucknow, told me women like that politician and Angoori were doing more harm than good. Verma runs a nonprofit in Lucknow called

Saajhi Duniya, meaning "a common world," which works to combat gender inequality, among other issues. She also founded an Institute of Women's Studies at Lucknow University, where she taught philosophy for thirty-nine years. "If you really believe in democracy, if you really believe in the rule of law, and assuring rights of individuals, then one can never ever support such movements even in the name of justice," she said. "Even if they fill a vacuum in the breakdown of law and order."

Verma pursed her lips as she decried the cults of personality around the Bandit Queen and Hindu goddesses of destruction such as Durga or Kali. After all, she said, Phoolan Devi was still a criminal.

After Phoolan Devi gave herself up to police in 1983, she was accused of forty-eight criminal offenses, including murder, plunder, and kidnapping for ransom. Thirty of her charges were attributed to "banditry." She got a private cell, but jail life was not easy. In her years behind bars, she survived multiple attempts on her life from fellow prisoners and watched the other men in her gang leave early. She told reporters she lived like a "rat" behind bars. When she developed an ovarian cyst, a prison doctor took the opportunity to remove her uterus without her knowledge. An Indian activist later asked why the procedure was done, to which the prison doctor laughed and said: "We don't want her breeding any more Phoolan Devis."

The Bandit Queen spent eleven years in prison before being released in February 1994, when a low-caste politician took control of Uttar Pradesh and exonerated her. Verma, the activist, didn't think women like Phoolan Devi deserved the public's absolution.

Despite the gender- and caste-based issues within India's courts, police, and panchayats, Verma said, she did not see Phoolan Devi and Angoori as heroines. To her, they were getting justice by committing another injustice, building a chain of violence that would never end. "It is very sad that the institutions have become so weak and so unhelpful that some feel like vigilantism" is the only answer, she said. "But it is brutal, and it will always remain brutal. Two brutalities don't make a right."

LONG LIVE THE GREEN GANG

> I have all the guns and the money. I can withstand challenge from without and from within.
>
> —Elaine Brown, who headed the Black Panther Party, according to her 1993 memoir, *A Taste of Power: A Black Woman's Story*

Ever since the incident with the girl and the engineer, Angoori worried. She worried about her cases and her women, and she worried about influence. But mainly she worried about money. Although one of her sons made a good salary, the Green Gang was draining more money than ever, because with the police turned on her, she had to bribe them to do their jobs. Also, the gang had swollen to thousands of women, and most of her members were desperately poor. Angoori still charged a joining fee of 150 rupees, but that was only enough to cover the cost of a cheap green sari and plastic membership card. New members often asked Angoori for food, clothing, and other necessities, which she gave them whenever she could. She still paid women a day rate of 100 rupees (about $1.50), but felt that was too little and wished she could pay more. The cases themselves were costly, especially if her women made multiple trips. She also had to pay her office rent. Soon, Angoori made the difficult decision to charge clients to solve their cases.

Despite Neelam's misgivings about Angoori, in summer 2018, the crime reporter still recommended the Green Gang to a young woman he met at a police station. Her story was full of twists and turns that Neelam thought only Angoori could handle. Her name was Rashmi Pal, and she'd fallen in love with a dark-eyed man who'd ruined her life.

According to Rashmi's account, she had sex with the man after he promised to marry her, and after they were intimate, he refused to wed. Rashmi loved him but told herself to move on, and ended up marrying another man. But then the dark-eyed man reappeared, she said, and began showing "objectionable" photos he'd taken of her to other people—seemingly to shame Rashmi's husband into leaving her. Rashmi's husband did divorce her, and she and her first love got married after all.

After marriage, their life together quickly turned ugly. Rashmi said her husband began to force himself on her, saying if she didn't comply, he'd upload her naked photos to the Internet. On top of that, according to Rashmi, he began having an affair with a female constable in the Uttar Pradesh police. The husband told me there was "no truth" to any of the allegations, that he did not want his name published, and that he'd never officially married Rashmi.

After all his threats, Rashmi decided she no longer wanted to stay with him. But, just like Priyanshi Rajput and Phoolan Devi, she did not think she could live without a husband. It was an awful saying, but it was true: *A woman without a husband is as good as dead.* She needed her husband to take her back. So, in 2018, Rashmi went to the police station to register a police complaint against him, hoping the courts would force him to stay with her. After receiving Rashmi's complaint, police arrested the man on charges of voluntarily causing hurt, criminal intimidation, and rape.

But within twenty-four hours he was released and the rape case was dropped. Rashmi was outraged. That's when she met Neelam in the station, who told her that perhaps the Green Gang could help.

Angoori met Rashmi in the young woman's small, bubblegum pink apartment in Tirwa, and told her she could help. According to Rashmi, Angoori charged her 21,500 rupees (around $300) for her services, a large sum for any Tirwa woman. Rashmi, who lived modestly, was confused at the high cost to solve her case. Angoori told her that to get the police to take action, the Green Gang would have to bribe them, so Rashmi agreed.

Not long after, Angoori and several other gang members showed up at the husband's house. They barged their way inside with their canes, demanding that he and his in-laws explain his bad behavior, and insisting he take Rashmi back as his wife. But the conversation only led to heated arguments. "They forcefully entered my house. They think they can go anywhere because they are female," the man told me later by phone. "I told them my case is in court. They work on half-baked information. How can they take action when you have the police and the courts?"

Angoori also went to the police to pressure them to do more on Rashmi's case, with no success. Rashmi was sure the man must have paid a higher bribe to the cops than she and the Green Gang did, which was how cases seemed to be decided. Her fate was now with the courts, but the courts would take years to resolve her case—if not her whole life. Angoori told her she was sorry, but there was nothing more she could do. Rashmi's voice rose in bitterness as she recalled the conversation. "I was 100 percent sure the Green Gang would solve my case," she said. Instead, she was thousands of rupees poorer and nowhere closer to a resolution.

Since the Green Gang hadn't helped her, Rashmi decided to get justice on her own. She went to the police station to confront the female constable about the affair, a visit that local media reported turned into a brawl. Still, her husband did not return to Rashmi. Rashmi's anger burned hotter with each passing day. "If my husband will not keep me, I'll murder him," she said with a faraway gaze. "I am very serious about this. I have no option. So I'll just murder him."

Angoori, wanting to distance herself as much as possible from the failed and drama-filled case, eventually returned most of Rashmi's money. "I dropped the case because I did not trust Rashmi," she said.

Angoori also had bigger problems on her mind. With dwindling resources and weakened influence, Angoori felt the gang was spiraling out of her control. Too many cases were going unsolved, and her members were beginning to grumble. She was also getting into regular fights with the new head of the Tirwa police, a mustachioed officer named Amod Kumar Singh. Singh sneered at Angoori and called her a "blackmailer with a criminal history." "As I remember, there is no positive impact they have had," he said. He added that Angoori only helped her Green Gang members and did not care about finding the truth, especially now that they were asking for money for cases. I pointed out that he and his officers took bribes from people all the time. But he said that was just how things were, giving me a crocodile smile full of teeth. He added that if Angoori wanted to change society, then she ought to behave better than them.

Finally free at the age of thirty, in 1994, Phoolan Devi had the same round nose and cheeks, but she'd gained weight and scars crisscrossed her face. At her surrender to police, when asked what she planned to do with her life, she'd coyly replied that she only knew how to use a rifle and cut grass. But now, after her release from jail, Phoolan Devi announced she was running for Parliament as a member of the Samajwadi Party, which even then was aimed at supporting the lower castes. One of her staffers said she did this to secure parliamentary immunity from further prosecution. But she told journalists a different story: "The time has come to do serious work for the people. And I think the best way to do it will be from the seat of power—the Parliament." When photographers took her picture during the campaign, she stared down the camera.

Phoolan Devi swept into office in 1996, when low-caste people were just beginning to gain more political might. She held the position the year Angoori was evicted from her home. Though the former bandit had been out of the spotlight for years, Phoolan Devi never lost her ability to woo a crowd. She spoke persuasively in her campaign speeches of helping women and the low-caste, promising that a vote for her meant the "days of exploitation are over"—because the lowly now had the power and the powerful would have to obey.

During her two terms in Parliament, the Bandit Queen, at last, seemed to live a stable life. Phoolan moved into a big bungalow in New Delhi, where she hung portraits of the goddess Durga on her wall. She married a portly realtor named Umed Singh, who cooked her meals. Her adopted Great Dane, Jackie, was pampered with chicken and fiercely protective of Phoolan. She worried about her safety, yet for half a decade, life went on without major incident. She told the media she found politics exciting because of how many people she had to keep happy.

Angoori was learning a similar lesson. Among the women who were increasingly unhappy with Angoori's failings was Urmila Sharma, a longtime gang member who had worked her way up to state general secretary of the Green Gang. Urmila was responsible for keeping track of paperwork and money, and her concerns with Angoori had grown over the years. She did not like that Angoori scolded poor women who failed to prepare tea or snacks at her arrival. She was troubled by the critical media coverage of the gang after the incident with the girl and the engineer. But Urmila was most upset that Angoori had taken so much money from Rashmi. As secretary, she knew Rashmi's case did not cost nearly that much. "I've worked so hard for the Green Gang, I don't know if it's day or night," said Urmila, who had come to believe that Angoori "is fooling everyone."

After much thought, in the fall of 2018, Urmila decided to try to oust Angoori as the gang's head. She thought the Green Gang needed new leadership to return to its roots: fighting for poor women who were harassed. Maybe, Urmila thought, she could even form a new gang, and all the Green Gang members would follow. She would call it the Narangi Gang, or Orange Gang—a saffron orange, the color of fire and purity. Unlike Angoori's, her gang would be pure and never motivated by profit. "I'll make them flat," Urmila said of the Green Gang, "and expose them in the market" in town.

Angoori soon got wind of Urmila's planned coup, after both Priyanshi and Sangita told her about it, as well as an elderly member whom Angoori sometimes used as a spy. The Green Gang leader held an emergency meeting with her core members. "How many women want to go with Urmila?" Angoori asked several dozen members assembled before her. The women were quiet or murmured that they would not leave with Urmila. "Urmila is saying, 'I have made this gang,'" Angoori continued, her voice wrathful. "I have called this meeting so that if any one of you thinks the same, then tell me. Today Urmila has said this, tomorrow Sangita can also say this. Urmila is telling other women of the gang that Angoori Dahariya did nothing, and it was her who made the gang and added members." She turned beseeching: "I am hurt after getting to know about all this. I have done nothing on my own. It was a joint effort of everyone."

The women listened silently, all eyes on their leader. Angoori went on: "If Urmila was this responsible, then why is she not here in the meeting? It is only me to call every one of you." No one replied.

Shortly after the meeting, Angoori expelled Urmila from the gang. Disloyalty could not be tolerated, even if Urmila had been with her from the start.

By the end of 2018, Angoori decided she needed to make an even more drastic change. *If you were in politics, then no one would have ever dared to touch you,* the king had counseled her years ago. She knew that if she fully joined politics a second time, this time would be very different. More than a decade later, she would no longer be a poor, lowly woman going from village to village with her hands folded in supplication, trying to convince rural people of idealistic policies that would likely never come to pass. Now, she had much to offer any political party, with the guaranteed votes of thousands of her women in the district of Kannauj, in Uttar Pradesh, a bellwether state with almost double the population of the next most populous state, and the most members in Parliament. Also, Dalits made up a fifth of the population in the state, and the party knew Angoori could rally the Dalit vote.

In Indian politics, officials were regularly accused of siphoning money, stealing state property, peddling influence for services, conspiring to commit crimes, and more. Angoori was aware of the stain that joining politics at this juncture would leave on her, with her women, and among the wider public, because everyone knew politics was corrupt. She tried to hide the decision from me when I was in Tirwa, until I learned of a political event she was planning. But as Milan Vaishnav argued at the Carnegie Endowment for International Peace in 2016, many people also accepted politics and crime as intertwined. "Voters in India strategically elect politicians who are tied to criminal activity," he wrote, "seek[ing] refuge in the hands of a strongman who can fill in for the state's various governance deficits." Angoori had become her own kind of strongman, even if she didn't want everyone to see it that way.

Angoori was increasingly convinced she needed the protection and support politics could offer her. She also felt she needed the power, for herself and for the thousands of Dalit women who followed her lead, because while their positions had improved as women, she wasn't sure much had changed in regard to caste. To keep making change outside the system, and to ensure the survival of the Green Gang, she believed she had to secure influence inside.

The year 2019 was a general election year. Every day, leading up to the elections, one political event or another would be held in the district. That time of year, no one could catch the scent of Kannauj's famed lemongrass, just the smell of burning plastic and the grease of the free samosas the politicians doled out. Tensions ran high as people argued about which party was made up of crooks. The rival, right-wing BJP had control of the state—and the country—but the Samajwadi Party still had a good chance to reclaim power locally.

And so, in November 2018, several months before the election, Angoori took 250 of her Green Gang women to the big city of Lucknow, where the important politicians lived, to demand a pension of 1,000 rupees (around $15) for all poor women in the state. Local journalists told me she did it as a "political stunt," to show her longtime ally, the Samajwadi Party, that she could easily gather hordes of constituents. By this point, Angoori claimed the gang had 14,575 members. While that number seemed high and was impossible to prove, the party was still likely to get thousands of votes with Angoori's help. Angoori didn't get the pension, but the Samajwadi Party told Angoori they'd love to have her campaign for them. At the same time, they gifted the Green Gang women one hundred hand pumps, which was impactful since about half of Dalit villages in the country were still denied access to water sources. The party also gave Angoori a special title: General Secretary of the Samajwadi Women's Wing in Kannauj.

That January 2019, Angoori announced to her Green Gang members that she was officially campaigning for the Samajwadi Party. She said she needed their help to get the political party back in office, with the promise that the party would give them the pensions they'd demanded. To start, she would hold a large event in Tirwa, and all of them were to come.

Sangita and Priyanshi organized the event together, calling Green Gang members to come to Tirwa from faraway villages, taking any transport they could. Angoori had impressed on her members how important it was that the party see the scale of their support, to vote for Yadav as chief minister of Uttar Pradesh, the same position he'd held before. It was not difficult to learn about the event, because it was the talk of the town.

The day of the Samajwadi Party event, scheduled ahead of the general election, dawned cool and bright despite Tirwa's perpetual haze. But the sun burned off any respite of cold air by mid-morning. A billboard in town was plastered with Angoori's face beside the faces of Akhilesh Yadav, his wife, Dimple, and other party bosses who controlled local branches. The billboard included Angoori's new title, and the event was described as a conference for the new Samajwadi Women's Wing, which would be made up almost entirely of Green Gang members. That morning, Angoori did not dress in her typical Green Gang uniform and instead donned an expensive chiffon sari in red and white, official Samajwadi Party colors.

The event was held outside in a dusty square in the center of Tirwa, with a red-draped stage up front. Hundreds of women showed up, not an easy feat for poor women without money to travel. One attendee, who worked as a washerwoman, told me she was happy to come and vote for the Samajwadi Party at Angoori's request, provided she got her pension in the end. All the female attendees sat on red plastic chairs in front of the stage, while the men stood awkwardly in clusters behind them. Sewa Lal, Angoori's husband, stood silently at the back. Red flags hung around the square, all bearing the Samajwadi Party's symbol of a bicycle, chosen because it's an everyday transport for rural people. Before noon, Angoori strode in surrounded by the leaders of her gang: Priyanshi, Sangita, and Ram Kali, who all wore red clothing. But while they were there to support the Samajwadi Party, the women wanted to make sure the party understood who they were. "Long live the Green Gang!" the women chanted as they raised their fists at her entrance. "Love live Angoori Dahariya!"

The event began with speeches by some of the lesser party bosses, who called for the Samajwadi Party to come into power again in Uttar Pradesh. The microphone cracked continuously, but the speakers continued undeterred. They praised Angoori for drawing such a large crowd. "When a woman starts speaking, they change history," one female party boss said, and attendees garlanded Angoori with marigolds. The politician also announced that they would collect bank account details that day for women's pensions, to be given out to every attendee at some undeclared future after they won the election.

Then Angoori took the mic. She castigated the opposition BJP for its unpopular policies, such as demonetizing the rupee, a move that had hurt many poor people. She joked that the BJP "worked only for cows and for bulls," because the party in 2017 had banned the sale of cow for slaughter, which led to multiple attacks on Muslims suspected of butchering cows, or on Dalits who were tasked with disposing of their carcasses. "I urge you all to work for the Samajwadi Party," Angoori went on, her voice authoritative but too loud on the scratchy mic. She looked out at the sea of faces, nearly every one of which she knew. Then she broke into a song from a Bollywood film, whose words she altered to suit the day: "Bahut pyaar karte hai tumko sanam," she sang, "I love you a lot sweetheart . . . I love you Samajwadi Party." Journalists in the back snickered at this profusive display, but most of Angoori's women nodded along.

When Angoori finished, Sangita again began the chant: "Angoori Dahariya zindabad!" "Long live Angoori Dahariya!" and the crowd joined in. Angoori smiled but inwardly felt herself falter. Over the last decade, she'd helped so many women. Now it felt like she was selling them out. Like cows, they trustingly followed her wherever she led. She just hoped her gamble was worth it—that she'd get the pension for her women, and that the police, seeing the support of the party and local party bosses, would learn to fear her again.

Sangita told Angoori that her speech was terrific, and that she had never seen such a crowd. "In the past, only men used to come for political rallies, but now, there are so many women," Sangita said, her eyes shining. Priyanshi nodded in agreement, her long braid hanging down her back. That night, Angoori's husband, Sewa Lal, also reassured Angoori, saying he would support her if she decided to run for higher political office, because he understood it would allow her to help more women. Angoori insisted she had no plans to run for anything, though it was clear she had bigger aspirations.

. . .

At a political event a few days after Angoori's event, Akhilesh Yadav was hounded by journalists for his alleged role in a mining scandal that had become national news. Dressed in a pressed kurta and vest and seated on a silk blue chair, Yadav laughed off the allegations, though they seemed likely to affect his chances as chief minister, and then quickly changed the subject.

When I took him aside to ask about Angoori's support for the Samajwadi Party, he praised the Green Gang and their actions. "Angoori is doing a great job. She is spreading awareness in the society, especially among marginalized people," he said. He added that the security of women remained one of India's biggest problems, and that Angoori was addressing it head-on.

Yadav said he didn't think it was right for Angoori to beat people but that he understood where she got her ideas. He described how female vigilantism was threaded throughout Indian culture and history, with Phoolan Devi's life story being taught in schools and Bollywood films regularly encouraging it, including a new movie called *Sonchiriya* that told of the exploits of the Chambal Valley bandits. He promised he'd push Angoori to act without her canes.

As Yadav spoke, several politicians seated nearby shook their heads. Abhishek Mishra, a former Samajwadi cabinet minister, spoke up to say it made sense for rural women to fight violence with violence. "The harder you press someone against the wall, the harder they rebound," Mishra said as he sipped his chai. "When there is exploitation, then there is rebellion beneath." Another party boss added that the Indo-Gangetic plain, where Tirwa is located, had always been turbulent, with some eight empires rising and falling there. "Rebellion is in our blood," he said.

Dimple Yadav, Akhilesh Yadav's wife who had been accused in the kidnapping case, no longer held the Kannauj seat. Unlike many of the disheveled male party bosses, Dimple's makeup was flawless, her hair coiffed, and sari pressed, as was expected for a female politician. She said she, too, understood why the Green Gang women combated violence with violence. She described how village women were not getting the help they needed and how crimes against women were rising. "Political parties should understand this," she said, adding that the women's phone line started under Samajwadi Party leadership. But she told me she understood that women in Uttar Pradesh still felt that canes were their only way to retaliate: "If the police are not listening, what can they do?"

On an ordinary day in New Delhi, in July 2001, Phoolan was on her lunch break at her bungalow when three masked men walked up to her residence and gunned her down. She had been in office for less than a decade; she was thirty-seven years old. Around her body, her front yard was covered in shell casings and the ground beside her neem tree stained with blood. She was rushed to the hospital, where Umed sobbed beside her gurney, but the Bandit Queen was already dead. Sher Singh Rana, the man who confessed to her murder, said he had killed her to avenge the massacre many years before at Behmai.

Angoori was not surprised by the ending to Phoolan Devi's story. A female vigilante upset many people doing the work she did. And a female vigilante who became a politician was forever a target. The week after her political event, Angoori felt exhausted and confused, like the quest for justice was impossible to get right. She was fifty-five now, the same age Phoolan Devi would be if she were still alive.

That week, a raspy-voiced Green Gang member named Gudden had come to Angoori's office, bruised and cut-up, complaining that another woman had beaten her during an argument over a drain. It was a minor complaint, so small that Angoori decided to respond to it alone. She was quiet as she rode by car to the nearby village, staring out at the passing fields of mustard flowers, paddy, and wheat.

When Angoori got out of the car, the villagers clamored over each other to share their version of events. They said the fight began over a makeshift bathroom that polluted the village water, which ran through a drain beside their thatched huts. Angoori shushed them. "A village is like a family, so why are we beating?" she lectured them, with no apparent irony. "Beating anyone is a wrong thing."

When a teenage girl showed Angoori cuts she said were inflicted by

Gudden, Angoori said they looked like old scars and that Gudden was likely the victim. "But how can you say we were beating her?" the girl cut in. "Were you here?"

Silence. At last, Angoori spoke. "You know I don't support anyone who is wrong," she said softly, as everyone in the village crowded closer to hear. Then she became stern, telling them to call her again only if they had video evidence of the culprit. Angoori instructed Gudden to get in her car, and they sped away.

On the drive back to Tirwa, Angoori berated Gudden, saying she knew Gudden was the guilty one. "If you know you are at fault, why did you start a fight?" she said. "I will never come again for you." But then Angoori said that because Gudden was a Green Gang member, she would ensure the police took her side. With the gang weakened, Angoori felt she could not afford to lose any members. It was just as the journalist Pankaj had feared. In the absence of hard evidence, and even knowing Gudden was in the wrong, Angoori favored her gang member.

At her home in Tirwa that afternoon, I asked Angoori whether she thought it was fair to favor Gudden, and Angoori said she did not know who was to blame in the drainage dispute. "It is very messy and very difficult to find truth," she said, her voice distant, as the sun set outside her window. Beside Angoori, her grandchild and a gangly puppy played on the floor. Perhaps she had unfairly favored her gang member, she added, but she had not used her canes on anyone. She did not see herself as nearly as corrupt as the many men in power in Uttar Pradesh. And it was better than doing nothing. Nothing was what the cops, courts, and politicians did.

In March 2020, the Indian government ordered a nationwide lockdown in response to the COVID-19 pandemic hitting India. No more than five hundred people reported having the virus thus far, but with 1.38 billion people in the country, many in densely packed cities, everyone knew the numbers could soon explode. Millions of people migrated to other states because they were abruptly put out of work or wanted to join family elsewhere. Angoori stayed put in Tirwa but shut her office in town because she could no longer meet clients in person. At first, she went out to the villages several times with her women demanding that noncompliant men wear masks. But soon, the Green Gang stopped its activities altogether. Her members were terrified of the virus, and no one wanted to leave home. After March, the lockdown in India was extended and extended again, and Angoori finally accepted the benefits of staying home. She increasingly felt the fatigue and joint pain of older age—she was fifty-seven now—and found she appreciated the rest. At home, she could spend time with her grandchildren, bouncing them on her knee or helping them raise the puppy they'd adopted after it was attacked by larger strays. When another wave of infections came, and a complete lockdown was reinstated in March 2021, Angoori did not even protest.

Instead, she spent time reflecting on the work the Green Gang had done. She felt that, since she had founded the gang, domestic violence incidents had declined in the region. Many women now threatened any man who tried to beat them, and that seemed enough to stop many aggressors in their tracks. Data-wise, it was unclear if domestic violence was up or down in Kannauj because advocates said more women were reporting.

Angoori, though, felt that little had changed when it came to caste, despite the Green Gang's work to help low-caste women such as Meena Devi, and all the thousands of Dalit women in her gang. Sujatha Gidla explained the stubbornness of the caste system in her 2017 memoir *Ants Among Elephants.* "Because your life is your caste, your caste is your life," she wrote. Caste followed a person from birth to death.

It didn't matter that caste was a "fiction," as activist Thenmozhi Soundararajan argued in *The Trauma of Caste,* just "a human creation set up to benefit a few at the expense of the many." It was a fiction with a tenacious grip. More low-caste women held positions of power these days, but many Dalit women still struggled to survive. The issue of untouchability felt intransigent to Angoori, like a truck stuck in mud.

By late 2021, the pandemic had stabilized. The following year was an election year for the Uttar Pradesh legislative assembly, and the Samajwadi Party asked Angoori for her help, as Akhilesh Yadav again ran for chief minister. The party hadn't done well in Uttar Pradesh in the general election in 2019, losing to their main foe, the BJP. Yadav decried the election as a "race between a Ferrari and a bicycle," with the Samajwadi Party as the lowly bicycle and the BJP with all the swag and money to buy ads and other airtime on TV. Although voter turnout for men and women was nearly equal for the first time in history, many women and Dalits outside Kannauj hadn't voted for the Samajwadi Party. The party again desperately needed the help of people who could bring out these voters, like Angoori. Angoori finally acknowledged she was interested in a party position, as a district president—or even a member of the legislative assembly.

That year, Angoori reactivated the Green Gang, whose women took to the streets with their canes and new chants: "Akhilesh Yadav Zindabad!" and "Long live Akhilesh Yadav!" Yadav, who was not Dalit but was from an officially "backward" caste, had again promised Angoori the pension for which she and her women had long lobbied. This time, poor women and their families were promised 18,000 rupees a year (nearly $250) in financial assistance—assuming he was elected. Yadav reminded voters that a Samajwadi policy from years prior had provided 6,000 rupees a year to poor families in the state.

Throughout the winter of 2021 and early 2022, the Green Gang stopped handling any women's cases. After all these years, Angoori felt her influence was better directed toward lobbying for the potential pension for her women, which would give them financial freedom and autonomy, rather than just helping out a few women here and there. She could not even imagine what would be possible if she secured a party position. So Angoori redirected her energy toward campaigning across Uttar Pradesh for Yadav, and brought her gang of women with her. They organized public meetings and knocked on doors, spreading the word about the prospective pension. In one village, a complaint was lodged against her with local police for "disturbing the governmental process," because someone reported she was trying to impede the opposition candidate from filing his nomination. But nothing came of it. Perhaps the police saw that she had stopped her usual Green Gang activities and was no longer a threat to them, or perhaps the Samajwadi Party protected her.

The local journalists who had long covered Angoori mostly stopped following her, uninterested in her political rise. They were more intent on looking for new female vigilantes, such as Sadhna Patel, a female bandit in her early twenties who had been operating in the ravines of Uttar Pradesh, until she recently slipped into the neighboring state of Madhya Pradesh to evade arrest. For months, Sadhna had been kidnapping, extorting, and committing armed robbery, including having robbed many traders and kidnapped a landowner's son for ransom. Police had put a 20,000-rupee bounty (or some $270) on Sadhna's head. Some people described her as the latest Bandit Queen, or the new female Robin Hood.

Meanwhile, Akhilesh Yadav, the man who'd once dismissed the Green Gang's actions as "poor people sometimes do these things," was now relying on the voices of people like Angoori to mobilize poor people in droves. Yadav had not grown up poor, since his father was a major politician, but that same father had likely impressed on him the impact that the poor vote could have.

If the Samajwadi Party came to power, Angoori was confident Yadav would help her and her women. In addition to the pension, and a possible party position for Angoori, he had promised to set up a big manufacturing center for women in Kannauj to have access to new jobs.

Loyal Priyanshi supported Angoori in her political campaigning, still hoping that her case with her husband would be resolved, and that other low-caste women like her wouldn't face the same struggles. But Priyanshi's situation had only worsened in the years since Angoori pressured Priyanshi's husband, Arvind, to take her back. In 2017—perhaps to get Priyanshi's court case against him dropped—Arvind filed a police complaint alleging that Priyanshi's brother had tried to shoot him. According to local media, Arvind fabricated the shooting with a firecracker he exploded in his breast pocket. Despite everything—the beatings, his affair, and now the faked shooting—Priyanshi told Angoori in her placid way that she still wanted to return to her husband. Her mother reminded her that divorce or remarriage was unheard-of in their village, and Priyanshi agreed she could not be the first one. Angoori promised her that, with enough time, she and her husband would be reunited.

"Keep patience," Angoori said. "For someday, I will get this case solved." But even Angoori knew this was no longer true. Priyanshi's husband had offered Priyanshi two lakh rupees (or nearly $3,000) for a mutual divorce, but as of 2021, Angoori still could not convince her to accept it. Instead, the case dragged on for its twelfth year.

In March 2022, the BJP triumphed in the legislative assembly elections in Uttar Pradesh over the Samajwadi Party, once again. Akhilesh Yadav would not come to power as chief minister again after all. There would be no car, money, or fancy position for Angoori, and no pension or industrial unit for her women. Angoori told me she felt sad and angry, and then a stinging regret. Around Tirwa, the Samajwadi flyers and posters began to tear and disintegrate in the wind. She believed the BJP must have cheated, and wished she had never asked her women for help campaigning. "I took the help of my gang in going to villages to convince people to vote for the Samajwadi Party," she said, "and until the last day of the election, I did whatever I could. But taking members without giving them any monetary benefit is also not right." She wondered if she had formed a nonprofit as the doctor had suggested so long ago—if she had done things the official, accepted way—she could have provided a better life for herself and her women.

The more Angoori thought about it, the more she felt she'd wasted time with the Green Gang. "I was not at home when my daughter and my daughter-in-law needed me," she said. "I was with my gang all the time, and I pumped in so much money to help people. I got nothing in return." She continued morosely: "And my members are poor and still do not have money."

Of course, she knew this was not entirely true. Angoori had the relationships she'd formed with her women—tough Ram Kali, serene Priyanshi, fierce Sangita, and all the others—plus the many battles they'd won. The Green Gang even helped some local men, including a bony farmer named Babaram Das, whose family was taunted by fellow villagers over a foolish rumor, leading his son to hang himself in shame. It was only after Angoori descended on the village that the villagers stopped their sneering.

Despite all the people she had helped, Angoori thought it was hard to feel any pride after she'd joined the multilevel marketing company Herbalife, which sells dietary supplements, to make more money for her family. Her husband tried to appease her, saying: "Whatever the family has become or how we have grown is all because of you." But this only made her feel worse. She wondered if perhaps the Samajwadi Party was the problem and she should join a different political party. She still thought she needed some party's support, both financial and political, to protect her women and herself. "I might get killed, or people may attack me," just like Phoolan Devi, she said. She, too, had upset many people over the years, and without protection, "anything can happen."

With the Green Gang officially inactive, its core women found other ways to earn money and spend their time. By the spring of 2022, Priyanshi was singing devotional songs called *bhajans* in the neighborhood and stitching clothes to sell and support herself, a quiet life that gave her a semblance of peace. Ram Kali had moved to another part of Uttar Pradesh after the pandemic began, to live with her daughter, something she had long wanted to do. And Sangita had become a full-fledged reporter, working for a hyper-local online news outlet. She paid little attention to her in-laws' demands, wore jeans with her kurtas, and continued to speak with an attitude. Angoori supposed that this was a success, though she sometimes worried that Sangita would take risks—even cheat on her husband—with her newfound confidence.

Looking back on its decade-plus of activity, Angoori maintained the Green Gang had never made a big mistake in its actions. Sometimes, the women did not make enough inquiries in cases or acted without having all the information, especially in the gang's later years. But in all the significant cases, Angoori felt she had done right. She was glad she had kidnapped the mother in Kachpura to get her to make a statement against the rapists. She did not regret beating the girl who hit her mother and loved the engineer. She was proud of setting the police station in Narangpur on fire.

If there was any mistake that haunted Angoori, politics aside, she said it was that she had beaten her children when her family was poor, when her boys were selling cardboard boxes that could hold saris or bangles.

She confessed that it wasn't true that she had never picked up a lathi before hitting her landlord during the eviction. When her children were young, she had used it on them often to keep them in line. "She beat us like we were going to survive for the last time," her daughter told me from their house in Tirwa, laughing. Angoori said this was wrong because they'd been weaker than her, and kissed her grandson on the head. If she had learned anything from the Green Gang, it was that canes should only be wielded against the powerful.

The Bandit Queen was dead, and the Green Gang had gone political, then disintegrated into the dust of Tirwa's everyday life. Still, other Phoolan Devis and Angooris continued to spring up across northern India. It seemed there would always be more. In Bahraich in Uttar Pradesh, an elderly woman called Bhanu Mati took on hooch makers with an old rifle, telling them that she'd shoot them if they didn't stop manufacturing alcohol. In the slums of Lucknow, a teacher named Usha Vishwakarma—furious after a fellow teacher tried to rape her, and after a girl she taught in the slums was molested by her uncle—formed a group of teenagers called the Red Brigade and taught them self-defense with martial arts and canes. And in Pilibhit district in Uttar Pradesh, a widow named Sahana Begum took a loaded rifle anywhere a girl was groped or sexually harassed, sometimes making men do sit-ups or ride a donkey with blackened faces as punishment, to make them feel shame. In Kannauj, Urmila continued to think about forming her own Narangi Gang.

Meanwhile in the jungles of the nearby state of Madhya Pradesh, police had finally found and arrested the twenty-something Sadhna Patel, who'd robbed many traders and kidnapped for ransom a landowner's son. One man recounted how she had chopped off his fingers. After her arrest, police paraded Sadhna before the cameras, describing her as "ferocious" and "terror incarnate." But the diminutive woman looked anything but. One official acknowledged "how innocent she looks," and how normal—which is to say that any woman could be her.

BOOK III
CICEK

SLEEPING LIONS

[He] never imagined I had grenades, .22 rifles and contact bombs in my closet. When he left for work, I took his pistol, and 'Bang bang bang!' shooting bullets into the air . . . I was very mischievous.

—A female member of the Sandinista National Liberation Front, which overthrew Nicaragua's dictator in 1979, from the 2018 documentary *¡Las Sandinistas!*

The drone strike hits the building at day's end, as the sun sets through the Syrian desert haze. Months later, Cicek* freezes the scene and plays it back. Her commander, Sosin, with whom she shares a birthplace, favorite music, and a dream, has just walked inside the building. It was Sosin who planted the clover in front of the new military office. Several civilians are midstep on the stairs. Cicek is outside smoking a Gauloises cigarette, as she often does throughout the day. A few other soldiers of the YPJ, or Women's Protection Units, have just left to go shopping. They ask Cicek to come, but she has an uneasy feeling and declines. She says she wants to stay close to Sosin.

It is August 2021, and the heat weighs like a heavy damask blanket on the region. Dozens of people displaced by recent attacks from Turkish militias are gathered at the new military office to ask for housing help, and are sweating in the heat. The sound of the missile is like a chainsaw revving, followed by a powerful explosion. The YPJ fighters are used to the constant insect-like buzz of reconnaissance drones. But this is different.

---

* Pronounced *Chee-czech*

After the drone hits, Cicek's world goes black. She doesn't know how long she is out. She wakes to the sound of a high-pitched ringing, then another fighter saying someone is crushed beneath the rubble. When Cicek opens her eyes, she realizes that the someone is her. She is pinned beneath heavy debris, and pain shoots from her leg up her back.

"Where is Commander Sosin?" Cicek asks, but no one answers. "Where is she?" her voice rises. They tell Cicek they need to dig her out and take her to the hospital. "I will not go to the hospital until I see Sosin."

At triage, Cicek refuses painkillers. The doctor tells her this is no time for valor. Her hip and leg are broken, and she needs an immediate operation because internal bleeding is filling her abdomen with blood. Three hours after the drone strike, Cicek still has not received word if Sosin is alive or dead.

Rewind to the early 2000s in Syria, a time of transition. President Bashar al-Assad had succeeded his father and proved he could be just as authoritarian, arresting activists and politicians. As the old proverb went: *When a cat wants to eat her kittens, she says they look like mice.* Under the second Assad's rule, the Ba'ath Party kept its stranglehold over Syrian politics, as it had since the 1960s. But the Assad regime was more stable than the government coups and instability that followed Syria's independence in 1946, and preferable to the decades of French rule that came before that.

Far away from the power plays of Damascus, in the northern Syrian district of Afrin, located snug on the border with Turkey, village life was serene. Olive trees crowded the countryside, and a wide river passed through the Arab-majority town. Nearly every house had a garden, where butterflies danced and children played. Men farmed the land and women stayed home.

Cicek Mustafa Zibo was the third of seven girls in her family and the troublemaker of the bunch. Her name meant "flower," but she was far from delicate, save for her mellifluous voice. She had thick chestnut brown hair, a strong nose, and broad smile. Her laugh rang out like a bell. In Afrin, girls were not supposed to act like boys, but Cicek did not care. Her mother called her "hot-blooded" because she was stubborn and liked to fight. Only boys were supposed to play football and ride bikes, but Cicek, who was short but strong, insisted she also do these activities. When her father left to work the land each day, Cicek demanded to accompany him and sit atop his tractor. By age ten, she was driving the machine and the family's motorbike. People in the village began to talk, telling her father, "It's not allowed for a girl to drive. It's taboo. Why are you allowing her to do this?" Cicek found the criticism absurd. Her mother would eventually give birth to a boy, but at the time there were seven girls in the family, and her father needed the help. Cicek's father kept letting her drive.

The men in her extended family continued to talk, which infuriated Cicek. "I used to see how a man came and went where he wanted, and laughed and screamed, and no one asked him why, or held him accountable," she said. "But when I laughed loudly, they said this was flawed." Cicek soon began to act out. She stole olives from trees "just to have a life." People in Afrin considered a tree as sacred as a child, but one day Cicek broke a branch anyway, and afterward avoided going home for days to put off a beating. She experimented with making explosives in her backyard out of a lemon, water, a bottle, and other household materials, which sometimes worked. On television, she watched and rewatched action films with thrilling fight scenes, such as those with Jackie Chan. Cicek also watched Syrian military parades on TV and dreamt of joining their ranks, even though she never saw female soldiers. Her mother did not tell her these dreams were foolish, for which Cicek adored her.

The family had two goats, and Cicek often took them out to roam. When an older man who owned a bread shop in town scolded Cicek's mother for letting her daughter traipse around the countryside, Cicek went to the bread shop to confront him. "Thanks be to God you're an old man or I'd make a problem for you," she told him threateningly, at just seven or eight years old. The man did not criticize her again.

Cicek was around eleven when she learned that her behavior could go too far. One night, trailed by other village children, Cicek wore a white dress to visit an elderly woman, pretending to be a ghost. "I have come to take your soul," Cicek said in a ghoulish tone. Frightened, the woman had a heart attack and died. Cicek was beaten for days and felt remorse for the first time.

As she grew older, Cicek dreamt of becoming a military doctor, a position she knew women were sometimes hired for in the Syrian military. But the more she studied, the more she disliked school. Her village was dominated by Arab families, with only four or five Kurdish families like hers, and at school, she was not allowed to speak Kurdish, her native tongue. Kurds, a stateless minority, were oppressed in Syria as in every other country where they lived in large numbers: Turkey, Iraq, and Iran.

Cicek's family were Sunni Muslims, just like the Arab families in town and the vast majority of families in Syria. But they were not hardliners, so her parents did not make their daughter wear a head covering at home. At her Arab-majority school, though, Cicek was forced to don a burqa with only a sheer slit for her eyes. She could not bear paying attention for long hours in the stiff chairs and heavy dress, and dropped out after seventh grade.

As Cicek continued to help her father work the land, tending to whatever local vegetables were in season, her questions grew. She wondered why her father owned no land while other families in Afrin were wealthy. "Why do some not have a loaf of bread while others live in complete luxury?" she asked. The treatment of women also continued to bother her. According to Syrian law, women were dependent on their fathers or husbands. She was especially bothered by never seeing women in the military. She constructed makeshift weapons in the backyard, but none were close to the real thing. She thought weapons would make her as strong as any man.

At thirteen, a neighbor's relative came to ask for Cicek's hand in marriage. Her mother rejected the offer because her daughter was too young, but Cicek knew other mothers gave their girls away at that age. She also knew that someday she'd be expected to become a housewife, as was the fate of many women in rural Syria. Cicek saw the home as a "mini prison" for women. She never saw abuse in her family, but she knew many women suffered through it. Marital rape was not illegal under Syrian law, nor was domestic violence. Even if there was no abuse, Cicek saw marriage as equivalent to becoming a servant. But whenever she talked to her sisters about it, they said marriage for women was a reality that could not be changed. Cicek thought they were just afraid of what people would say.

As she got older, Cicek began asking her parents more about being Kurdish. Kurdish strangers whom her father called "hevals," or "friends," sometimes visited when passing through town. Her father warmly welcomed them and used it as an opportunity to tell Cicek about the Kurdish struggle. Kurdistan's land had been split into multiple countries by the Sykes-Picot Agreement of 1916 (and ensuing treaties), which Britain and France secretly drafted to gain their own spheres of influence amid and after World War I, to partition the Ottoman Empire. The agreement would stoke resentment in the Middle East for decades to come, especially among the Kurds, who were left without a state to call their own.

Nearly a century later, from their home region of Afrin, Cicek's parents were quietly taking part in the fight for the rights of Kurds like themselves, who numbered between 25 and 35 million. One of the largest stateless peoples in the world, the Kurds had long represented a threat to the countries in which they lived—Iraq, Iran, Turkey, and Syria—and as a result were the targets of persecution. Kurds of her parents' generation had painful and still vivid memories of the massacres of Kurds in Iraq and Turkey, a large-scale chemical attack on Kurds in the city of Halabja, Iraq, and Kurds being buried alive in the Iraqi desert.

In Syria, a 1962 census to weed out "alien infiltrators" had stripped one in five Kurds of citizenship. The Kurdish language, publication of Kurdish books, and the registration of Kurdish names were also banned in the country, and many Kurds did not have full voting rights. Syrian Kurds were also not allowed to celebrate their holidays, such as the Kurdish New Year of Newroz—no costumes, dancing, or merriment— but they celebrated in secret anyway. Newroz was a holiday that memorialized a mythological victory over tyranny, which made it all the more meaningful to Kurdish families like Cicek's.

In his poem "Counting," Kurdish poet Sherko Bekas wrote that if a person could count, one by one, all the immeasurable leaves in a garden, fish in a river, and birds in migration, then the narrator could count "all the victims of this beloved land of Kurdistan!" But while Kurdish history was filled with pain, there had also been myriad Kurdish rebellions. In another poem, Bekas suggested that if four children from different backgrounds were asked to draw a picture of a man, the Turkish, Persian, and Arab children would draw the man's head and body, while the Kurdish child would draw the "gun on his shoulder."

When Cicek asked her father more about the Kurdish struggle, he told her about a man named Abdullah Ocalan, who was the Kurds' ideological leader. In the late 1970s, Ocalan and other Kurdish college students in Turkey had formed a Marxist group called the PKK (Kurdistan Workers' Party) that was dedicated to the establishment of an independent Kurdistan, and which would later launch an armed struggle. The PKK's insurgency was brash and violent, using suicide bombings, kidnappings, and assassinations to stand up for the rights of the Kurds. As a result, the United States and European Union had designated the PKK as a terrorist group. Ocalan was captured in 1999 by Turkish forces, which saw his ideology and the Kurds' growing power as among Turkey's greatest existential threats. Turkey considered Ocalan so dangerous they gave him a death sentence, which was later converted to life imprisonment. Ocalan was jailed on a remote island off the Turkish coast and the stories about what happened to him there soon grew—that he was its only prisoner (which may have been temporarily true), and that he alone was guarded by 1,000 men. In photos, Ocalan looked to Cicek like a genial old uncle, with a bushy mustache and twinkling eyes. The aggressive persecution of Kurds and of Ocalan made little sense to her. "These kinds of things became question marks for me," she said.

The more Cicek learned about Ocalan's ideology, the more she liked it. Even from his island prison cell, Ocalan, a brilliant thinker with a cult-like following, kept issuing updated guidance to the Kurdish revolutionaries. At first, Ocalan told the Kurds to fight for an independent state. He later revised this plea, saying that instead the Kurds should call for autonomous rule wherever they were, while being inclusive of residents from other backgrounds. A hungry reader of history and philosophy, Ocalan also emphasized women's roles in the revolutionary struggle, writing in a later paper that "the 5,000-year-old history of civilization is essentially the history of the enslavement of women," and that it was time for women to defend themselves. PKK women, who were wielding weapons in Turkey, had been saying this and organizing on their own for decades. An early founder of the PKK, Sakine Cansiz, wrote in her memoir, *Sara: My Whole Life Was a Struggle*: "[My mother] often said, 'If only you hadn't been a girl!' and every time she did, I loved femaleness more."

Ocalan's ideology seemed created for Cicek—that women could fight and be powerful, that Kurds have rights, and that class and ethnic differences could be overcome.

In 2011, as the antigovernment protests of the Arab Spring spread across the Middle East, demonstrations also broke out in Syria against the rule of President Bashar al-Assad. In northeast Syria that January, a local man named Hasan Ali Akleh set himself on fire in protest of the repressive government, and in March a group of teenagers in Syria's southwest wrote graffiti that read: "It's your turn now, Doctor," referencing Assad's occupation as an ophthalmologist. The teenagers were arrested and tortured, with even their fingernails removed. By July, more than 100,000 people had protested across Syria. Although the unrest was intended to unseat Assad, it would also help make a Kurdish revolution possible.

Kurds in Syria had been restive for years, most notably during the Qamishli riots of 2004, which began after Arab fans at a soccer match began waving around images of Iraqi leader Saddam Hussein, who had committed genocide against the Kurds. In anger, Kurds burned down the local office of the Ba'ath Party, to whom both Hussein and Assad belonged, leading to a brutal crackdown by regime security forces.

But not until 2011 had the approximately two million Kurds living in Syria seen the real possibility of revolution. As the rebellion against Assad spread across the country, underground Kurdish parties joined together to officially declare a Kurdish militia in northern Syria, where many of Syria's Kurds lived. The militia was named the People's Protection Units, or YPG, and while they were directly inspired by Ocalan's ideas and the work of the PKK, they claimed the PKK did not create them and that their goals were different. The PKK, which Turkey designated as terrorists and claimed were still trying to overthrow the government, had deadly clashes that year with Turkish forces. Meanwhile, the YPG was focused on consolidating Kurdish areas and defending them, to create an autonomous homeland in Syria.

With Syrian forces busy battling rebel groups in conflicts that would eventually become the Syrian civil war, the YPG was able to capture Kurdish-majority towns and cities across northern Syria without much conflict. By 2012, Assad, overwhelmed by internal enemies and hoping for Kurdish support, granted citizenship to thousands of Kurds and allowed the Kurds control of much of northern Syria—including Cicek's home district of Afrin. The next year, the YPG, in the spirit of Ocalan and the PKK's beliefs around gender equality, announced the formation of an all-female militia called the Women's Protection Units, or YPJ. It would operate in parallel with the men's units, under the same leadership and with the same mandates.

Cicek's life was changing at a dizzying speed. One minute, her future was to be a housewife who rarely saw the world beyond her village, listening to her father's stories about how they lived in a community with few rights. Now, Kurds like her were suddenly in charge in the region, and Kurdish women were wielding guns as if they had always done so.

In the winter of 2013, Cicek, seventeen and bold as ever, learned that the YPJ would be passing through her town. Since the announcement of the all-female militia earlier that spring, she could think about little else. She'd heard units were being established in every district in northern Syria, and that hundreds, maybe thousands, of women had already joined. They were tasked with protecting the newly autonomous Kurdish-majority region and, as Syria continued to destabilize amid protests, faced the rising threats posed by Syrian rebel groups and Islamist terrorists taking advantage of the country's power vacuum. Assad's regime was partly responsible for this, having released hundreds of Islamist militants from prisons in mid-2011 in an effort to show the dangers of nonsecular rule. Cicek could not wait to see the YPJ women and find out if they looked ordinary or somehow superhuman.

She stood anxiously on the side of the road in her village as the female warriors approached. They wore camouflage and smiles and cradled Kalashnikovs instead of children. Ribbons and scarves were tied in their hair, and their excitement was contagious. "At that moment, I wanted to be one of them, and I began to imagine I was," Cicek said. She imagined what it would feel like to carry a weapon of her own, walk with confidence, and be feared by others.

Cicek went home that night and told her parents she was joining the YPJ. They expected the news, knew her stubbornness, and did not try to stop her. Her father told her it was an honor and a "gift to the party," the PKK, to have her join and help the Kurds defend themselves. Her mother told her daughter she'd bitterly miss her but gave Cicek her blessing. A week later, Cicek left home for a training base elsewhere in Afrin. "I went to the YPJ and started my new life as if I was born again," she said.

When she joined, she chose a new name, as did most every recruit, as a way of separating the old self from the new one who had joined the revolution. She chose: *Viyan*. It was not a name with a delicate meaning, like Cicek, or "flower." Viyan meant "demand" or "desire," like a wish a person had all their life that somehow, unexpectedly, has been granted.

Cicek was sent to a two-month YPJ training not far from her home village, with about thirty other recruits. Some were young, just thirteen, fourteen, or fifteen years old. Some had joined with parental permission, while others fled impending child marriages or strict households. International human rights groups would soon criticize the YPJ for accepting—or even recruiting—child soldiers within their ranks, but Cicek felt the West didn't understand what the girls were running from, or toward. She thought they didn't understand that women also wanted to fight.

It was bitterly cold and rainy that winter and the recruits all slept outside in the chill. But Cicek was too excited to care. She and the others peppered the senior fighters with questions: *Tell us everything about the YPJ. How do we fight? What is the situation at the front line? Are the fighters all close to each other? How do you address people if they are older than you? How do we use a weapon?*

Cicek was surprised to find not just Kurdish women in the YPJ. There were also Syrian Arabs and Armenians, and later, people joined the YPG and YPJ from all over the world. They came from France, Britain, Greece, Spain, the United States, and other places, attracted by the principles of the Kurdish revolution, which was not just to establish an autonomous region, but also one that was democratic, egalitarian, and feminist in its rule. The revolution suggested an alternative not only to the autocratic regime of Assad, but also to the democratic capitalism of the West. At training, Cicek learned that the fighters all referred to each other as hevals—"friends" or "comrades"—the same Kurdish word her father had used for the Kurdish strangers who visited her home as a child. Some of the hevals called her Viyan, but more of them would call her Cicek (though most of the other fighters went by their new name). Even if Cicek had a soft meaning, it had a hard sound, and it suited her better.

Instructors started by training them on YPJ ideology, which Cicek did not initially like because the classrooms reminded her of school. But the content was very different. Her instructors described to them the plans for this new autonomous region they had begun calling Rojava, which means "the land where the sun sets," or "West," because the Kurds hoped someday Rojava would be the western limb of a reunited Kurdistan. They explained to the recruits the democratic confederal system that Rojava was trying to implement, which would be bottom-up instead of top-down, with decisions made by local, interlinked councils. They taught them that society had once operated as a matriarchy until 5,000 years ago, when power changed hands from women to men. (Many Western historians disagree with this notion.) They said that it was important to have egalitarian rule, or else one group or another would always be oppressed. Some of the young women said the glut of new information gave them headaches, and Cicek agreed. But it also made her feel more educated, mature, and confident than she'd ever been, especially since she'd dropped out of school.

One other essential part of training was called "jineology," which means "the science of women," an ideology developed by Ocalan. Jineology classes went deeper for the students on the possible birth of the patriarchy. They taught that early societies had worshiped mother-goddesses and that it was only later—after the division of labor and production, with men controlling the surplus of goods in the city-state—that men took control. Ocalan said he wanted to kill what he called the "dominant male," which was embodied by autocrats like Syria's Bashar Al-Assad or Turkey's Recep Tayyip Erdogan. In order to kill these strong men, he believed, women must be mobilized. The teachings of jineology were meant to embolden women like Cicek to critique and fight the power systems around them while they physically fought them. Mobilizing women was also a convenient way to double the number of Kurdish revolutionaries fighting for his cause.

While she was moved by the doctrines, Cicek much preferred the physical training that followed. The recruits ran up and down mountains and learned to weave in and out of trees. They climbed single file for many hours without sleep, with more than thirty pounds of equipment in their rucksacks. They walked silently down the mountain in the dark of night. There was an old, well-worn saying that *Kurds have no friends but the mountains,* which expressed how they felt repeatedly abandoned and betrayed as a people, and had no safe retreat but the mountains. The Qandil Mountains were headquarters for the PKK. Mountains had surrounded Cicek's village in Afrin growing up, and she felt comfortable there.

Even in the physical training, the recruits learned some ideology, including Ocalan's "theory of the rose" behind self-defense—that a rose has thorns not to hurt but to protect. The instructors told them that violence should never be used offensively or to provoke fear, as Cicek had learned the hard way from the older woman she scared to death. Violence was for self-defense and self-defense alone. "If you don't know how to protect yourself, you will be killed," one instructor told her.

After this lesson, Cicek was handed a Kalashnikov, the automatic rifle of Russian origin, with 7.62mm x 39mm rounds that could tear through a body. The rifles were cheap, reliable, and available on the black market all over the Middle East. The recruits were taught to take apart the gun and put it back together again. They learned to shoot with and without sight. Cicek was surprised at how simple and effortless it was to shoot a gun. It was like the dialogue in that popular American movie *G.I. Jane,* when a journalist asks a female senator whether women, being often physically weaker, are equipped to join the military. The senator replies: "How strong do you have to be to pull a trigger?"

According to Cicek, her first twelve shots hit the target.

After training, Cicek became a driver for the YPJ. She was one of the few female fighters who could drive, having learned by operating her father's tractor and motorbike as a girl. During this time, she closely followed the news of the Islamist groups' spreading influence. Multiple groups with different origins operated in the region, but by early 2014 the so-called Islamic State of Iraq and Syria, or ISIS (also called IS, ISIL, and Daesh) held the most power. With their black flags, black clothing, ski masks, long beards, and ideology of terror, ISIS announced plans for a worldwide caliphate that would have domain over Muslims everywhere. They were Salafi Muslims, the word *salaf* meaning "past" because it was the past—the seventh century, specifically—to which they wanted to return. They preached that nonbelievers should be wiped out or made subservient while women should be utilized or controlled, and they used ancient Islamic texts to justify their behavior.

Cicek watched the TV reports of the public beheadings, stonings, and rapes of civilians by ISIS, all done in the name of Islam. But it wasn't any Islam Cicek knew. Although Cicek was a Sunni Muslim, she was not devout. She watched the ISIS militants shout "Allahu Akbar!" or "God is most great!" as they executed a Muslim victim, which made no sense to her. *They do not know the meaning of humanity,* she thought.

Cicek was uncharacteristically afraid as she watched these reports, and sometimes cried in confusion after they were over. "Why are they doing this?" Cicek asked an older heval, who told her, "It is for this that we are training. We have to be well-prepared to face these dark powers."

The hevals reminded her that they were fighting against ISIS to keep hold of Rojava, the new, autonomous region that the Kurds now held in northern Syria. The Democratic Union Party, the largest Kurdish political party in Syria and the political wing of the YPG and YPJ, officially declared Rojava autonomous from Syria in January 2014. Kurds across the region had long hoped for something similar in Turkey and Iran, with little success, but Rojava was a point of light.

That January, Rojava also ratified a constitution, enshrining gender equality and religious, cultural, and political freedom as inalienable rights for all residents. It could not be more opposite the ideology of ISIS, who in May 2014 kidnapped nearly two hundred Syrian Kurdish college students, sent them to a jihadist school, and threatened beheadings if they escaped. In June, ISIS declared the Syrian city of Raqqa as their capital, where they began enforcing strict interpretations of sharia law, on pain of death. And in August, ISIS militants attacked villages and towns near Sinjar Mountain in Iraq, abducting thousands of Yazidis, a religious minority, some of whom identify as Kurds, and raping many Yazidi women.

The YPG and YPJ ultimately came to the rescue in Sinjar, carving out a corridor for the Yazidis to safely escape from the mountains of Iraq into Syria. Cicek followed all of this on TV the way she had once watched her Jackie Chan action films and Syrian military parades. But the Kurdish-led militias were now the real-life heroes.

That September, ISIS launched a full-scale assault on the Kurdish-majority city of Kobani in northern Syria, just south of the Turkish border. The origin of the word *Kobani* is unclear, but the word would soon be on people's lips around the world, in songs, poems, and on television news bulletins. Kobani had 400,000 residents, the majority of them refugees from the Syrian civil war, and ISIS militants had sent thousands fleeing on foot again with swaddled babies in their arms and overstuffed bags on their heads. As YPG and YPJ soldiers began defending the city, some without even a gun, Cicek was glued to the television. If ISIS captured Kobani, the dream of an autonomous Rojava would be dead, and the jihadists could have the run of the region.

"I want to go and join them in Kobani," Cicek told the senior hevals. She enjoyed driving her fellow fighters, but was ready to see action.

The hevals denied her request. Inexperienced soldiers had already been killed in the first days of Kobani's fighting, and the commanders thought she needed more training. "I don't care," Cicek told them. "I'm going." She insisted until the senior hevals grew tired of her arguments and told her she could join a battalion of some fifty fighters, who were leaving the next day from Afrin.

Kobani, a city of tightly packed apartment buildings and Arabic-style one-story houses, is surrounded by small hills and plains. The tendrils of the city's sprawl follow the outlines of its major roads. In August, when Cicek arrived, many of the city's inhabitants—mostly Kurds but also Syrian Arabs and Turks—had not yet fled. Cicek washed her face and hands in a house in Kobani controlled by the hevals, knowing it was the last time she'd be clean for a while. Then she changed into dark-colored clothing because she did not yet own a YPJ uniform. A senior heval told her to take a position outside a nearby building with a male YPG soldier, rifles in hand.

"This is the first time for me in battle," Cicek told the male comrade in a low voice as they settled in beside one another. "I have never shot anyone or killed anyone before." "No problem," he replied, as Cicek remembered it. "Just load your weapon and try to shoot." Cicek loaded. She thought of her mother and unexpectedly felt tears well in her eyes. She was still only seventeen. Then she thought of the ideology she had learned at YPJ training—that all mothers in Syria were their mothers, not only their biological ones. They were fighting for everyone to be free, not just their own family. *I have bigger things to think about, higher principles,* Cicek told herself. She aimed. She worried, afraid the bullet might ricochet back at her and accidentally kill her comrade. "You'll be all right," he said. "Just shoot at the enemy when they come, and you'll feel encouraged to shoot more."

She reminded herself that if Kobani fell, ISIS might take her home region, and that her village could be next. They could behead her father, rape her mother, and sell her sisters for sex. The ISIS militants were still a distance away from their positions, but her comrade told her to fire for practice. Cicek fired all thirty rounds in her rifle's magazine and exhaled with relief. "How do you feel now?" he asked. She laughed, feeling the tension release from her body. "I shot a lot of bullets. I think I'm ready."

Fighting began in earnest that afternoon and stretched until five a.m. the next day. It poured rain most of the night, a heavy rain that soaked the fighters to their skins. Cicek did not shoot anyone but fired often to let the enemy know they were there, "so that they will not dare attack us," she said. She found she loved shooting in battle, because "it gives me energy, it gives me power." When the clashes ended, Cicek felt an overwhelming exhaustion come over her. Her clothes were leaden with rain. She passed out in a YPJ-controlled house and woke up two hours later to the smell of breakfast. The other soldiers had prepared olives with thyme and olive oil along with chai, all of which reminded her of home. Over breakfast, Cicek chatted with the other fighters, telling them that she was from Afrin, the land of olives, and that she could drive a car, which was unusual for women. They told her that her skill would be put to good use in Kobani.

It was the last full conversation she'd have for days. More ISIS militants suddenly appeared, at first in small numbers, sneaking from street to street, then in larger groups with heavy weapons: tanks, machine guns, and mortars, which they had bought with money made from oil production and smuggling. The YPJ didn't have that kind of funding or artillery. They had only secondhand Kalashnikovs, grenades, and some makeshift tanks they'd made from pickup trucks. But they were trained guerrilla fighters, and nimbler than the ISIS militants.

Like other guerrillas around the world, Cicek was taught at Kobani to keep her last bullet so, in the event of capture, she could kill herself instead of being raped by the enemy. The Tamil Tigers in Sri Lanka, who also fought for their own independent state, similarly kept a cyanide pill around their neck. Death was better than the violation.

On one of Cicek's early days in Kobani, she watched from a rooftop as ISIS militants drew near. The men were dressed in black gallabiyahs, or long tunics, and were quiet as they crept past an abandoned elementary school. Cicek found their silence unnerving. Then she got a message by walkie-talkie: there were wounded comrades in a nearby house who needed help. Cicek conferred with her fellow fighter. For several minutes, they argued about who would run to the house first. Whoever did so would be at risk of being shot by ISIS, and both of them wanted the more dangerous job.

"I'll go first," Cicek told the male heval with her usual stubbornness. "And if you don't let me be the first, I'll leave you alone here for good." After he agreed, Cicek ran down and across the road safely. But the nearby house appeared to be empty. Like an increasing number of structures in the city, there was a big hole in the wall, which YPG and YPJ fighters made with hammers so they could easily run from one building to the next. Cicek wondered if her wounded comrades were just outside the building, but when she leapt through the hole, she found an ISIS fighter standing there alone. His face froze, and Cicek recoiled. They both stood with their rifles lowered, unmoving. If either raised their gun, they knew it could mean death for both of them.

By this time, Cicek's male comrade was worried she'd been gone too long and left to find her. He arrived noiselessly behind the ISIS fighter and motioned to Cicek his plan: he would count to three, then Cicek should throw herself down to the ground, and he would shoot the ISIS fighter in the back. *1, 2, 3!* Cicek threw herself flat, and her male comrade shot the ISIS fighter more than a dozen times—the first to kill him, and the rest for good measure. Cicek watched the man's blood splatter brightly across the dusty ground, the first death she'd seen up close.

A message came across the radio: the wounded fighters had been located. The two of them returned to a heval house to eat a meal a local family had prepared: kibbeh, fragrant meat fried in grain flour. "Look how I could save you," the male soldier joked to Cicek as they ate, knowing it would irk her. Cicek nodded curtly. Her only regret was that she wanted to be the one to kill the ISIS fighter.

• • •

Weeks of battles followed in Kobani. For many days the ISIS militants were raucous and loud as they approached the YPG and YPJ, shouting "Allahu Akbar! We are here to behead you!" Many days it rained. Cicek's military coat, pants, and boots, her makeshift uniform, were often soaked. Between battles, she hurriedly cleaned her face and hair, which hung nearly to her knees and which she tied back tightly. But she couldn't always get rid of all the blood. She was hungry but rarely felt it. She was tired but didn't feel that either. If a soldier acknowledged their exhaustion, their vulnerability could get them killed.

Tanks had already destroyed many of Kobani's one-story houses, whose backyard gardens were razed to dirt. The city's tall concrete apartment buildings were punched with holes or had been reduced to rubble. The smell of decomposing bodies was everywhere, like sweet rotting meat. Even when there was an hour to eat, usually a meal of canned meat or kibbeh, many fighters could not work up an appetite because of the persistent smell of death. But on the contrary, Cicek boasted to the other fighters, "I can eat anywhere, even close to a dead body." To her, it was a simple matter of forgetting. If a person tried hard enough, they could even imagine themselves up in the olive trees of Afrin.

It was impossible to get into a rhythm in battle because every day was different. Sometimes the fighting was constant, escalating for a whole day, and then the fighting would deescalate for several hours or days. Sometimes it was ground combat, while other times ISIS snipers attacked from above or used suicide vehicles to blow themselves up, and as many YPG and YPJ soldiers as possible. ISIS even had night vision technology and heat-seeking missiles.

The Kurdish-led militias had developed clever systems of defense and attack to make up for their smaller numbers. The forces communicated via walkie-talkie, sometimes with the use of codes, because both sides were tapping each other's lines. When they ran out of ammunition, they told the other hevals over the radio that they needed "food." The code made sense, darkly, since many of them would eat bullets in the end. Whenever ISIS captured a Kurdish fighter with a radio, the hevals changed the codes. Sometimes, a male YPG fighter with long hair and a beard would put on a black gallabiyah and go undercover among ISIS militants to ambush them. The female YPJ fighters would follow with their Kalashnikovs and grenades and finish the job. Then they would all celebrate their success.

Before and after battles, the fighters listened to music, "revolutionary songs that gave us the power to fight," Cicek said. There were new songs just written about Kobani and the YPJ. "I'm a Kurdish girl, eyes dark and tall," one song's lyrics went. "Experience became my education." Sometimes the fighters danced as they went into gunfire. After a battle finished, the women were always hyper and laughing—a release valve to the absurdly high levels of stress.

But some moments stopped their dancing short. One day in Kobani, Cicek saw ISIS militants dragging the corpse of a captured YPJ fighter in the dust behind their car. Cicek had seen the woman before. She was from Rojava, though Cicek could not remember where. Her hair was light, almost blond. The sight made her stomach turn, more than the smell of death ever had. Cicek was also sickened when, at Kobani, ISIS exploded animals with IEDs to kill the Kurdish fighters.

Soon Cicek developed a taste for revenge. She wanted retribution for all her new friends that ISIS had killed or wounded. Just last year, she had been tilling the fields with her father, her biggest problem being the gossipy older men in town. Now she slept with one eye open for death. A few weeks into her time in Kobani, she got her chance when a bearded ISIS fighter ran toward her through a hole in a house. Cicek, who was inside the building, held her Kalashnikov steady. By this time, she had heard that ISIS militants were afraid of being killed at the hands of a woman because that meant they would not go to heaven and get their promised seventy-two virgins. She could see the fear in the man's eyes as she raised her rifle and shot him in the heart, then in his belly. Cicek shot him again and again, though she knew he was dead, "just to enjoy killing him, to release my anger," she said. She described killing him, the first life she'd taken, as "so joyful."

The fighting remained heavy in the days that followed. Cicek said that after killing that first ISIS fighter, she shot and killed around a dozen more. She got her period around that time and had to wash herself clean in vacant houses between battles. There was so much blood everywhere it hardly mattered.

Not long after her first kill, the YPJ fighters near Cicek's position captured several dozen ISIS men. When the women searched the militants' bags, they found ammunition, paraphernalia for injections, and pills, Cicek said. Later, it would come out that ISIS militants relied on an illegally manufactured version of Captagon, an amphetamine that made a person euphoric, to keep them fighting for days. Cicek remembers swaggering up to the captured jihadists. "Guys, do you want me to kill you?" she said, with the bluster she'd acquired from surviving several weeks of war. They shook their heads. "Well, I'm not going to kill you," Cicek went on, and began moralizing instead: "Because you do not have a weapon in your hand. If you captured us, you would kill us without mercy. But this is not what we learned, and we will not kill you that way." Instead, Kurdish-led forces jailed many of the captured ISIS militants.

In their decades-long campaign to secure rights for Kurds in- and outside of Turkey, the PKK had killed thousands of Turkish state security members and some civilians, though the Turkish state had undoubtedly killed more. While the PKK felt their killings were justified, the YPG and YPJ wanted to prove it was different from its predecessor. They wanted it to be clear that they were not the terrorists—ISIS was.

As ISIS's influence spread across Syria and Iraq, with a territory of 34,000 square miles, and Kobani now surrounded by the militants on three sides (with Turkey on the fourth), the United States decided to intervene. ISIS was a kind of American creation, after all; the American invasion of Iraq in 2003 led to the birth of the extremist network al-Qaeda in that country the following year, which, like a shape-shifting jinn, ultimately led to the formation of ISIS. As Lydia Wilson, a researcher at the Centre for the Resolution of Intractable Conflict at the University of Oxford, wrote in 2015 in the *Nation*, the jihadists are "children of the [U.S.] occupation, many with missing fathers . . . filled with rage against America and their own government." ISIS was the first group, she wrote, "since the crushed Al Qaeda to offer these humiliated and enraged young men a way to defend their dignity, family, and tribe."

In September 2014, against the wishes of Turkey, which saw the YPG and YPJ as terrorists just like the PKK, the U.S. House of Representatives voted 273 to 156 to give the U.S. military the authority to train and arm partners fighting ISIS on the ground. The U.S. promised the YPG and YPJ intelligence as well as aerial support, for which Cicek was grateful. She knew the guerrilla fighters could handle the ground but not the air. She and her hevals soon stared up at the sky in Kobani, waiting for the promised U.S. Air Force B-1B bombers to appear.

As they waited, one day in the city blended into another, and one week into the next. Every hour of Cicek's days was spent in ruined houses amid the detritus of former lives: torn mattresses, toppled tables, and laundry still on the line. The ghost houses reminded Cicek of what they were fighting for, which in her mind was peace and security for the Kurds, and for everyone to live with full rights in northern Syria. At last, only five days after the vote but after what felt like forever, the bombers arrived. From above, arriving B-1B bomber pilots saw a city that had become a cratered wasteland.

Later that month, Cicek and her comrades entered an apartment building that the U.S. had hit by airstrike. The building had fallen in but some of its skeleton remained. Cicek told her comrades she would do a thorough check to ensure everyone inside was dead. She found ISIS militants' bodies strewn across the floor, including one man whose body looked intact but lifeless. As Cicek turned to leave, she felt someone catch her long ponytail. The man had a firm grip and pulled hard. Cicek screamed, elbowed the ISIS fighter hard in the stomach, and ran. Outside, her comrades asked what happened. "There's a man still alive in there," Cicek heaved. The hevals went inside and killed him, or Cicek returned with them and shot him in the stomach. Some of the killings would blend together in her memory in the end.

The U.S. conducted many more airstrikes on ISIS positions after that. Sometimes, the YPJ fighters were so close they were also injured in the strikes. One day, Cicek and the other hevals received orders to climb up to a crumbling building's second floor, using a ladder because the stairs in the building were destroyed. An airstrike was planned for nearby ISIS militants, and the hevals would be safer if they were upstairs. Cicek and the others held their breath, awaiting the *pssshh* and *boom!* of the airstrike. *If the building falls, we will go down in the rubble,* she thought. She and the others began to pray. They put their hands on the building's wall as if to keep it from falling.

The airstrike was precise, and the building held. The other soldiers shouted and Cicek ululated, a wavering, high-pitched call. People wailed that way at weddings in Syria to greet a bride and groom's arrival, and the YPJ fighters had started doing it, too, no one quite sure where it began. To Cicek, ululation was both joyful and a message to her enemies, "that whatever you do, we still have the power to fight and enjoy ourselves at the same time."

Because of Cicek's notable wails, because she was stubborn and inserted herself into so many battles, and because she was a talented soldier with a lot of kills, her comrades often said her name over the radio. ISIS militants, hearing the same name repeatedly, began to describe her on their walkie-talkie channel as the soldier they were determined to kill. They boasted that the fighter Cicek was as good as dead. But Cicek did not care. Her weeks in Kobani had emboldened her far past the audacity she'd had as a child. She no longer thought of her mother during battle or cried at ISIS's acts of terror. The YPG and YPJ had captured enough ISIS militants to distribute helmets and bulletproof vests to all their fighters, but Cicek and the others did not wear them. They were guerrillas, and they needed to stay light. One day, Cicek said, she casually jogged past gunfire on a side street of the city just to see it, even though she had no assignment in that area.

"You have cold blood," one of the hevals told her, meaning she was fearless and dispassionate, almost callous in her fighting and in her kills, which numbered nearly a dozen by this time. It was the inverse of the "hot-blooded" description Cicek's mother had given her as a child. "You should leave Kobani and go somewhere else where you are safer," another comrade advised, since ISIS had become determined to kill her. But Cicek was not afraid. As a child she had admired the Syrian military, made explosions in her backyard, and stood up to local men for a reason. This was what she was born to do.

By early October 2014, even with U.S. support, the YPG and YPJ guerrillas were starting to lose the battle of Kobani. The ISIS militants' heavy weaponry—tanks, artillery systems, and Howitzers—plus their willingness to do anything, no matter how deranged, put them at a clear advantage. The jihadists boasted that they would celebrate the upcoming holiday of Eid in the mosques of Kobani. Turkish president Recep Tayyip Erdogan, also invested in a Kurdish defeat, warned America: "Kobani is about to fall . . . I am telling the West: dropping bombs from the air will not provide a solution."

The YPG and YPJ soldiers grew desperate. That same month, ISIS militants surrounded a group of Kurdish fighters including Arin Mirkan, a YPJ commander in her twenties with dark eyes and a sunny smile, on Mishtanour Hill, which overlooks Kobani. But instead of surrendering, Mirkan, who was strapped with explosives, exploded herself along with a number of ISIS militants to become the first known YPJ suicide bomber. Cicek found Mirkan courageous.

The PKK had used suicide bombers for years, and it was an honor in the YPG and YPJ to die as a shahid, or martyr, for the cause. The vast majority of martyred fighters did not die intentionally, and perhaps the concept of martyrdom helped their families cope with their loss. Even with so many sacrifices, later that October, ISIS planted its black flag atop Mishtanour Hill to signal its victory over the area.

Down in the city of Kobani, a group of ISIS militants surrounded Cicek and a dozen other YPG and YPJ fighters, who were inside an Arabic-style house. Then there was an explosion—likely an airstrike from U.S. forces, which were trying to target ISIS—and all the hevals could see, breathe, and taste was dust. Broken furniture in the house caught fire and rounds from ISIS began whizzing through the air. Two of Cicek's comrades were wounded, and Cicek felt a sting in her thigh. She hunched over in pain and began to run. She felt a sting again, this time at the back of her left rib and inside her stomach, the bullet's diagonal direction like a bee twisting and turning as it flew.

Cicek kept running until she got to a heval safe house, away from the gunfire and dust. As she looked down at herself, she thought distantly, *Oh, there is blood on my body.* Hevals in the house crowded around her. As Cicek had done for countless wounded comrades, the hevals took off her scarf and tied it around her leg. They applied a bandage to her stomach, but blood began seeping through it. It was nighttime in Kobani, and battles still raged nearby. Cicek told them she could continue fighting. With all the adrenaline coursing through her body, she felt little pain. "But are you okay?" the hevals asked. "I am okay. I expected this to happen," she replied, though she could feel herself growing weaker.

Then: another house, another airstrike. This time, a far larger explosion. The other fighters fled but Cicek could not run and told them she'd stay behind with the protection of her rifle and two grenades. The hevals promised to get her later. After they left, Cicek could hear people speaking Arabic outside the house, which likely meant ISIS militants were near. She staggered deeper into the house to find a hiding place and dropped behind a washing machine in a bathroom. Crouching behind it, she put her Kalashnikov in her mouth. If ISIS found her, she would throw the grenades at them and shoot herself instead of surrendering. The walls spun. Cicek thought she heard Kurdish, but perhaps it was still Arabic—she was not sure.

After some time—maybe minutes, maybe hours—the fighting slowed and Cicek's comrades found her. They were incredulous that she was still alive, certain she would have been shot or kidnapped by ISIS militants. She was parched and asked them for water, but they told her she could not drink anything because of her injuries. She urgently needed a hospital.

Cicek's vision went in and out as she was driven out of the city. She thought that no matter what happened next, she would never forget Kobani: *Everywhere I go, I will tell people what happened there.* Her life as a girl among the olive trees seemed like a distant dream. The events of

Kobani had swallowed everything. She was aware of the other hevals beside her but not conscious enough to speak. They told Cicek they were taking her across the border to Urfa, Turkey, just two hours by car if a crossing was open, where the hospitals were better and many Kurds lived.

Cicek was hospitalized for the remainder of the battle of Kobani, forced to watch her comrades fight from afar. A doctor told her she was lucky to survive two rounds, likely from an ISIS belt-fed machine gun, especially the bullet that had split open her stomach. By November, ISIS had lost so many militants it called for thousands more to help, and the YPG-YPJ felt the tide was turning in their favor. But while the Kurdish-led militias were winning, they had also lost hundreds of fighters, maybe more.

In the Urfa hospital where Cicek was recovering, news of ISIS atrocities flashed across the TV screen, and on the doctors' phones. The *Guardian* reported that month that a woman and eight-year-old girl were found dead, raped by ISIS, their hearts carved out of their chests and placed atop their mangled bodies. Cicek, who had thirty-five stitches in her belly, which the bullet had opened in the shape of a *T*, vowed vengeance for every woman ISIS hurt.

PICTURES ON THE WALL

Women! Get up off your knees;
We knelt beneath the feudal's rule;
We were only speaking tools.
Now we as well as men have guns
And one day we'll be free.

> —From "Marta's Song," sung by Tigrayan female insurgents
> from the Tigray People's Liberation Front, which has fought
> Ethiopia's government for decades

There is a popular legend among the Kurdish guerrillas, and perhaps every detail of it is true. In 1991, a young woman named Beritan joined the PKK in the mountains of Sirnak in Turkey, with its rugged peaks and dusting of snow. A year later, Beritan was appointed to lead a group in battle, despite her lack of experience. At the time, the PKK was fighting Turkish-allied Iraqi Kurdish forces who were trying to squash them, as they both battled for territorial control. Beritan's group summited a hilltop, where the enemy outnumbered them. Beritan ordered her group to retreat and save themselves, saying she'd stay and fight to the last bullet. After she fired her last rounds, the opposing forces ordered her to surrender. Instead, Beritan climbed atop a boulder and threw herself off the cliff.

Beritan became an instant symbol of resistance over surrender. It is said that, after she jumped, the men who'd come to capture her laid down their arms and stopped their attacks. A movie was made about her, songs were written, and countless babies named after her. Many YPJ fighters also assumed Beritan as their new name.

One of them, born Randa Mohamed Ibrahim and renamed Beritan, had already fought several battles with the YPJ when Cicek joined the militia in Afrin. She joined the YPJ because as a child she'd watched the Syrian regime arrest her father, a Kurdish activist associated with the PKK. This Beritan was tall and lanky, with wispy, coffee-colored hair, nerdish glasses, and a quiet, careful demeanor. After she joined, the YPJ trained her to make landmines, which were set in the road to sabotage the advance of ISIS militants. By the time Cicek traveled to Kobani to fight, Beritan had already built hundreds of mines in a tiny room where her throat burned from the urea and smoke. She had already battled ISIS in several cities, including one where an ISIS car bomb just missed killing her, so close she could smell the burning bodies like barbeque. Beritan had already applied and been rejected to become a sniper: she was a careful person, but she had a temper that exploded without warning, and a temper could get a sniper killed. Also, Beritan had fallen in love with a YPG soldier—even though relationships between the two groups were forbidden.

In 2013, a year before Cicek was shot and injured in Kobani, Beritan, who was twenty and a relatively new fighter, was sent to a YPG-YPJ base in Tal Tamr, about four hours from Kobani. Beritan kept to herself at the Tal Tamr base, as she often did in new situations, until a male YPG fighter named Shiar approached her. Beritan had noticed him already because he was one of those people who always had energy and morale. "Why are you angry?" Shiar asked Beritan by way of greeting. "I'm not angry," she said, still looking serious. "No, no, you are angry," he insisted and laughed. His teasing annoyed Beritan. They went back and forth until she finally allowed herself a small smile. Shiar grinned and left her alone.

The next day, Shiar approached Beritan to pester her again. This time, Beritan allowed herself to laugh and they soon became fast friends. Shiar began calling her "Barry" and Beritan began noticing small details about him: that he was short but had a sturdy body and that, instead of sleeping normally, he sat with his back to the wall, eyes closed, before often waking up to exclaim, "Oh! I have more work to do." Beritan noticed that even though Shiar had black circles under his eyes from how much he worked and how little he slept, his eyes always twinkled.

Whenever Shiar left the base, he let Beritan know where he was going, because if he was going to the front line, a person might never return. One day they received word that ISIS militants were swarming a nearby village. As all the hevals prepared to leave, Shiar told Beritan as they stood in a group that she should not go. Beritan was furious. *How can he make me feel small in front of the other hevals?* she thought. Beritan was one of the YPJ's more experienced fighters, who had built and exploded mines and targeted many ISIS fighters, yet here he was making her look like a foolish girl. The behavior reminded her of her brother, who had not wanted Beritan to join the YPJ because he found it shameful for a woman to fight. She hoped Shiar was not that kind of man. Later, Shiar approached her to apologize, but Beritan ignored him until he took her by the wrist. "Beritan, I'm sorry," he said with sincerity. "The truth is, I didn't want you to go there because I wanted to protect you." Beritan softened a little. *Oh, he likes me,* she thought, and her face burned. "Okay," she said, "but just don't do that again."

It was considered a distraction from battle to form romantic attachments. Marriages and babies were for women outside of the YPJ. If a woman got pregnant, she would not be able to fight. In *Freedom Fighter*, a memoir by former YPJ fighter Joanna Palani, who is Danish and Kurdish, Palani writes of the penalty for a woman getting pregnant: a female fighter may have to marry the man or be sent to a camp in the mountains for punishment. Beritan had never heard of such a penalty, but she knew her commander would castigate her about Shiar if she found out.

It was the same for women during World War II, as a female sergeant major described to Svetlana Alexievich in *The Unwomanly Face of War*. "At the front, love was forbidden," the sergeant major said. "We cherished our love and kept it secret." She went on: "I think that if I hadn't fallen in love at the war, I wouldn't have survived."

Beritan kept talking to Shiar and thinking about him despite the risk. He was a salve for the cruelty of war, and an itch that gave her both pain and pleasure, and would not go away.

Meanwhile, in December 2014 in Urfa, Turkey, not far from the border with Syria, Cicek stewed and plotted how to escape from the hospital so she could return to the fighting in Kobani. The hospital was advanced, and her stomach was healing fast from her bullet wounds. When the senior hevals visited her several weeks later, Cicek told them she was ready to get back to the front line. "I'm good. I can carry weapons," she said, but they disagreed. They told her that if she was antsy in the hospital she could recuperate in a local Kurdish family's home.

On television at the family's house, Cicek watched the Kurdish-led forces begin to retake Kobani. Still, ISIS had seemingly inexhaustible resources and victory was far from promised. After two weeks, Cicek could not bear to watch from afar anymore. She told the local family she must return to Kobani, even though her stomach had not fully fused. "I should go, I should go," she said repeatedly, insisting until they gave in. On New Year's Eve 2014, the family told her she could join a group of Kurds traveling from Urfa to Kobani but not to tell her commander until she was there.

When Cicek arrived in Kobani later that day, the mood was celebratory. ISIS had been mostly defeated in the city, though many surrounding villages remained under jihadist control. The commanders, however, were furious with Cicek. One senior heval, also renamed Viyan, told me of Cicek later: "She is a troublemaker. She always wants to make problems. She just cannot stay in one place." One of her commanders nodded in agreement. "But she is also very strong and very brave," Viyan went on. "In fighting, she is excellent, because she does not know fear. She fights like a person whose eyes are closed to fear. She just does it, unafraid of ISIS or any mercenaries."

Cicek's reputation had grown even as she was recuperating. Viyan said she heard stories about Cicek from the front line where she "tried to sacrifice her life for her comrades. And she did it smiling. Even when bullets were coming for her, she smiled. To lift the morale of her fellow fighters."

In Kobani, the senior hevals examined Cicek's stomach, whose skin was red and barely held together by its sutures. They had already lost many soldiers in the city and did not want to lose one more. But Cicek refused to return to Urfa, so they begrudgingly sent her to a local house for wounded YPJ fighters instead. Cicek was amazed at the Kobani she saw outside her window on her drive to the house. The city was quiet and mostly cleared of ISIS fighters. The battle had reduced it to rubble, but it was free.

In the house for the wounded, Cicek met about ten other YPJ women, all with lesser injuries than hers. Most fighters wounded by gunfire were still in hospitals. The other women at the house had shrapnel in their bodies from explosions, as did Cicek, but she considered those minor wounds. Like Cicek, all the wounded guerrillas in the house wanted to return to combat as soon as possible, since the battle for Kobani's villages wasn't over.

Cicek would never forget her New Year's Eve in the house for the wounded. "We celebrated because the whole city was ours," she said. The women gave each other whatever objects they could find in the house as gifts: socks, perfume, a scarf, and necklace. They used boxes and paper for makeshift wrapping, and while their clothes were dirty for a New Year's Eve party, they did not care. They sang songs about Kobani and liberation. Theirs would be a society that would be feminist and democratic, proud and free. Those who could danced until early morning, when they fell asleep exhausted and happy.

In January 2015, the U.S. and other allies carried out airstrikes over the last ISIS positions in Kobani and elsewhere in Syria and Iraq. The YPG and YPJ drove any remaining ISIS militants out of the city. The Kurdish-led militias announced the operation to retake the villages around Kobani, which Cicek was told by a senior heval remained "infested" with jihadists. In the house for the wounded, the women became restless, knowing their comrades would soon need their help.

"Why are we just sitting here?" Cicek asked another wounded female fighter, who suggested that if the senior hevals did not send them to the front lines soon, they should "make problems for them." Cicek agreed. When a senior male heval came to see them, Cicek punched the woman's injured leg, while the woman punched Cicek's belly until it bled. "If you do not take us to the front lines, we will do this," said Cicek, as if she was still the little girl threatening the older man in his bread shop. The senior heval was furious and told them to stop acting like children. He said if they continued to act immature, he'd send them back to the hospital in

Turkey. Cicek and the other woman quickly backed down. At least they were close to Kobani's villages and the action in the house for wounded women.

Then, on January 26, 2015, the YPJ officially declared Kobani "liberated." YPJ and other Kurdish flags were raised all over Kobani, including on Mishtanour Hill, where Arin Mirkan had blown herself apart and ISIS's black flag once had flown.

After two weeks in the house for the wounded, Cicek was cleared to rejoin her fighting comrades, but only as a driver because of her injuries. She was sent to the east front line of the operation, where she met a woman named Buhar, who was older than her by about a decade. The two immediately took to one another. They hugged each other warmly, as if they had been friends all their lives, and began telling jokes over tea. Buhar, who had mischief in her smile, showed Cicek the fragments of a bomb in her lower back, while Cicek showed Buhar her Frankenstein belly. Buhar asked Cicek to teach her to drive, which Cicek promised she would do after the operation for the villages was over. Despite what they'd both been through in Kobani, Buhar was unrelentingly positive, with an energy Cicek described as "strong and vital." Buhar also wore a black scarf with bright flowers around her head, as Cicek and many of the other fighters did. She had a habit of biting her nails.

One day, Buhar woke Cicek from a nap in one of the village houses. She asked Cicek to make chai, saying guests were on the way. Cicek assumed some senior hevals were en route to give them orders, but when no one appeared after the chai was ready—one black tea bag with several heapings of sugar, the way Cicek liked it—she asked "Where are our guests?" and Buhar laughed. "Our guests are ISIS," she replied. "I heard by walkie-talkie that they are coming. But I guess they are not here yet." Cicek laughed along with her. While they waited for the enemy, the two women sat down to relax over their tea and talk.

Many days in Kobani's villages were spent waiting for battles to begin. Another day, Cicek and Buhar entered a deserted house where they found a broken perfume bottle. They both leapt at the chance to spray themselves with something sweet-smelling to cover the stench of dead bodies and sweat. Back at the house with the other hevals, several women told them they smelled strange. Cicek and Buhar looked at one another. Flies were pestering the other fighters but fell dead when they came close to the two of them. Another heval cried out that they had sprayed themselves with pesticide, not perfume. Cicek and Buhar, red-faced, broke up laughing along with their comrades, who made fun of them for weeks.

Their next assignment was to hole up in a local two-story building, which had a fan but no electricity. They decided to get a stick and turn the fan by hand. All the villages were hot and full of flies, and the fan would keep the bugs away, too. When Cicek got tired of turning, it was Buhar's turn. But when Buhar sat down to turn the fan, the chair collapsed. The women, Cicek just seventeen, and Buhar in her late twenties, laughed until their stomachs hurt.

Soon Cicek was assigned to drive in the villages for a famed commander, about whom a documentary was being made. In *Commander Arian*, released in 2018 by Spanish filmmaker Alba Sotorra, a commander named Arian tells an interviewer about a twelve- or thirteen-year-old girl who was kidnapped from her neighborhood, raped and impregnated, then killed by her family in an honor killing. It was a double tragedy that woke Arian up to misogyny in her community. Like Cicek, she was impressed that the YPJ gave women an escape from that kind of life.

Commander Arian was famed for her feats in battle and her hard-nosed demeanor. In the film, when a recruit named Sozdar tells Arian she wants to leave the YPJ and go home to her family, Arian pressures her to stay. "What kind of life do you want?" Arian asks. "The life of a slave? A life with no meaning? A life where nobody appreciates you as a woman? Or a life with difficulties, but that belongs to you? . . . Which life do you prefer?" "I will think about it," Sozdar replies. "It's just for a while. Then I'll come back." Arian is not convinced. She coldly tells the young woman to make a decision one way or the other. "Make your decision . . . but don't say 'I will stay,' and spoil our lives or hate your life here," the commander goes on. "This is the life of martyrdom." It was the life of knowing you could be killed at any moment for the cause. It was the life of choosing, as a girl or young woman, to prove yourself in a world of men. But when Sozdar tells her commander her back hurts, Arian puts her hands on the girl's back to massage it.

Cicek admired how Arian could be both stern and kind in equal measure. They parted ways earlier than expected when YPJ fighters in multiple villages did not have enough munitions to deal with ISIS ambushes. While Commander Arian left to deal with the problem, Cicek was told to stay put and drive the other hevals. But with Commander Arian gone, Cicek told them she'd had enough of driving. "I'm a fighter, not a driver," she said. Buhar was being sent into an ISIS stronghold in the nearby villages, and Cicek was desperate to accompany her. The senior hevals, who had heard of Cicek's legendary stubbornness, told her no. Although the YPJ sought to be as nonhierarchical as possible, commanders and senior hevals still assigned the more junior hevals their positions. Mid-argument, ISIS militants besieged a nearby village and Cicek saw her chance. She told a male comrade headed out with Buhar that she was coming along, whether he liked it or not. She climbed in the back of his truck and told him to pile some bags over her body. With Cicek well-hidden, they drove off toward ISIS territory, with Buhar in the car ahead.

The women soon found themselves in Korke, a large-sized village of cement and mud homes outside Kobani, surrounded by open plains. The commanders had gotten word that ISIS forces would attack them in the village that evening, likely expecting their dark clothing and ski masks would camouflage them in the velvet black of night. Still, it would be easy for the hevals to pick out the militants if they approached on the open plains, which meant it also would be easy for ISIS to see any movement of the YPG and YPJ fighters. Their goal was to hold Korke and not let ISIS advance.

When Cicek found Buhar, the two women shared an embrace. It was March 2015 and brutally hot for that time of year. Buhar told Cicek to snap a picture of her with another heval's phone ahead of the night's battle. "Because maybe I will become a shahid today," Buhar said, using the word for martyr and only half-teasing. "If so, you will need it to remember me."

As the women stood guard that night, Buhar joked that it was too hot for ISIS to attack. Then, as if she'd summoned them, a group of militants suddenly appeared like ants in the distance. Buhar, who was a sniper, climbed atop an Arabic-style house with several other YPJ fighters while Cicek stayed below. The men were getting closer fast. Soon, the militants were upon them, and some of the ISIS men climbed atop empty houses to position their snipers. Within minutes—two, five, maybe ten? Cicek wasn't sure—a YPJ soldier on the roof called out that Buhar had been shot. Cicek glanced up and saw her comrades tying Buhar's scarf around her head wound. *No, no, no,* Cicek thought. A bullet to the head was often fatal. But Buhar, with her bandage tied tightly, sat up again on the roof and shot her rifle. *Okay, it must be a light injury,* Cicek thought.

Minutes passed, maybe an hour. Time in battle expanded and contracted seemingly at random, never faithful to ordinary time. More ISIS militants arrived, and Cicek shot her Kalashnikov more times than she could count. Men swarmed the garden behind the house where Buhar was on the roof. Next, they entered the downstairs. It would be only a minute or two before they were up on the roof with Buhar. Cicek kept shooting as was her duty, knowing her friend was in peril.

Later, Cicek would learn that Buhar had told her comrades to save themselves because she did not have the energy to escape. "I'll just keep shooting until I run out," Buhar said, before her comrades threw themselves off the roof. One female fighter broke her back from the fall. Cicek, just fifteen or so feet from Buhar, saw ISIS militants stream onto the roof as bullets whizzed past her. Then she heard a senior heval give the go-ahead for an airstrike to the U.S. forces by radio. As the heval called out the house's coordinates, Buhar remained on top of the roof, still shooting. With a powerful explosion, the house was struck and collapsed. The ISIS militants were killed, and Cicek knew Buhar must also be dead.

Cicek blinked and thought to herself: *So now we'll just go and bring the bodies. Maybe I will just find Buhar's parts and collect her.* But when she found Buhar lying amid the rubble, her body remained whole, with no blood on it at all. It was as if when the rocket hit and the roof caved in, Buhar had floated down to earth like an angel.

When Cicek removed Buhar's scarf from her head, she saw a sniper had shot her in the skull. It was a miracle Buhar had stayed upright shooting for so long. She remembered their photoshoot from earlier that day. *She was martyred as she predicted she would be,* Cicek thought with pride, then numbness as her friend's body was carried away. Buhar would later be buried in a graveyard for martyrs, but Cicek would still be fighting in the villages and could not attend. Though Buhar had been older than Cicek, she was as playful as a teenager and funnier than any heval Cicek knew. Her picture was hung on the wall in a local YPJ building, as so many of the martyrs were.

After Buhar's death, ISIS, which had once seemed terrifying to Cicek, was reduced to their reality: a collection of angry, poorly trained men. The YPG-YPJ did not need drugs to keep them going—losing and protecting their friends and family was all the motivation they needed. Cicek felt her chest grow tight every time she thought of Buhar on the roof or them laughing together over tea. Cicek now understood it was the Kurdish-led militias who were more resilient, nimble, and better trained. It was they who actually believed in their cause.

In the city of Kobani, Cicek had shot about a dozen ISIS militants. In the operation for the villages, she estimated that she'd killed between fifty and sixty men. Her marksmanship kept improving. She was as gifted a shooter as Hannie Schaft, the Dutch resistance fighter who, with two other women, sisters, formed an assassination cell to kill Nazis. According to lore, Hannie's last words were "I'm a better shot," after initially only being wounded by her executioner. Cicek said she killed many militants with the precision of an assassin, and admired her handiwork every time.

At Beritan's base in Tal Tamr, it was almost the holiday of Eid, and she planned to take a break from the fighting to go home to Darbasiyah and see her family. She did not want to leave Shiar, but he told her not to be silly. "Don't worry, Barry," he said. "I won't go to the front line without you." They were both senior enough now to have cell phones, so they could still communicate while she was away.

Beritan disliked Darbasiyah because it was flat and dull, and not known for anything in particular. In Darbasiyah, her family lived in a simple mud house with religious surahs hung on the wall. They sat in a circle to eat their meals, often big bowls of chicken and rice prepared for hours by her sister or mother. Beritan called Shiar to check in as soon as she arrived. She could hear the sound of heavy clashes through the phone, so discordant from the mundane reality of Darbasiyah, where she woke up daily to the sound of roosters crowing. "You promised not to go to the front line without me. You lied to me," she told him, upset. "Come back and fight, Barry," he replied without apologizing. Beritan hung up the phone.

Afterward, Beritan chastised herself. If she were a simple woman living in her humble village, it might be acceptable for her to hang up on a boyfriend who distressed her. But Shiar was in battle, and she felt it was wrong to cut their call without knowing if they'd speak again. She knew that anything could happen. Once, she'd gone to set out a simple road mine and was ambushed by the enemy while relaxing and eating mortadella. And Shiar was in a far more dangerous place. She continued to chide herself as she and her sister went into town for holiday shopping. Beritan's sister noticed her foul mood and insisted Beritan call him back.

"We are still fighting," Shiar said this time, giving no indication of how the battle was going. Beritan could hear heavy artillery in the background. She called him three more times that evening, and each time, he gave no significant update. "Barry, just come back tomorrow," he said finally with exhaustion, "and then I'll send you back home after another day." *No.* Beritan was irritated again, and was still angry that he'd lied to her about going to the front line. She could not just go back to Tal Tamr at his beck and call as if she were a traditional woman. "I'll go after Eid," she told him, and fell into a restless sleep.

At five a.m., Beritan's phone rang. "Heval Shiar has been martyred," a friend told her, the words slicing the room in two. Beritan sprang from her bed and left Darbasiyah immediately. Tal Tamr was only a few hours away. At the base, she found all her comrades crying, as Shiar had been widely admired. "Let me go to the position where he was martyred," Beritan told the senior hevals, who said it was too dangerous there. It was Beritan's turn to be stubborn. She insisted on going, saying she did not believe that Shiar had been killed. Shiar was a talented fighter and had planned to fight for the cause his whole life. They had spoken three times the night before. It seemed impossible that he was dead.

After Beritan returned from the front line, she went through Shiar's belongings at the base, where she found his grenades and a pen he'd loved. She told herself she would keep the pen forever but never use it because she did not want it to run out of ink. And she would change her name so that forever afterward she would be called "Beritan Shiar." Her old name of Randa held far less meaning.

Like Cicek after Buhar, Beritan hardened after Shiar's death. She met many more male and female hevals but did not let anyone get close. She focused only on the fighting, which was easier to do after she was sent to a northern Syrian town called Tell Abyad (later renamed Girê Spî), where ISIS was committing unspeakable crimes. In Tell Abyad, Beritan saw men in cages, blank-faced women who'd been raped, and children who cowered when approached. The YPG and YPJ forced ISIS out of the city soon after she arrived, and she said that she and the other hevals offered the townspeople water, food, and sweets, to show them they were not the monsters ISIS was. On days like that, Beritan could forget Shiar, but only for an hour or two.

The YPG-YPJ forces eventually won the operation for the villages around Kobani. Cicek herself traveled to Tell Abyad to celebrate, which is an hour or so from Kobani and a major thoroughfare to the rest of northeast Syria. In Tell Abyad, the YPJ raised their flag to signal their total victory over the area. Thousands of residents who had fled Kobani remained sheltered elsewhere, but some returned to their houses, where they took stock of the damage, unfurled their bedrolls, and found a way to restock their pantries. "I can't describe how happy I was when I saw people returning home safe and happy again," Cicek said.

That June, the jihadists tried to stage a comeback in Kobani, but the YPG and YPJ fighters quickly dispelled them. ISIS was no longer the ferocious fighting force it had claimed to be, not in reality or in people's imaginations. Their power had dwindled after their loss at Kobani, against all odds, to the Kurdish-led forces. Even though the forces had U.S. backing, and there were more male fighters than women, the YPJ was integral to the victory and they knew it. At the Tell Abyad round-about, as women shouted and ululated and sang songs of liberation, Cicek could think only of Buhar, while Beritan grieved Shiar not far away.

Buhar was saying one day Kobani will be liberated and we will all celebrate, Cicek thought. But Buhar, like Shiar and so many others, had been reduced to a picture on the wall.

THE WRATH OF OLIVES

This is not a declaration of war. War has been upon us for decades. A war which we did not want, and did not provoke . . . This was only a warning . . . and we will issue no further warnings . . . We are not one group, but many. We are in your city. We are in every city. Your repression only strengthens our accomplice-ship and resolve.

—Communique from Jane's Revenge, an anonymous group that claimed credit in May 2022 for firebombing an antiabortion center in Wisconsin ahead of the U.S. Supreme Court decision overturning *Roe v. Wade*

It was August 2015, less than two years since Cicek stood alongside the road in her village and watched the female warriors of the YPJ pass by. Those two years had seemed like ten, and it felt as if she'd aged that much. Her long, fine hair was always greasy these days, her skin no longer soft and unlined. Her body was baked by the sun and split apart by metal and lead. But her eyes still had the same roguish glint.

That month, the YPG and YPJ announced they controlled twice the territory in northern Syria as the year prior, and estimated that their collective force was 40,000 fighters strong. In October, they also announced a new name. With the U.S. as partners, and in conjunction with Yazidi and Arab militias, they were now the Syrian Democratic Forces. The moniker made it more palatable for the U.S. to fight alongside the Kurds in their battle against ISIS without upsetting America's powerful NATO partner Turkey. It sought to differentiate the Kurdish-led militias in Syria from the PKK, which Turkey saw as terrorists.

But Turkey was upset. The country saw the Kurds as a major security threat and had for decades. The Kurds were a people that the Ottoman Empire and then Turkey had suppressed, displaced, imprisoned, and killed. In response, the Kurds had armed themselves and killed Turkish people—experts estimated that more than 50,000 people had died in the PKK-Turkey conflict on both sides since the 1980s. Responding to the Kurdish militants had cost Turkey trillions of dollars and significantly lowered their GDP. Many ceasefires were called, sometimes for years, but later broken. Turkey's army was enormous compared to the number of Kurdish guerrillas, but the Kurds did not care.

That fall, the human rights group Amnesty International released two reports that accused Kurdish groups of committing serious crimes in northern Syria. The reports found that as the YPG and YPJ retook areas from ISIS, they forcibly displaced and demolished the homes of local Arabs, and also that the Democratic Union Party, or PYD, the leading Kurdish political party in Rojava, practiced arbitrary detention and unfair trials. But a subsequent United Nations Commission found no evidence that Kurdish groups ever targeted Arabs, and YPG-YPJ leadership argued the reports had been politically motivated. Cicek said the allegations made no sense to her, since she fought alongside Arab comrades, and saw Rojava's goal as protecting the rights of all ethnic groups to live peaceably together.

As Turkey stewed, the Syrian civil war dragged on, and ISIS clung to its diminishing caliphate, the Kurds kept trying to develop Rojava. While forming a new government, Rojava was split into "cantons," or administrative areas. All governing bodies required 40 percent representation of women, which was enforced. Governance was democratic and shared, though the leading political party, the PYD, which had originally been established as a Syrian branch of the PKK in the early 2000s, held the most sway, operating in a coalition with the smaller parties. A coed university was opened in Rojava's big city of Qamishli after decades in which many Syrian Kurds were unable to study in their native tongue. Later, a town called Jinwar for women and children would be founded, welcoming women who had lost their husbands to war, did not want to marry, or had escaped marriages characterized by domestic and sexual violence. Despite the chaos of war—perhaps because of it—Rojava was continuing its feminist, egalitarian experiment.

That fall 2015, the *New York Times Magazine* published a piece profiling Rojava, describing it as a "dream of secular utopia in ISIS's backyard." The piece made clear that Rojava's vision was radical not only for the Middle East, but anywhere in the world. "We're fighting for our ideas," a teacher at a local academy told the magazine. "Ideas, like people, die if we don't fight for them." Other publications in the West soon picked up on the piece, including *Slate*, which was astounded to find that a region in northern Syria, "ruled by militant feminist anarchists," wasn't getting more attention. Anthropologist David Graeber, one of the few Americans who did pay attention to Rojava from the start, told me by phone that this aspect of the woman's revolution alone was just "an amazing historical fact." We spoke in February 2020, when I first began intensively researching the region and the YPJ after years of following the female fighters' exploits from afar. To him, Rojava was one of the most important and hopeful experiments of all time, and especially for the modern era, when he felt so much of progressive politics revolved around a "mood of international despair." For Graeber, who died suddenly just months after we spoke, Rojava was a blazing bright spot amid the war and bloodshed in the region.

In the canton of Afrin, where Kurds and Arabs both lived, Cicek's mother, Asiya, joined a local commune that responded to regional needs, such as building and repairing hospitals, schools, and roads. "We are making the area more beautiful," Asiya told me by phone. "The cause has become like blood in our body that we cannot do without. I promise to protect it until my last drop." Cicek's mother sounded just like a YPJ fighter; many people in Rojava talked that way now. The idealism of the revolution was contagious. Afrin had so far been spared from violence by ISIS but Cicek worried it could be next.

By 2016, Cicek had been sent to Manbij, an Arab-majority city in northern Syria that ISIS marauders had controlled for the last two and a half years. By the time the Syrian Democratic Forces—involving the YPG, YPJ, and U.S. forces—arrived in Manbij that year to clear out ISIS, many civilians had tried to flee the jihadists' control. Cicek shivered when she thought of her time in Manbij.

In Manbij, Cicek's friend Amara, a YPJ comrade who was always laughing, went to receive a young burqa-clad mother with a baby in her arms, thinking she was fleeing ISIS for the safety of the Syrian Democratic Forces. But when Amara took the baby, who was just four or five months old, the Arab mother pressed a button beneath her burqa and blew herself up, also killing Amara and her baby. Later, another local woman told the YPJ fighters that ISIS had forced the mother to wear an explosive belt, saying that if she didn't detonate herself, they'd do it for her with a remote-controlled device. Perhaps the mother had thought her baby would survive in Amara's arms.

In Manbij, Cicek saw ISIS militants shoot a man, a civilian, in the head to prevent the Syrian Democratic Forces from advancing. "We killed one," came the announcement from the ISIS side, as Cicek remembered it. "And we will kill more if you advance or attack us." She saw ISIS shoot a woman in the back as she ran away. The woman's body launched forward and fell to the ground. Then she saw two heads at a roundabout, their bodies nowhere to be found.

Later, Cicek was patrolling a four-story building, from which she could see an ISIS-controlled area at ground level across the way. She watched ISIS fighters force a man in black pants and a blue shirt, with white hair and a white mustache, to his knees. He could be any older man she knew: her uncle, her father. From her vantage point, Cicek could not see his expression, hear if he was crying, or make out if he said a final few words. But she could see an ISIS militant take out a knife and—perhaps with a grisly sound, a breaking of bones in his neck, she was too far to hear—behead him. Her YPJ comrades considered shooting the militants to stop the beheading, but too many civilians were nearby to do so safely. The Syrian Democratic Forces were having trouble advancing at all in Manbij because residents could be killed in the crossfire, and because of the landmines and explosives ISIS had planted everywhere. Afterward, an ISIS fighter held the man's head by his hair like a prize. Senior hevals told Cicek the beheadings were strategic by ISIS, to make the civilians too terrified to flee to the Syrian Democratic Forces' side.

Sometimes, when there was a break in the fighting, Cicek walked alone through the city streets, where all she could see were corpses and ruined houses. It was overwhelming to her. "Sometimes in Manbij, I would sit under a tree or in a corner to cry," Cicek said. "I could not take seeing all the destruction." She had once cried over ISIS, missing her mother, and the death of her beloved Buhar. Now, Cicek cried in sheer helplessness that despite everything they'd protected, ISIS could still destroy so much. She listened to sad songs whenever she drove around Manbij, gazing into the passing windows of destroyed houses and wondering what they had been like before the war. She imagined people eating at a table, getting dressed before a mirror, and laughing in front of a TV.

It was so hot in Manbij that even the water from the tap was warm, and Cicek soon developed a high fever. The dead bodies and high temperatures of the city proved too much to handle. She could not move, so the hevals sent her to a nearby doctor for treatment. When Cicek returned, she learned that the Syrian Democratic Forces had freed Manbij from ISIS, whose remaining militants had fled in a convoy of vehicles. Other towns and cities had also been "liberated," as the hevals called it. This included Al-Shaddadah in northeast Syria, where it was said ISIS had been selling Kurdish women into sexual slavery at the entrance to town.

Before leaving Manbij, Cicek was driving with her comrades when she saw a man beating his daughter with a plastic tube. The hevals stopped their car to ask what was going on. "My daughter won't go to school," said the father, annoyed, according to Cicek. "Anyway, it's my daughter and it's not your business." The hevals suggested he explain the importance of attending school to his daughter instead of beating her. They also warned him that if they saw him beating his daughter again, they would put him in jail.

A few days later, Cicek and the hevals drove by the man's house a second time, and again saw him hitting his daughter. This time, they intervened. Instead of taking him to jail, they brought the man and girl to a "Mala Jin," or "Women's House," a network of women-run houses formed in Rojava in 2011, and with which the YPJ worked to help local women. At the Mala Jin, women could report issues they were facing at home, including domestic and sexual violence, forced and child marriages, polygamy, and more. With the rise of technology in Syria, new problems like digital sexual harassment of women were also on the rise, and an issue the Mala Jin handled. The workers of the Mala Jin were trained in both Syrian and Rojava law, reconciliation and mediation, social work, and data collection. If needed, the Mala Jin escalated the problem to the courts or the police.

In 2014, Rojava had passed a "Women's Law" that outlawed many old practices that were harmful to women and children, such as polygamy, the dowry system, and the exchange of two daughters between families for their sons. But large swaths of northern Syria continued to rely on religious and tribal codes, which were rooted in the idea of honor. As University of Ankara political scientist Handan Caglayan wrote in a 2012 paper in the *European Journal of Turkish Studies*: "The main characteristic of the social structures under the patriarchal belt [in the Middle East, North Africa, and South Asia] is the strict control over women's behavior. In question is a strong ideology which relates the honor of the family to women's chastity."

Dozens of Mala Jin soon popped up across northern Syria. On any given day at the Mala Jin in the city of Qamishli, about fifteen women came in with various complaints. While I was at the center, a teenage girl reported that a boy was coercing her to have sex with him by threatening to release a naked selfie she'd sent. A Roma woman, her skin pink and raw, told me she'd set herself on fire because her husband beat her regularly and ordered her brother killed. "I got tired" of all the violence, she said. "He is the reason I burned myself." Another woman described how her husband and in-laws had beaten her when she was pregnant, causing her baby to die in her womb. A man also came to the Mala Jin to report that his wife would not let him see his daughter on Eid.

When the Mala Jin system first started in Rojava, scattered reports emerged that some women were going overboard—that several had felt so empowered by the Mala Jin that they'd beaten the husbands who abused them. Behia Murad, who runs the Mala Jin in Qamishli, acknowledged these incidents may have happened at the start. "Maybe in the beginning, the women were overusing their power," she told me. "But also in the be-ginning, when a husband heard his wife wanted to go to the Mala Jin, he directly divorced her. And the men were also asking, 'How can a woman solve our problems?'" After several years, she said, the Mala Jin system had improved. "Now, even a lot of men come to us with their issues."

Cicek was stunned by some of the stories she heard at the Mala Jin. One woman complained her husband was beating her, but the same woman also planned to marry off her nine-year-old daughter to a sixty-year-old man. Cicek felt this story perfectly encapsulated how difficult it was to implement social change in the region—with one step forward came another step back. Cicek said the Mala Jin worked with the couple to stop the husband's abuse, and the YPJ took the daughter into their custody, as they sometimes did if a girl's rights were being violated, often in coordination with Rojava's police. The nine-year-old girl was shaken and traumatized—and now part of a militia—though Cicek insisted she would not fight until she was sixteen.

After these experiences, Cicek realized that while the YPJ had been focused on fighting ISIS and its crimes, gender-based violence was still rampant among her own people. "We saw our people doing the same thing our enemy was doing," she said. "You're shocked when you're lis-tening to these stories, because people are suffering, suffering, suffering and not talking. Then they finally talk, and you discover how big the problem really is."

By 2016, Western journalists were intensely covering the story of the YPJ's war against ISIS, as they had ever since the battle of Kobani. Every-one wanted to report on the female fighters who wielded Kalashnikovs while wearing colorful scarves or ribbons in their hair. As journalist Gayle Tzemach Lemmon recalled in her book *The Daughters of Ko-bani*, Kobani's proximity to Turkey meant Western journalists could safely cover the fighting from just across the border. Reporters filed im-age after image of "young women in braids with flowered scarves, star-ing down the barrels of their AK-47s," she wrote, and "the longer the cameras rolled, the stronger—and more compelling—the narrative of the plucky ragtag militia taking on the savage global terrorists became." Every YPJ fighter I met, however, told me they were pleased about the positive international coverage, which ensured that Ocalan's ideology would be spread far and wide, and that the U.S. military would continue to support them.

But the Western press also sexualized the guerrillas. They dubbed one nineteen-year-old YPJ fighter the "Angelina Jolie of Kurdistan" for her striking good looks, while another blond fighter, who was reportedly killed, was nicknamed "The Angel of Kobani." Sensational stories spread, such as that ISIS had a $1 million bounty on the head of former YPJ fighter Joanna Palani because she had killed a hundred or more ISIS men. Palani later told reporters she'd never counted her kills but that the number might be accurate, while the bounty story appeared to be fabricated.

Dilar Dirik, a prominent Kurdish activist and researcher of the Kurdish women's movement, published an essay as early as 2014 critiquing the Western media's "myopia" in how it covered the YPJ. She argued that reporters were focusing on the gloss instead of exploring the deeper reasons why women were taking up arms. "No matter how fascinating it is—from an orientalist perspective—to discover a women's revolution among Kurds, my generation grew up recognizing women fighters as a natural element of our identity," she wrote in *Al Jazeera*. Dirik cited the stories of Kurdish female fighters Kara Fatma Khanum, who in the nineteenth century led a battalion of three hundred men against the Russians, and Leyla Qasim, a Kurdish activist executed at twenty-two by the Iraqi Ba'athist regime in 1974 for being involved in the Kurdish student movement. Before Qasim was killed, the young activist reportedly told the judge: "Kill me! But you must also know that after my death, thousands of Kurds will wake up from their deep sleep."

Western coverage of the YPJ would also soon come under fire for being too praiseworthy and uncritical of the Kurds. In a 2018 blog post entitled "Romancing Rojava," guest writers British-Assyrian journalist Mardean Isaac and Assyrian artist Max J. Joseph argued that the news media was ignoring the way the Kurds were imposing their ideology on Assyrians, an ethnic group indigenous to the region. Rojava's self-administration denied such claims, saying peaceful coexistence of people from different backgrounds was core to their revolution. But some Assyrian schools seemed to have been replaced by Kurdish ones. Major media outlets did little at the time to investigate if the claims were true, at least in comparison to its exoticizing coverage of the female fighters.

As academic Richard C. Reuben wrote in a 2009 paper entitled "The Impact of News Coverage on Conflict," traditional war reporting is "oriented toward violence, propaganda, elites . . . and victory." In the case of Rojava, its coverage seemed heavily influenced by Kurdish propaganda about what Rojava was or could be, and propaganda put out by its critics. On my trips to Rojava, I found myself struggling to sift through all the propaganda, to find reliable news sources and less-biased experts to get to the heart of the matter. I came to the story late, but this gave me the opportunity to read reams of news stories and research that already had been published on Rojava. By the time of my arrival in 2021, the U.S. had already betrayed the Kurds in announcing it would pull troops from northern Syria, and American blunders in the region were under more of a microscope.

As early as May 2017, however, the *New York Times* reported that American-led airstrikes had killed at least 352 civilians in Syria and Iraq since the start of the war against ISIS. The military confirmed the deaths, but Airwars, a nonprofit group tracking civilian harm in the region, suggested the number was eight times higher. One airstrike in northern Syria alone that year killed hundreds of civilians, who had been sheltering at a school near where ISIS militants were hiding. A local journalist who covered the strike recalled that day to me later: "There was the sound of a plane. A shhhhhhheeeww boom sound. Some of the people died because they were stuck under the rubble. Others were eaten by dogs."

The majority of the coverage in 2017, though, was still telling the other story, the prettier one, which was also true—that young women like Cicek, brave and brazen as lions, were killing jihadists in northern Syria, one by one.

In 2017, a video was posted to YouTube from Raqqa, the Islamic State's professed capital and center of operations, and reshared by the BBC. In the video, a young YPJ fighter stands at a window in a cement house with a Kalashnikov on her shoulder and blue scarf around her head. After a bullet flies just past her ear, the woman laughs in disbelief at her close call and sticks out her tongue. The video soon went viral. "Close to piercing her eye!" one commenter wrote on YouTube. "And she laughed, too," another replied. Other commenters could not believe the video was real.

By October of that year, the Syrian Democratic Forces declared victory over ISIS in Raqqa, where the militants had run a sex slave market and displayed heads on stakes of those they'd killed. The capital of the caliphate had fallen.

Cicek was sent to Raqqa just before the battle's end. On victory day, she said, young kids ran to the female soldiers for bread, candy, soft drinks, and water. Men asked her for cigarettes because ISIS had forbidden smoking. Women took off their veils and abayas in the streets, a dress code ISIS had strictly enforced. Many girls who were ISIS brides had escaped, and some tried to join the YPJ. According to Cicek, the commanders told anyone under sixteen that they were too young to fight.

But a United Nations report the following year, which focused on child soldier recruitment in Syria, suggested the YPJ was still allowing minors in its ranks. It found 137 underage girls were recruited to its force between 2013 and 2018. In Turkey, dozens of Kurdish parents took to the streets to say their children had been stolen from them to fight for the PKK, and that some were taken to the YPJ—protests that Turkey then used as propaganda.

The YPG and YPJ weren't shy about calling the spreading of Ocalan's words "propaganda work," and Cicek often said everything she did was for "Serok Apo," a nickname for Ocalan that translated to "President Uncle." Ocalan's photo—with his trademark bushy mustache and eyebrows, and puckish grin—was ubiquitous in Rojava. It was on billboards and signs and in portraits hung on walls, like Mao or Lenin. A cult of personality had existed around Ocalan for decades, although it was unclear how much control Ocalan retained over the Kurdish fighters from prison.

Cicek argued that Ocalan's ideology had spoken to her as a girl and the person she had always been: stubborn, combative, and idealistic. She pointed out that people in the West also adopted ideologies she saw as problematic, namely capitalism, which she felt turned everything into a commodity. Cicek, like the rest of the YPJ fighters, did not wear makeup, buy objects for herself beyond the necessary, or own a phone. She did not understand the appeal of consumerism or the desire to accumulate. It was Ocalan who taught her how to live as a woman, unafraid of any man. Without his ideology, she believed she would be living like the conservative Syrian Arab women who lived in her village, covering her face and relegated to the home or fields.

By this time, Ocalan's teaching of jineology, or "the science of women," had spread to at least eight cities in Rojava, where it was taught in college programs and master's classes and even at an all-boys high school. Though some male fighters grumbled about the classes, others told me it changed their thinking. One fighter, Dilbrin Rumailan, raised his hand in a class in Al-Hasakah to say that he previously didn't understand why women needed freedom. He hadn't liked his sister to leave the house, or his wife to visit her family for more than an hour or so. But after taking the classes, he told his female instructor, who was named Roken 23 Doshka, after the machine gun, "I see that even the woman has a life, an ideology, and her own independent personality . . . I realize I misbehaved and offended her."

When I sat down with Aldar Khalil, a co-chair of the leading PYD political party in Rojava, I was surprised to find that he had also studied jineology. After taking the classes, he told me, "Even I started to criticize myself as a man." Khalil, who had fought in the PKK, said he was ashamed he'd once believed only men could fire a gun: "I hated myself as a man, how we treated women before, and how we couldn't respect her and give her proper rights."

In several jineology classrooms I visited, images of the mythical Shahmaran were hung. Shahmaran, half-snake and half-woman, was a symbol of wisdom and healing for the Kurds. According to myth, the creature was ultimately betrayed by a man she loved and killed. In a way, the story of Shahmaran was a distillation of jineology's teachings—on the capability of women and the danger of men.

In her book *A Road Unforeseen*, feminist academic Meredith Tax argued that, due to feminist teachings such as jineology, Rojava was likely the best place in the Middle East to be a woman. That is, unless a person is queer. As Zoza, a twenty-eight-year-old Syrian-Kurdish transgender woman who grew up in Rojava and later went to Toronto as a refugee, told the website The Intercept in 2017: "Rojava never was, and never will be, a welcoming place for queer people." Very few people identified as transgender or gay, and the subject was almost never discussed.

In the YPJ, and even sometimes outside of it, sexuality of any kind was discouraged in favor of an independent life. Roz Abdulbaki Ali, a twenty-two-year-old woman who graduated in jineology from the University of Rojava in Qamishli, told me that after studying its teachings, "My dreams are no longer related to marriage, the house, and the man." It was as if she was channeling Cicek, who once said, "Cooking, cleaning, having kids, being a wife, I can't tolerate this kind of life."

Also hung in jineology classrooms were portraits of the Sumerian goddess Inanna, one of the mother-goddesses Ocalan described as being worshiped in society before patriarchy was born. Inanna was a formidable goddess who ruled the underworld, earth, and sky. She also oversaw the growth of plants. As women across Rojava sought to rebuild cities ravaged by war, a female co-op called the Inanna Agriculture Cooperative was established in Afrin in 2016. The women sowed onion, garlic, chickpeas, and other beans in a collective, as a model to grow the rural economy of northern Syria. Just as Rojava's governance was shared and cooperative, so, too, did the women hope its economy would be.

Several years earlier, in 2014 in the northeast Syrian city of Qamishli, Beritan sat beside her bedridden male comrade, Haroun, whose hands had been mangled by a mine. By this point, Beritan could not count the number of landmines she'd constructed by hand. Haroun had been in the town of Jazaa when it happened, which at the time was overrun by ISIS militants. In Jazaa, a sniper hit Haroun in the shoulder and a mortar strike affected his vision. But it was the mine that damaged him the most. One of his hands was disfigured, while the other was almost totally gone. Beritan knew intimately the damage that mines could do.

As Beritan sat beside Haroun's bed, he slipped in and out of consciousness, remembering flashes from the day. He had been driving and then stopped the car. His hands were on the dashboard. Then a blast—or an explosion. His hand separated from his wrist, while his comrade's head flew one way and his body the other. Haroun could remember little else. He was aware that a friend, a woman named Beritan with a low and calming voice, sat beside his bed. He had fought beside her in several battles, and she always struck him as different from the other YPJ fighters. Beritan was mature, self-possessed, and never haughty. He liked the way she talked to the other hevals. He slipped into darkness again.

Beritan remembered one night as a teenager when she gazed up at the night sky. She had just learned the Arab folktale of the two star-crossed lovers, Layla and Majnun, and that night she had seen two stars touch just as she drifted off to sleep. She had been a romantic then. But she wasn't interested in that kind of love anymore, not after losing Shiar. In Kurdish, another way to say "I love you" is "Without you I have no heart." Beritan no longer believed in that kind of love, the kind where two people were fated to be together, and passion that so excited and tormented a person it made them lose sleep. Beritan told herself that if she ever loved again after Shiar, it would be a friend, someone who made her feel calm. Someone she could talk to about everything from battles to her love of animals, whom she could share a meal with or play a song to on the tanbur.

Haroun woke up. Beritan was still there. He knew the rule in the YPG about not dating anyone in the YPJ. Beritan was his friend and probably came to see him because she was a generous person. But Haroun had his sights on something more significant than dating. He wanted to get married, especially after his parents had recently reminded him, "We will pass away someday, and you should have a friend to be with you." Beritan knew how to keep a person's spirits up. Beritan was here beside his bed. He did not see any woman better than her.

Beritan liked Haroun for similar reasons. He was kinder, gentler, and seemed more innocent than the other YPG men, some of whom immaturely made fun of the female fighters. Whenever they fought together, Haroun said it was like visiting a house where he knew he was always welcome. Beritan might describe love that way. Love, she'd decided, was not about sex or obsession, but about two people who cared for and protected one other. It was about the feeling of home. She spoke to Haroun at his bedside even though she did not think he could hear her. She was glad she had come.

After years of tension and a week of pointed threats, in January 2018 Turkey began bombing Cicek's home of Afrin, as she had long feared an enemy would. Then Turkey sent its soldiers to invade on the ground. Turkey called their offensive, unironically, Operation Olive Branch.

It all started after Turkey saw how much land the Kurds had gained in northern Syria, and after the U.S. announced it would train and arm 30,000 members of the Syrian Democratic Forces. Both seemed like a direct threat to Turkey, and Turkish president Recep Tayyip Erdogan was furious. "A country we call an ally is insisting on forming a terror army on our borders," Erdogan fumed in a speech in Ankara. "What can that terror army target but Turkey? Our mission is to strangle it before it's even born." The YPJ already had forces in Afrin and soon sent more. But this would not be like fighting ISIS. Turkey was the eighth largest military superpower in the world, with nearly 750,000 active and reserve soldiers, compared to about 60,000 fighters in the YPG and YPJ forces combined. If Turkey wanted to take all of Afrin, it could, assuming the U.S. and Syria did not stop them.

Eight days after Operation Olive Branch began, a YPJ fighter named Avesta Habur tossed a grenade down the hatch of a Turkish tank, blowing herself up and killing two Turkish soldiers. Like Cicek, Habur had joined the YPJ at seventeen from the canton of Afrin. A little more than three years after Arin Mirkan at the battle of Kobani, YPJ had what may have been another suicide bomber, though likely there were more that went unreported.

By February, Cicek convinced her commander to send her to Afrin. Afrin—her birthplace, the homeland of her parents and grandparents, a place she saw as "holy ground"—was under siege. Afrin was a big district, stretching more than fifteen hundred square miles and with hundreds of thousands of residents. Her family was safe so far, but Cicek knew that could change soon. She imagined Turkish mercenaries invading her village, boots stomping into her parents' home, and her sisters violated by faceless men in uniform.

Cicek began to feel calmer as she and a group of fellow fighters approached Afrin, heading to the front line by car. She was always more composed when heading into battle, when she was preparing to fight instead of passively watching events play out on TV. Cicek was driving the car, a Mitsubishi pickup truck. They were making their way up a mountain called Jabal al-Ahlam, or Dream Mountain, which was south of the city of Afrin. Cicek was in her element, driving fast and telling the other hevals about the natural beauty of Afrin, since most of them were not from the area. She spoke of the lovely cool weather and the olive trees as far as the eye could see. "Everywhere you go you can see trees," she said. "There is green, there are mountains, there is everything." She went on and on. She said Afrin was more beautiful than anywhere in Rojava.

As they approached a police checkpoint, her hevals put on a YPJ song, and Cicek got a queasy feeling. She opened the car's windows and heard a voice. Time slowed down, and then the truck blew apart. The three hevals in the back threw themselves out of their car doors, while the YPJ fighter next to Cicek jumped out of the window. Cicek found herself jammed behind the steering wheel. Her door was locked and she could not move. She also could not hear, likely because of the roaring sound of the explosion. Nor could she see, blinded by the smoke and dust.

Cicek told herself not to struggle or move. If the enemy saw movement, they might order another drone strike. Once the situation calmed down, she would escape. She heard a man's voice call out to her before he opened the door and pulled her out from behind the steering wheel. "Just walk with me," he said. Cicek stumbled, struggling to hear or see. "But who are you and what is your name? I need to know who is taking me out," she said. He identified himself as a heval.

Cicek thought the drone strike had only messed with her eyes and ears, but now she felt a burning hot sensation on her abdomen where she had been wounded before. When she felt her face, it was covered in blood. *Is the blood from my eyes or my stomach?* she thought. She wasn't sure. Maybe she had shrapnel in her belly. The heval deposited her under the shade of a tree. Cicek knew that she would not be going to Afrin's front line to fight after all.

Her comrades gathered around her. Their uniforms were scorched in the explosion, so that two of them were almost naked. Cicek, with her stomach bleeding, was the worst off of the bunch. She rubbed her eyes and made out the outline of their truck, which was in fragments. "If you saw the car then you would never believe that we survived this explosion," she said later.

Cicek stayed for nine days in a local hospital to get the shrapnel removed and four stitches in her stomach, in the same place the previous doctor had given her thirty-five. She also had a broken hip. Her mother, Asiya, came to visit and gave her daughter a bright red-and-blue scarf of her own to keep for luck. Her mother was now working on a second local committee to help solve disputes that arose in the community. She was worried about but proud of her daughter.

At the same time in Afrin, a Turkish missile struck and killed Anna Campbell, a YPJ volunteer soldier from the U.K. A photo of the young woman who'd volunteered to help the Kurds, with blond hair and blue-green eyes, was soon published all over the world. Campbell's father told the BBC he was "in pieces" over losing his daughter, but that she had known exactly what she was doing. "When she heard about the political experiment in Rojava, this seemed to her to be the way the world should be," he told the British public broadcaster. "The social organization at all levels, the equality. She wanted to help protect that."

Though Rojava was focused on developing Rojava, an overwhelming task, many thought it could be a model for autonomous rule and direct democracy elsewhere. From Basque separatists in Spain, to the Irish Republican Army, which wanted to end British rule in Northern Ireland, to Cooperation Jackson, a network of Black worker cooperatives in Jackson, Mississippi, all had exchanged lessons with revolutionaries in Rojava. Women from across the world, like Campbell, were attracted to its ideals.

Campbell died at twenty-six. And by that March 2018, Turkish-led forces would have much of Afrin.

After Afrin, Cicek had vision problems for months, so that she was no longer such a good shot. She began sleeping facedown so that if they were ambushed, she would not be hit again in the stomach. Her dreams became vivid and unnerving, often featuring the sound of a drone hovering as it had in Afrin or swarms of ISIS militants arriving in Kobani. Whenever Cicek dreamt of drones, she was hit by a missile and woke up. She described her nightmares to one of her hevals, who advised her to "think of good things before sleep, to forget ISIS and the fighting." Even if Cicek fell asleep after conjuring happy moments—her with Buhar, her mother, or in the olive groves of her village—she still had the same sinister dreams.

Her family soon fled their village in Afrin. They moved into a refugee camp for displaced people in Shahba Canton, an hour from Afrin city. As Cicek heard the news, a YPJ Press video reminded fighters, "Before you were a member of your family. Now you're a member of your nation."

Cicek was sent to various doctors for her eyes, hip, and stomach after the drone strike in Afrin, including a doctor in Sinjar, Iraq. Leaving the grand, idealistic experiment of Rojava for the first time in years, she thought to herself, *Rojava is my whole life*, and she was not afraid to die for it. From a hospital recovery room in March 2019, after a year of recovery, Cicek watched the Syrian Democratic Forces announce on television the total territorial defeat of ISIS at last.

ISIS, whose sniper had killed Buhar, whose IED had killed Amara, and whose militants had killed so many comrades she'd lost count, was vanquished. But the victory felt anticlimactic, because Cicek had learned that when one enemy fell, another often rose in its place. Turkey now occupied Afrin, and the United Nations and international nonprofit Human Rights Watch warned of increasing human rights abuses there: forced displacements of Kurds, the rapes of local women, and extortion and kidnappings of men. Local media reported that as part of Operation Olive Branch, Turkish mercenaries set fire to thousands of Afrin's beloved olive trees.

Meanwhile, an extremist group in Afrin calling itself Ghadab al-Zaytoun, or "The Wrath of Olives," began publicizing its violent efforts to fight back. The Wrath of Olives group boasted of kidnapping and executing Turkish mercenaries, and also of killing local Kurds suspected of cooperating with the enemy. "Since day one of the Turkish occupation of the Afrin region, we warned that those who agreed to work with the occupation would be considered as traitors and informers against the sons of our people and have a similar fate to the killed soldiers," a Wrath of Olives statement read that June.

In an analysis for the investigative journalism site *Bellingcat*, open-source researcher Alexander McKeever suggested the Wrath of Olives could be a front group for the YPG and YPJ to carry out more extreme actions with which it might not want to be publicly associated. The forces publicly denied being affiliated with the group, and soldiers like Cicek would never be told if it were true—nor could she get back to Afrin to find out.

Instead of being sent back to Afrin after her recovery, Cicek was assigned to Al-Hol, a sprawling, sometimes lawless refugee camp in northern Syria that held tens of thousands of captured ISIS families. Most of the inhabitants were militants' wives, the women's niqabs and hijabs framing their frightened eyes, and their children.

Cicek was assigned to an Anti-Terror Unit of commandos whose responsibility was to patrol Al-Hol. The majority of the women Cicek met claimed they'd joined ISIS only because their husbands had, after the jihadists seized their cities or towns. It was difficult to parse who had enlisted in the group by necessity versus choice. Cicek came across many foreign-born ISIS wives who said they were forced or indoctrinated into participating. Shamima Begum, a British-born Bangladeshi woman who left the U.K. at fifteen to join ISIS, had married an ISIS militant, and was now at Al-Hol. She'd had three children with her ISIS husband, all of whom died. Stories emerged that Begum had been one of the strictest enforcers of ISIS's morality police, and that she had stitched people into suicide vests. But Begum maintained she'd joined the group out of the folly and ignorance of youth, and that some of the reports about her were false.

Cicek started smoking regularly for the first time at Al-Hol, even though she thought cigarettes tasted better in battle. She found that cigarettes made her need to eat less often and helped with her anxiety. Memories of her battles tormented her, and it was also unsafe and unpredictable at Al-Hol. ISIS sleeper cells—former militants planning the group's resurgence—were all over the camp. Escapes from Al-Hol and violence on the grounds were common. One day, Cicek was accompanying two female police officers on their usual rounds when they saw dozens of shoes lined up outside a tent. Inside, about a hundred women were preparing to behead an Indian woman because she'd reported an incident to the police. Cicek and the two policewomen arrived "just in time to rescue her," Cicek said. "We threatened them: 'If you don't leave the woman alone, we will kill you all.'"

Some days at Al-Hol, Cicek drove security patrols. She preferred to do the drives alone, so she could survey the camp's population without the chatter of other commandos or policewomen to distract her. If she missed a single worrying detail, a woman could die. One day, she received a report of a woman using a hammer to crush another woman's head, and the woman was killed before anyone could intervene.

That summer of 2019, a woman's corpse was found in a sewage tunnel at Al-Hol. The body had been decomposing for at least a month so that the face and body were deformed. When camp officials said they needed a body part to test the woman's nationality, Cicek said she volunteered to retrieve it. She figured it was no big deal after all the dead bodies she'd encountered. She found no flesh on the body, only bones. There was no sickly smell. She did not know if she had taken an arm or leg in her plastic bag, but it did not matter. There were so many anonymous victims now, and little plan of what to do with the remaining women and children at Al-Hol, because some of their countries did not want to take them.

On October 6, 2019, U.S. president Donald Trump announced, without any warning, that he was withdrawing American troops from northern

Syria, which would essentially green-light a Turkish incursion there. He did not tell the Kurds, America's partner in fighting ISIS, beforehand. Instead, he weakly told Turkey not to do anything "off-limits."

Within three days of Trump's announcement, Turkey launched airstrikes on border towns in northeast Syria, in an operation the country dubbed Operation Peace Spring. "Behold the 'great and unmatched wisdom' of President Donald Trump," the *Economist* wrote sarcastically at the time, noting that the offensive threatened to revive ISIS and "condemn Syria to yet another cycle of slaughter." It also threatened to destroy the entire Rojavan experiment in democracy and lead to a humanitarian crisis.

Former and current top U.S. military officials denounced the proposed withdrawal, which they saw as a stark betrayal of the Kurdish-led militias who had sacrificed so much for the U.S. by fighting ISIS on the ground. Cicek had mixed feelings about the news. "It's not their war," she said, remembering how four U.S. personnel had been killed in Manbij in 2019 by an ISIS explosion. "So it's their own decision if they want to stay or not. But what made me upset and angry is: Why did they give Turkey the green light to attack us?"

Her voice grew harder, her hands gesticulating her frustration. She believed the U.S. had "opened the air for Turkey," meaning it was no longer stopping Turkey from flying through airspace it controlled to launch Turkish attacks. "And if they do that, we cannot defend ourselves," she said. "We have the weapons and morale to fight on the ground but not in the air. It's too hard for us to fight off airstrikes. If you want to take back your troops, fine. But just don't give them the sky."

After Turkey launched Operation Peace Spring, Cicek was sent to defend Ras al-Ayn, a border city in northeast Syria with so many natural waterways its name translated to "the head of the spring." She arrived on the second day of the operation and was assigned to the heavy weapons team. She was given a thermal weapon sight, which was mounted on a heavy weapon, a device she had never been trained to operate. The sight could find sources of heat in the total dark, and she used it to target approaching Turkish vehicles and tanks.

The YPG and YPJ urged all civilians in Ras al-Ayn to evacuate because many more airstrikes were expected. Cicek thought Turkey was cowardly to rely on their drones, jets, and rockets, with only minimal troops on the ground (and most of them Turkish-backed forces instead of Turkish nationals). "If they do not use the air they cannot advance even one step," she boasted. In fact, Turkey's armed forces were large enough to outmatch them on the ground, but Turkey seemed unlikely to launch a full-fledged invasion, which NATO would not support.

Although more than 200,000 people evacuated the Syrian border towns during Operation Peace Spring, many others refused to leave. "This is our land, our home," several families told Cicek, who replied that she would not force them to go, though some did not have any weapons to defend themselves when the Turkish troops came. Cicek had never been more convinced of the necessity of having a weapon and knowing how to protect oneself. As Kurdish activist Elif Sarican told me by phone, "In the case of the Kurdish movement, you have the second largest NATO army [Turkey] out to annihilate you. If you want to stick to nonviolent methods, you will literally be annihilated. Nonviolence is a privilege."

On October 17, 2019, eleven days after Trump announced the U.S. troops' withdrawal from the region, Turkey agreed to pause the operation after pressure from U.S. officials. But Rojava's health authority said at least 218 civilians had already been killed, and Cicek knew it was only the beginning.

After he recovered in the hospital, Haroun was scheduled to go to Bashur, Iraq, to get more treatment for his maimed hands. Doctors in different countries had proposed various solutions: transplant flesh from his stomach, put in a metal implant through surgery, or give him entirely artificial hands. He currently could not write, hold a glass, or move fingers on either hand. He had hoped to visit an excellent hand doctor in Italy, and the hevals had even offered to pay. But as a Syrian citizen, Haroun could not get a visa, so he was going to Iraq for several months of treatment instead. Beritan told him she would drive him toward the border.

By this time, Beritan and Haroun were secretly dating. They had even discussed marriage. Since marriages were not allowed in the YPJ, Beritan would have to leave the militia. She had already fought for years, and she agreed that the front line was no place for a mother. As for Haroun, he was no longer an active soldier because of his injuries. They talked about building an ordinary, peaceful life together: Haroun would open a shop, while Beritan would work in Rojava's self-administration or police force. They just needed the permission of their families, whom they had not yet told.

When Haroun got in Beritan's car for the drive toward Iraq, he began to cry. It was rare to see a Syrian man shed tears, and Beritan did not know what to do. She stayed silent and lowered the volume of the music, driving slowly to their destination to give Haroun time to speak. She did not know if he was crying about his hands or something else, and did not dare ask. When she parked the car, Haroun got out without saying a word. Beritan was confused and called him. "Why are you crying?" she asked. "Because I'm leaving you," he replied, "and I don't know what will happen." Beritan could not believe that she was the reason, not his hands or the never-ending war. "No, come on," she said, trying to calm him. "You will go and have a fine trip and come back and I'll be here."

The more Beritan had gotten to know Haroun, the more she felt they shared something pure. They did not get to see one another often, but when together they talked for an hour straight. They did not play games and treated each other with admiration and respect. Once, Haroun had asked Beritan about her last name, "Shiar," and she said it was the name of a friend who was martyred. She did not tell Haroun that she'd loved Shiar, and he did not ask her any follow-up questions. They never seemed to have enough time for her to tell him the whole story.

Under the Turkish occupation of Afrin, some women had started disappearing, and others reported rape at the hands of the Turkish-backed militias and mercenaries. In 2018, a video emerged of one mercenary mutilating the half-naked dead body of a YPJ fighter named Barin Kobani. "That's our revenge against the pigs of the PKK," the man says in the video as the woman's organs fall out of her body. "Man, she's pretty," another man leers. Later, YPJ officials said Barin Kobani had blown herself up, but it was not clear if that was a story to save face.

Meghan Bodette, a Washington D.C.–based researcher of Kurdish issues, began tracking the kidnappings and disappearances of women in Afrin in 2019 in an effort she called the Missing Afrin Women Project. Bodette relied on data sourced from human rights monitors, nonprofits, local media reports, and activist networks. Her spreadsheet listed the names of missing women, locations where the incident happened, any sexual violence or torture that allegedly took place, and which militia or police force was reported to have taken them. Though men were also going missing, "Turkey was very clearly targeting women," she told me. Bodette cited the case of Hevrin Khalaf, a Kurdish-Syrian politician who was killed by a Turkish-backed militia in October 2019. An autopsy report showed Khalaf was beaten over the head, hit with sharp objects on her legs, dragged by her hair, and shot. "It doesn't get any more clear that *that* is what they think of women," she said.

The U.S. State Department's 2020 country report on Syria warned of the kidnappings of women by Turkish-backed militias, torture and rape of minors taken into custody, and forced marriages of Kurdish women. At the same time, Turkish mercenaries continued to raze more of Afrin's olive fields, including the area around Cicek's village.

That year, Cicek was sent by the YPJ to Shahba Canton, where her family was living in a refugee camp, but avoided going to see them. "I didn't want to go and see my mother in that situation, in the camps," Cicek said. She was in denial of how difficult life had gotten for her family and could not bear to face the reality. But eventually Cicek met her mother, and they embraced and talked for hours. She saw there was an olive tree outside their humble camp dwelling, at least, with its familiar gnarled trunk and silvery gray-green leaves. In Shahba, she saw that her family's fate was in her hands, and Cicek, now twenty-three, had never felt like less of a child.

WE ARE A PEOPLE

Trim and dark-eyed, Miss [Leila] Khaled, a 24-year-old teacher who speaks English fluently, was seized at Heathrow Airport on Sunday after trying to hijack a New York–bound Israeli airliner carrying 145 passengers . . . "I am a fighter, just like any other of the Palestinians who are determined to regain Palestine," [Ms. Khaled said]. "We were sorry for the inconvenience we caused to [the passengers], but the world must know we are a people and we are a people entitled to rights."

—*New York Times*, September 9, 1970

Sunrise in Rojava. It is Eid again, and crowds gather in a graveyard for YPG and YPJ martyrs under the gray-pink sky. A mother sobs as she caresses a photograph on a headstone, while an elderly woman beside her stares off into space, letting her cigarette burn down to ash. Nearby, children run after tossed sweets. Male soldiers with rifles stand atop sandbags at the edges of the graveyard, patrolling. The front line is not far away.

At midday along the road from the graveyard, Bedouins lead their sheep to pasture, while people squat in parched fields to harvest barley with scythes. Clouds of dust rise behind passing motorcyclists, who ride with their scarves tightly wrapped around their faces. In the distance, tunnels stretch across the horizon like angry welts in the earth. They were dug as a place from which to conduct military operations, in preparation for more incursions by Turkey. But the tunnels do not make people feel safer.

In the city at the golden hour, light bathes Abdullah Ocalan's face on each of the billboards: Ocalan looking jovial, Ocalan reading a book, and Ocalan standing in front of a mountain scene. Downtown, dozens of concrete apartment buildings sit unfinished, construction abandoned because of war. The city is quiet for the holiday, but on most days, it bustles: women doing their evening shopping, men stopping for shaved meat. Several of the remaining American soldiers carry themselves like saviors, showing a small boy their big weapons. Alley graffiti beside them reads: "Women are life, don't kill life."

At night on the border, a couple hours east, a sliver of moon hangs in the haze. The Tigris River moves fast under a rickety bridge used for the border crossing between Iraq and Syria. Invisible lines mark the divide between two mud hut villages that share family members and look much the same. In the distance, across the Turkish border, the night is lit up by a constellation of lights, while in Rojava few lights are visible or, in some places, there are none at all.

In May 2021, at a new headquarters for the Syrian Democratic Forces, YPJ general commander Newroz Ahmed, who holds the militia's highest position, sat in a front room when I arrived, her television turned to Jin TV. Jin means "women" in Kurdish, and Jin TV is a station run by women and devoted entirely to women's stories. Ahmed said she watched it often. The room was a simple one, meant to receive journalists or hold other meetings, and it was nicer than most of the offices at the other YPJ bases, with blue recessed lighting and tan faux-leather couches, instead of humble pillows on the floor. A heval with a prosthetic foot sat across from Ahmed and me while a gray-and-white kitten dozed in a cardboard box on the floor.

I had many lingering questions for Ahmed, who was in her midforties and unassuming except for her knowing stare. When I asked how close the YPG-YPJ and PKK remained, I was surprised to find she made no effort to obscure their ties, as the Kurdish-led militias had done for years. Instead, she freely admitted that Ocalan's ideology was their ideology; that many PKK comrades had joined their revolution in Rojava, and that she and PKK leaders sometimes exchanged ideas. "If they want us to say that the PKK is bad, we will never say this," Ahmed said, arguing that the PKK was fighting for Kurdish rights just as the YPJ were. But she maintained that the PKK was not running the show here in Rojava. They were the PKK's siblings, not its children.

Plus, she argued, the YPJ was constantly evolving. At the beginning of the revolution, she said it had been challenging in the chaos to control who joined the militia, with women and girls of all ages and abilities picking up guns to fight ISIS. As battles raged, she claimed, it had been impossible to verify every fighter's age, but since the international outcry they had become more careful about that. With so many comrades lost—11,000 or more—she said they had also become choosier about who they recruited: "We don't accept everybody, we want them to be elite, unique people." And they no longer accepted married women.

Ahmed estimated that the YPJ had about 5,000 soldiers as of 2021, about the same number as when they fought ISIS, though the international media had regularly inflated that number. Before, they had rapidly lost and gained fighters, while today the force's size was more stable. She said she wanted every YPJ soldier to be well-trained, put on a two-year contract, and paid a salary. The guerrilla force was becoming almost like a professional army.

It was clear Ahmed envisioned the YPJ being a fierce militia for years to come. But she told me she also hoped to turn its focus to another battle: the continuing fight to transform the chauvinist mentality within Syrian society. Rojava was trying to model itself on new, feminist ideals, but violations at home and within communities continued, and so she believed all Syrian women needed to learn how to defend themselves. "Our aim is not to just have her hold her gun, but to be aware," she told me. "And this is even harder than the military operations."

As Ahmed spoke about all the converging problems in Rojava, she seemed overwhelmed. The list was long: the mentality in Syria toward women and minorities, the rising economic crisis due to the ongoing conflict, the uncertain political situation with the Syrian regime, the potential resurgence of ISIS, Turkey's threats of invasion, and, worst of all, the possibility that they were trapped in a forever war.

It felt safe and quiet here in headquarters, in the heavily fortified Syrian Democratic Forces base, where American soldiers had a presence.

After the intense criticism that greeted Trump's proposed withdrawal, he had changed course and said American troops would stay.

But I knew that Ahmed and the other YPJ commanders were a target almost anywhere else. Turkey had started picking off members of the YPJ leadership one by one, just as the government of Mexico had once picked off leaders of the Zapatista movement for indigenous rights, a movement to which the Kurdish struggle was often compared. In a 1994 interview, Major Ana Maria of the Zapatistas told a comrade, "They grabbed our leaders. They put them in jail. They dragged them along with horses to torture them." Turkish proxy forces did not jail or torture YPJ commanders, and instead announced they had been "neutralized"—a few by this point, but many more to come—usually via drone strike from the sky.

Ever since her injury at Afrin, Cicek had been grounded from battle to recuperate. She begged her higher-ups to send her somewhere, anywhere interesting, preferably to the front line. Instead, they assigned her to be a driver for Commander Sosin Birhat, a well-respected commander in the YPJ, who oversaw a base in the northeastern Syrian town of Tal Tamr. Cicek had met Sosin in a follow-up training a year or two before, and immediately both feared and admired her. Sosin had joined the Kurdish rights movement in 1996 and had been a commander in the YPJ since 2014.

I met Sosin in the spring of 2021. She was slight but commanding, with intense dark eyes, soft olive skin despite her middle age and experience, and a tone of voice that was not to be trifled with. People spoke of her as a legendary commander. She reminded me of a description I'd once read of Nanny of the Maroons, who at the start of the eighteenth century led formerly enslaved Africans to fight against British authorities. The Jamaica Information Service described Nanny as a "small, wiry woman with piercing eyes," whose "cleverness in planning guerrilla warfare confused the British." Sosin was like that: clever, strategic, and intimidating.

For once, Cicek was afraid to joke around or talk back to a commander. She found herself quiet around Sosin instead of brash, wanting to hear and understand everything the commander had to say. "When you listen to Sosin talk, you would like to go and sit next to her, and pay more attention to whatever she is talking about," Cicek said. "And when you are in discussion with her, you will be completely convinced of whatever she is saying."

It was Sosin who had requested Cicek as her driver. The young fighter, just twenty-three, was a famed driver in the YPJ because of how many battles she'd driven hevals through without injury. Still, Cicek was not the obvious choice at this point, given that her eyesight remained poor from the drone strike in Afrin, and that she now drove automatic because switching gears manually was too difficult with her leg and stomach pain from Kobani. But Sosin had heard that Cicek was restless to get to the front lines and asked for the headstrong young heval as her driver.

"Why are you always trying to fight?" Sosin asked Cicek on her first day in 2020, her voice gentle but chiding. "It's in my nature," Cicek replied, and they both laughed.

After that, Cicek was always by Sosin's side. Cicek remembered how she'd found the commander so intense in training that she could not imagine talking or joking around with her. Now, they bantered and spoke without pause on their long drives. They both loved the same revolutionary music and songs from Afrin, where they both were born. Cicek continued to want to hear everything Sosin said. And whenever Cicek had a problem, Sosin always seemed to arrive with a solution. Not long after moving to the base in Tal Tamr, Cicek was upset after receiving news that another friend had been killed. Sosin appeared suddenly in the doorway and asked Cicek in her usual, direct way, "Why are you sad and angry?" Cicek crumpled, telling her a comrade had been martyred. "If we lose one of our friends, we are certainly suffering a big loss," Sosin said. "But if you're not sacrificing your body for the cause, how can you serve our people?"

Cicek nodded and felt better. They never discussed PTSD, which most of the fighters likely had, but YPJ pamphlets that were passed around talked about small ways to reduce stress: have less cigarettes and coffee, make sure not to stay isolated. Cicek never felt alone when she was with her commander. Sosin was hardcore on the ideology, but Cicek appreciated that. Her commander helped her focus on the big picture—the effort to not just defend Rojava, but also reshape society—which helped Cicek to not repeatedly see her lost comrades' faces in her mind.

Despite the violence just an hour away at the border, Cicek's base at Tal Tamr was often idyllic. Songbirds chirped in the mornings, and crows cawed in the afternoons. A shaggy white dog often trotted by for food. The base itself was an old, one-story cement building that had once belonged to the Syrian regime. Graffiti praising the regime at the entrance had long ago been crossed out. The building had a kitchen, meeting room, bedroom, and outdoor bathroom, the perfect setup for a small base. Pine trees surrounded the courtyard, where the fighters had set up a makeshift volleyball court, and the smell of sap was strong. The wind blew gently even in the summer. An occasional dust storm spiraled in the distance. On sweltering nights, the women slept outside.

One day, at the base in 2020, Cicek was helping Commander Sosin carry a heavy battery when she felt the stitches in her stomach burst open. "Migo!" she shouted, a childlike exclamation, and fell to the ground. Sosin rushed Cicek to the hospital. "Why are you doing stupid things like carrying a battery if you have that wound?" Sosin chastised Cicek as they drove, though it was clear she was concerned about her heval. "You should take better care of yourself, Cicek."

Later, as Cicek lay in a hospital bed, Sosin tried to drive her point home. "Cicek, listen to me," she said. "We are friends, we are hevals, we are the same. Don't put obstacles between me and you." Cicek nodded. She knew it was true, because Sosin was a humble commander who cooked and made her own tea. She should not be so stubborn. "We are equal, Cicek, and I'm telling you: take care of yourself," Sosin said.

When several hospital staff entered the room, one asked Cicek if she was Sosin's daughter. Cicek blushed. She looked nothing like her slight, intense commander, with her own broad face and shoulders, and impish attitude. But it was an honor to be compared. "She is not my mother,"

Cicek said, and boasted, "I can stay away for twenty years from my mother in Afrin. But I can't stay far away from heval Sosin for more than a few minutes." She didn't say the rest of what she was thinking, which was: *I want to stay close to Sosin for always. I want to spend the rest of my life beside her.*

After Cicek returned to the base, Sosin gave her more duties, though she told me she did not think Cicek had it in her to be a commander. At least not yet. Cicek was a fearsome fighter and excellent at raising morale among her comrades, but she was still too stubborn and reckless. Instead, Sosin made Cicek a training officer and assigned her to teach a four-day intermediate training course at the nearby, historic Sugar Palace. On the first day, Cicek instructed the trainees to run stairs in the wind, including a stubborn heval who refused to go. "Count the steps, and then you will find it easy," Cicek told her. At the end, the heval told her breathlessly: 184.

It was freezing and rainy on most of the training days, so Cicek had to work hard to keep up morale. She worried the cold would be brutal on her stomach but found it easy to ignore the pain once they started moving. She applied the same thinking to her hevals, pushing them to get faster, stronger, and smarter. With uncharacteristic patience, Cicek showed them how to better wield their Kalashnikovs and BKCs, the machine gun whose bullets had torn open her stomach in Kobani. She taught them how to prepare for ambushes and launch attacks in the dark of night. On the rainiest day of the training, Cicek instructed the hevals to crouch in the mud with their bags on their backs and run. Their clothes became as heavy with wet as hers had been in battle. She felt she had to train them for every possible situation because no one knew what kind of battles lay ahead. Cicek remembered how she could barely fire a rifle on her first day in Kobani. These women would be far more prepared to face the more serious threat of Turkey.

With Cicek's sun-weathered skin, chain-smoking habit, and many injuries, she seemed an impressive veteran to the less experienced hevals. They looked at her as she had once looked at Commander Sosin, with a mix of admiration and fear. "Do you know how many times I was supposed to die from ISIS?" Cicek asked them. "How many?" they replied, eyes shining. "Twenty-one times." Twenty-one close calls that should have killed her. "We are surprised you did not become a shahid," a "martyr," one heval said. Cicek grew somber: "The purpose is not to die, but to live, to protect yourself and others."

When the women grew grumpy from the repetition of training, Cicek invented challenges, such as putting stones on the chests of hevals, who had to protect their stones from attack. After training finished each day, she played Kurdish and Arabic music, handing the hevals containers of water to use as drums and encouraging them to sing and dance. She urged the women to huddle around the fire under the old palace turret, which was covered in graffiti and filled with old cigarette butts. She told them that the palace had been grand in the time of Saladin, a Kurd who was the first sultan of Egypt and Syria. Each night after training, the women slept deeply under the stars.

As they left Sugar Palace on the final evening of the training, a passing man asked the crowd of women who they were. "We are the children of Saladin," Cicek intoned, "and we are haunting his grave." She could not help herself. The man hurried away, and all the hevals laughed. Of all the trainers, Cicek was their favorite.

Around this time, Beritan was also instructing young hevals in Al-Hasakah, near Tal Tamr, and had finally told her parents she wanted to marry Haroun. She visited her village and showed her mother Haroun's picture on her phone. "From the picture, he is good," her mother said, her scarf drawn tightly around her face. Haroun looked tall, thin, and handsome in his photo, striking with his dark hair and beard and hazel eyes. No mother would say no to such a picture. Beritan added, in her quietest voice, "But there is something else. He is disabled, and he doesn't have a hand." Her mother drew back and shook her head. "Then I will not accept it," she said. "A disabled man cannot be your husband."

Beritan pushed back on her mother. She said she would talk to her father, who would better understand. But her father deferred to her mother, and even some of Beritan's siblings opposed the union. "Why will you marry a disabled man?" one of Beritan's sisters asked her. "In the society, they will talk." Beritan shook her head and bitterly replied, "No one has destroyed our life except this society. The society who says: 'You will do this or that.'"

Beritan did not consider disobeying her family. She told Haroun she could not bear to hurt them, but that she could still convince them of the union. Especially her father. Her father always understood.

But in spring 2020, the COVID-19 pandemic spread its tentacles around the world, and though it didn't impact the younger fighters much, Beritan's father contracted the virus. He died within four days of his diagnosis. Beritan was so angry at the news that she smashed her Samsung phone into pieces. If she were to text Haroun to tell him, the shards of the screen would cut her fingers.

Back in Tal Tamr, a group of men delivered a refrigerator to Cicek's base in May 2021, when I was there for a visit. All the women sprang up to help, including Cicek, because Commander Sosin was not there to chide her. Despite the YPJ's triumphant battles against ISIS, local men remained doubtful of the female fighters' strength, so the women took every opportunity to show them. COVID was widespread in Rojava in 2020, but vaccinations had reached the region by this time, and the situation had stabilized.

It was mostly new recruits at the base with Cicek—half a dozen young women in their early and mid-twenties, plus a late-twenties woman with a goofy demeanor named Zeynab, who had joined the YPJ after Turkey bombed her hometown. Zeynab was Kurdish but had grown up in an Arabic village, and she spoke a confusing mix of both languages all the time. She had thick, raven-black hair, a big gap between her two front teeth, and walked with a limp from an injury she'd gotten in YPJ training. Cicek loved Zeynab's "comic personality," and immediately took her under her wing. The two joked around and told stories over tea, or Zeynab read Cicek's fortune from coffee grinds, which was an old gypsy tradition. Cicek always snorted at the predictions.

Sometimes, Zeynab talked more seriously about what had happened to her family in her hometown of Ras al-Ayn. Days after Trump announced the withdrawal of American troops from northern Syria, Zeynab's family were warned that Turkish airstrikes were imminent. "We didn't believe it at first," Zeynab said. It seemed absurd that their tranquil garden of flowers, trellised grapes, and fig and apricot trees could suddenly be wiped out. "But then, at four-thirty, airplanes started targeting the area," Zeynab went on. "So, we left around eleven in the night and went into the desert." From their car, Zeynab's family watched mortars rain down over their village. Zeynab later learned that Turkish-backed militias, who arrived after the airstrikes, burned down her family's house because they had an Ocalan photo on their wall.

Soon after, Zeynab told her mother that she was joining the YPJ. Even though her family was supportive of the Kurdish cause, her mother vehemently opposed the idea because two of their extended family members, both men, had already died in the YPG. But Zeynab pushed back. "We have been pushed outside of our land, so now we should go and defend our land," she said with newfound courage. "Now I have a purpose—and a target."

Cicek loved watching Zeynab grow at the base in Tal Tamr. When Zeynab first joined the YPJ, Cicek said, the new recruit was afraid of heights and strangers, and did not know how to express herself. But several months in, Zeynab knew "how to talk to you and deal with people," Cicek said. "And she always wants to go to the front line." Cicek warned Zeynab that the front line was full of loss, but that she'd endure it if she never lost sight of the love of Rojava.

To keep themselves busy on slow days, when they were not sent to the front, the women drank tea or instant coffee and talked. Zeynab always prepared the drinks, saying she enjoyed the task. No one had phones at the base because Turkish drones could find them that way. No one seemed to miss them. They ate simple, delicious meals: hot dogs, hummus, ramen noodles, fries, and overcooked leafy greens—wartime food. They kept the base squeaky clean. In the backyard, the women grew grapes as Zeynab's family had once done. An old TV hung on the wall, and because Zeynab had grown up in an Arab village, she sometimes liked to watch Bollywood romances and serials.

The women hardly ever talked about boys or men, which they told me is because they'd joined the YPJ to be equals, not fall in love. They reminded me that being gay was taboo, haram. There were no laws at all discussing queerness in Rojava, despite the progressiveness of the rest of the constitution. Cicek told me the idea of dating at all seemed silly to her, especially while they were at war. The women at the base sometimes annoyed one another, but there was little cattiness, petty talk, or gossip. Too much was at stake for that. The only fear the women at base had, even Cicek, was the rat that sometimes scurried through the building.

On infernally hot days in Tal Tamr, the women found inventive ways to stay cool, as Cicek and Buhar had done in Kobani's village with the fan they turned with a stick. One afternoon when Sosin was away, Cicek started a water fight. She filled a bucket with water in the courtyard and began throwing it at the younger hevals. Grinning, Zeynab held the hevals' heads under water for Cicek's attacks. The young women giggled helplessly, still girls underneath it all. With everyone soaked to their skins, Cicek turned on Arabic music from the car radio and they danced arm in arm.

That night, the crickets started up their calls like little sirens. The women laid their mats on the ground outside, and I lay down to sleep beside them. There were very few lights in the distance, and it was quiet minus the call of the crickets, the growl of a distant motorcycle, or the occasional howl of a dog in the distance. The women could see the stars and even a few constellations. They took turns on watch to look and listen for Turkish drones, which increasingly hovered over Tal Tamr for surveillance. One woman chain-smoked that night to keep herself awake, on watch, until morning. The pain in Cicek's legs woke her up, but she turned over and tried to ignore it. When she fell back asleep, she dreamt of mortars, like the ones that hit Zeynab's village, then of planes and her car being struck in Afrin. In the mornings that followed, Cicek tried to write some of her memories down in a journal. But she was unhappy with what she'd written and burned its pages.

In Afrin, Cicek's family had moved out of the refugee camp and into an abandoned house an hour away from the shelling. Without being able to farm, her father struggled to financially support the family. After Cicek learned of her family's situation from the hevals, she became stern with the recruits, telling them to pay close attention to news reports of the Turkish-backed militias' alleged violations in Afrin, including rapes, arbitrary arrests, and murders. "If those people come here, they will do the same to us. That is why we are fighting," Cicek told them, as a senior heval had once told her about ISIS. "We will not accept that. We will hold our weapon and stand against them."

But Cicek herself hardly watched the news. She could not stomach seeing footage of people crying in Afrin or the fields of razed olive trees. Because Commander Sosin was also from Afrin, she and Cicek talked constantly about what was happening there. "I will feel so sad if I am martyred, and I do not live to see Afrin liberated," Sosin said. The commander was twenty years senior to Cicek, but often vulnerable with her driver these days. Cicek nodded. She understood the desire to live just to see Afrin freed. She and Sosin almost always thought the same way about the Kurdish struggle. "If there is any chance for me to go and fight there," Cicek replied, "I will be the first."

The drone strike hit the building at day's end, as the sun set through the desert haze. Cicek would later freeze the scene and play it back. Her commander, Sosin, with whom she shared a birthplace, favorite music, and a dream, had just walked inside the building. Cicek was outside smoking a Gauloises cigarette, as she often did throughout the day. A few other soldiers had just left to go shopping. They asked Cicek to come, but she had an uneasy feeling and declined. She said she wanted to stay close to Sosin.

It was August 2021, and the heat weighed like a heavy damask blanket on the region. Dozens of people displaced by recent attacks from Turkish militias were gathered at the new military office to ask for housing help and were sweating in the heat. After the drone hit, Cicek's world went black.

When Cicek woke up in the hospital, the hevals told her that Sosin had been martyred, along with three other hevals. *You lied to me,* Cicek thought furiously. They had known Sosin was dead but kept it from her when she asked, after she'd been pulled from the rubble. The hevals realized Cicek would not go through with the operation if she knew, because she wouldn't want to live without Sosin.

As people murmured around her hospital bed, Cicek grew livid. She refused food until the doctor told her that if she did not eat, her condition would deteriorate, and she'd have to stay in the hospital for over a year. Cicek did the minimum to stay alive, remembering that her commander would want her to keep fighting for a free Rojava. She was still in the hospital during Sosin's funeral, for which Zeynab braided her raven-black hair and was not goofy for even a moment. Sosin's death forced all the hevals in Tal Tamr to grow up faster.

A few weeks later, Zeynab had a vivid dream about Sosin, in which the commander placed a white wedding veil over Zeynab's face. Zeynab told the other fighters at the base that she thought it prefigured her own death, because people in Syria were often buried in white shrouds, and white was the color of death. One heval thought it was a sign of a marriage to come but Zeynab disagreed.

That afternoon, Zeynab was sent to the front line, where she had only been a few times and where she'd been asking to return to for weeks. She was thrilled and grinning as she left the Tal Tamr base in her flak jacket, her Kalashnikov in hand and a belt of ammunition slung across her chest. Zeynab was reportedly making tea for the other soldiers at the front line when she was hit by a drone strike and killed.

Cicek was still in the hospital when she heard the news. This time, she felt only numb. Zeynab's death made little sense to her. Sosin was a seasoned commander, someone Turkey would want to target and eliminate. But Zeynab had not yet fired a rifle in battle. Cicek reminded herself that Zeynab had wanted to go to the front line, that she had insisted and insisted, and that the hevals at the base said she'd flashed her gap-toothed grin as she sped off in a truck heading north. Cicek reminded herself that when any woman put on the YPJ uniform, she knew she could be wounded or killed. Zeynab had known that, too. Still, it seemed like a senseless loss.

On Zeynab's grave, the hevals placed a white veil to represent Zeynab's dream, and as a sign that she was with Sosin now. Zeynab's mother, Zulekha Juma Rashid, said she had wanted her daughter to wear a veil at her wedding someday, not bury her with it underground. In Rashid's mind, her daughter was never going to be a guerrilla fighter forever. "She was not only my daughter, she was my friend," she wailed as she looked through photos of Zeynab at home. Only days before, her daughter had brought her grape leaves from the Tal Tamr base to cook for dinner. "I don't know what [Turkish president] Erdogan wants from us," Rashid cried. "We lost our home; we lost our city. We live in very difficult conditions . . . And today my beautiful daughter Zeynab. What is this injustice? We are tired."

After Zeynab's death, Cicek demanded to leave the hospital and return to her base in Tal Tamr. The new base commander offered her a transfer elsewhere in Rojava, but Cicek was insistent she be back with her comrades among the pines. After losing Sosin and Zeynab there, she could not go anywhere else. For the first time, Cicek felt she was losing hope in the cause—and hope in everything. She had wanted to die with Sosin, and now she felt unmoored. "I refuse to go away from the place where my friends have been martyred," she said. "Whenever I walk around Tal Tamr, I remember what happened there. And I don't want to forget."

Some 6,000 miles away in Washington, D.C., Amy Austin Holmes, a researcher and fellow at the Wilson Center, a think tank, pored over data from the Turkish-Syrian border. For several years, Turkey had justified its series of operations inside Syria by saying the YPG and YPJ were terrorists who threatened the country, just like the PKK terrorists they'd feared in-country for decades. Holmes wanted to put that assertion to the test, by looking at how many attacks were initiated from each side.

For months, Holmes analyzed Armed Conflict Location & Event

Data (ACLED), which maps political violence and protest worldwide. She studied 4,000 events on Turkey's border with northern Syria from January 2017 to August 2020. Holmes found something startling: Turkey and Turkish-backed militias had launched over 3,300 attacks against the YPJ, the YPG, the Syrian Democratic Forces, or civilians, compared to 22 cross-border attacks initiated by the Kurdish-led forces over three and a half years.

Of those twenty-two attacks, she could not independently verify ten of them. As for the remaining twelve, she found that they happened between October 2019, when Turkey launched Operation Peace Spring, and August 2020, when they retrieved the data, so she deemed those self-defense.

Holmes was dismayed. Turkey's claims were mostly taken at face value in the American foreign policy community, especially since Turkey is a NATO ally of the U.S. But Turkey's claims did not hold up once she had subjected them to empirical scrutiny. She published her findings in a 2021 Wilson Center report. "To put it bluntly, Turkish intervention [in northeast Syria] was based on a lie," Holmes told me by phone. "Turkey promised to safeguard religious and ethnic minorities and protect civilians [in their operations]. But they did not do that." Turkey's goal, as everyone knew, was to stamp out YPG and YPJ and its alleged terrorism entirely. Though Turkey had signed a ceasefire agreement with the American president, Donald Trump, after the uproar over his proposed withdrawal of troops from the region, Holmes found that Turkey violated the ceasefire over eight hundred times in the first year after it signed.

Holmes also found something else striking in the data: a town called Tal Tamr, far outside of the area Turkey said it controlled, and an area with a large YPG-YPJ presence, had been attacked by Turkish drone strikes or shelling every month.

After Sosin's death, Cicek began trying to keep a diary in Tal Tamr. "I picked up the pen to write my sufferings," Cicek wrote, finding a poetic voice she did not know she had. "The pen cried before my eyes gave tears." She tore out the page and pasted it to the journal's cover. Inside, she glued a photograph of Commander Sosin and wrote underneath it: "Heval Sosin was—and still is—a very different person." Cicek was at a loss for how to describe her commander. She had so much to say about Sosin but little way to say it, so she tried to make sense of Sosin's death in free verse: "In each memory, there is hope. And in hope, there is a meeting. In each meeting, there is a departure." She and Sosin had met, spent a beautiful year or more together, and then Sosin had abruptly left her. "In each departure, there are tears. In tears, there is love. In love, there is a spirit of comradeship, and in each spirit of comradeship, there is sacrifice." The sacrifice was that Sosin was dead.

Cicek felt the urge to burn the diary again. She turned to another page and wrote: "I ask Death, is there anything stronger than you? He answered quietly, 'Losing someone, you miss them every moment.'" Underneath, she added a quote she said she took from Ocalan: "I wanted to burn my body as a light for the dark way." And then, "Şehîd Namirin." *Martyrs never die.*

The more Cicek wrote in the journal, the more chaotic her penmanship became. By the fifth page of the journal, her writing was a scrawl. "You can forget about your wounds"—in this case, her eyes, arm, legs, and belly—"but you will never forget the words of your heval." *We are friends, we are hevals, we are equal,* Sosin had told Cicek, as she recovered in the hospital from lifting the battery in Tal Tamr. *I'm telling you: Take care of yourself, Cicek.*

Cicek also wrote about Zeynab, and those words came more easily. She wrote that Zeynab was the only daughter in her family, and from Ras al-Ayn; that Zeynab was kind and selfless and did not know that she was a little strange, and that she never got bored when Zeynab was around. As Cicek wrote, she switched from the past to present tense, as many do after losing a loved one, as if Zeynab were still alive: "She had high morale to empower all her friends. She didn't want to annoy anybody. She has the kindest heart." Cicek listed Zeynab's favorite meal (mahshi, or filled zucchini), her favorite color (black), and her goal in life (to face the enemy). Though Zeynab was new to the base, Cicek wrote, "Whoever saw Zeynab thought she had been serving with us for more than ten years because she respected everyone and she had a nice way of behaving with people. Everyone loved her. She was laughing most of the time."

Cicek could find the words to explain the loss of Zeynab and her grief over her friend. But her sorrow over Sosin was different, too immense to speak. Cicek thought that Sosin and Zeynab were likely together now, which made her feel a little better. Zeynab, her funny yet courageous heval, was with Sosin, her brilliant, intense commander, her equal and her comrade, a woman she had loved and longed for in a way she could not define.

On the last page of her journal, Cicek added a Post-it note like an afterthought: "Death is better than a life without suffering." Cicek had suffering in spades, but she also had meaning and a purpose: a revolution for the rights of women and the Kurds, and for a better world. She knew Sosin would not want her to lose sight of that.

10,000 LEAGUES

Don't tell me women / are not the stuff of heroes / I alone rode over the East Sea's / winds for ten thousand leagues.

— Nineteenth-century Chinese poet and activist Qiu Jin,
  from her poem "Capping Rhymes with Sir Ishii from
  Sun's Root Land"

In nearly all utopian societies, there is a moment when things go wrong. For the revolution in Rojava, it did not come from women wielding guns, which they did adeptly and which even some of the most conservative Syrian men came to accept. Instead, the revolution soured for many northern Syrians in 2021 when the region spiraled deeper into an economic crisis. The reasons were many: a decade of war had stretched the self-administration's resources thin; warmer temperatures and less rainfall imperiled wheat production; and Turkey cut off the water supply of the Euphrates River, further bleeding northern Syria's fertile farmland dry. And although oil pumps dotted the landscape of the area, producing 15,000 barrels of oil daily that should have made Rojava rich, the self-administration said it barely made any money from the resource.

Aldar Khalil, co-chair of the leading Democratic Union Party of the self-administration, said that as a result of wartime sanctions on the Syrian regime by Europe, U.S., and other countries, they could not sell to other countries, "so we are forced to deal with smugglers who abuse us to sell our oil." He said the other 40 percent of the oil went to the Syrian regime, whose currency had become nearly worthless, and whose president, Bashar al-Assad, continued to hold on to power a decade after the uprising began.

To many, the promises of a democratic, egalitarian, and feminist revolution began to seem foolish when they did not have any bread. People grew upset even with the Kurdish-led militias that had so heroically vanquished ISIS. Rojava's residents lacked essential services, but watched the YPG and YPJ build tunnel after expensive tunnel, popping up like giant molehills in the earth. Khalil admitted to me that 60 percent of the self-administration's budget went toward the military but said that it was out of necessity. He gave the example of Afrin, Cicek's home region, into which the self-administration had poured money for development. "Then in a short time it was occupied by Turkey and we lost everything," Khalil said. "So we need to protect ourselves first. Then we can start building."

Still, even some of the most disgruntled Rojava residents said they preferred the self-administration over the rule of ISIS, Turkey, or the Syrian regime, which had mercilessly squashed dissent and whose economy was in no better shape. In May 2022, after more than a decade of a bloody civil war, Syrian president Bashar al-Assad freed hundreds of detainees from prison, but many could not remember who they were because of the extreme torture they'd endured. In the city of Qamishli in northeast Syria, people played tic-tac-toe on the pedestal of the once-sacred statue of Assad's father, Hafez al-Assad. The Rojavan self-administration was still better than the rule of a dictator or Salafists.

Across the border in Iraq, some Kurds were skeptical of the Rojava revolution. In Iraq in 1991, Kurdish people had risen up against dictator Saddam Hussein's Ba'athist regime, expelled the Iraqi army from parts of the north, and, the following year, established their own Kurdistan Regional Government (KRG), which was autonomous from the rest of Iraq. The KRG had a similar population and physical size as Rojava.

Unlike Rojava, the KRG chose a top-down political approach, electing a president and prime minister, and adopted a capitalistic mindset in terms of developing itself. One Kurdish woman, who fled northern Syria at the start of the civil war with her family, and lived in the KRG, was harshly critical of the self-administration in Rojava. "The roads are damaged, and there is no improvement. All this oil is making millions of dollars, yet they take from everyone and it's all for nothing," said the woman, who did not want to be named for safety reasons.

The woman was disgusted by Abdullah Ocalan and the ideology the Syrian Kurds were fighting for. She did not see it as idealistic to be engaged in a forever war with enemy after enemy, no matter the cause. She saw it as criminal. "Fuck Apo [Ocalan]. He is an animal," she told me, spitting out her words with distaste. "He took so many beautiful men and women who have died. If we were there, my children would have to go and fight."

As for the YPJ women, she saw them as brainwashed.

Most YPJ fighters did not have phones, so the women kept their memories on personal flash drives instead, taking photos on the more senior hevals' phones or cameras. At her base in Tal Tamr, Cicek scrolled through the contents of her drive on a borrowed computer. Among its contents were several videos the hevals had made of Cicek when they assumed the Afrin drone strike had killed her—it was common for hevals to make martyr videos to honor their dead. In one video, Cicek wears a baseball cap and a bulletproof vest as colorful graphics fly by. In another, flower petals rain across her face. A third video animates a photo of Cicek as a recruit, sitting in a car in uniform, looking impossibly young. All three videos are set to dramatic music to remind the hevals of the immense sacrifice that the martyr Cicek has made, and the enemy's brutality in taking her. Cicek laughed as she rewatched these videos, at how she had escaped death yet again.

But mostly, Cicek collected photos and videos on her drive of happier times, including of the training Sosin had assigned her to lead at Sugar Palace: her hevals with mud on their faces and army-crawling through dust, and a video of Cicek firing her rifle and shouting at the trainees to run. As Cicek's eye focuses on the sight, she squeezes the trigger and absorbs the recoil into her shoulder.

There were pictures from her earlier days in the YPJ, too: Cicek huddled in a blanket beside a heval, standing atop a mountain with her arms thrown open in joy, and posing, grinning, beside a DShK machine gun that is larger than her. There was also a photo of her mother, Asiya, with her headscarf on, smiling in that bright-eyed, closed-mouth way she always did. It had been many months since Cicek had seen her.

Cicek also saved her favorite songs on the drive, both Kurdish and Arabic, to play on long car rides from Tal Tamr. Among them was Lebanese singer Roro Harb's romantic *"Haremni,"* which translates to "Deprive Me," and is about never forgetting those who have departed. "Force me to wear the clothes of forgetfulness," the lyrics go, "but I swear I won't forget you. If they burn my heart with fire, I swear I won't leave you." No matter how many Turkish drone strikes hit Tal Tamr, Cicek swore she would not leave the base where her comrades were killed.

In the months since Sosin and Zeynab had died, Tal Tamr had transformed into a kind of front line, with shelling and airstrikes occurring every week. Cicek was still at the same base, and the building where Sosin had been killed had been turned into a garden. One day, Cicek and her comrades were running from village to village to escape the latest shelling, diving into the dust whenever artillery struck. When they finally made it to a safe place, they laughed "because we looked like creatures made from dust," Cicek said. She told the younger recruits to always laugh that way, especially after battle. "You have to enjoy your life," Cicek said. "If you lock yourself in sadness, you will not move. You will be stuck." Buhar had taught her that a person cannot suffer all the time.

Cicek also thought that a person had to take notice when something miraculous happened. On another day at the Tal Tamr front line, shrapnel and bullets flew by the YPJ fighters. Cicek's hip still hurt from the Afrin drone strike, so she could not break into a sprint. But a friend offered to make a slow run together for another village so they would not survive or die alone. They made it across, but a drone hovered over them in the next village, striking one house and then another. By radio, Cicek told the hevals at the base that the shelling was too heavy for them to make it home that night. She was sure they both would die.

Then, the women heard a bark and a shaggy white dog appeared, one they did not recognize. It was scrawny like all the dogs were in wartime. The dog began trotting off into the distance, looking back to see if they were coming, and Cicek suggested they follow him. The two women ran after the scrawny dog until he led them to a safe location, after which they returned to the base. Cicek was amazed. Everyone at the base had lost hope they would survive, but here they were safe and sound because of a starving animal. War was full of miracles like this. Cicek thought every-day life was, too, but it was only in war that a person noticed.

That May 2021, Beritan and Haroun met in a cafe in Ain Diwar outside Derik city in northeast Syria, breaking YPG and YPJ rules. A couple of local journalists and I went along with them, which made the meeting less suspicious. On the drive to meet him, Beritan fanned herself to keep cool and grasped her hands together in nervousness. She wore her square glasses, and her hair was pulled up in a silver-and-turquoise clip.

They both grinned when they met, Beritan with her naturally kind smile and Haroun with his prominent teeth showing, and his thick, dark hair brushed off to one side. He shook her hand formally with his better hand. The cafe had a view of the Tigris River and was famous for its food, so we ordered a feast: fattoush salad with pomegranate sauce, tomato and cucumber salad, hummus and pita, and kebab including chicken and lamb with cooked onion and pepper, plus fresh blackberries for dessert. Afterward, they sat under a leafy overhang, close enough to touch but not. They spoke in a stilted way at first, finding their way back to one another.

While they were apart, Haroun had sent Beritan a photo of himself with his hand in a cast, holding a pink flower. "Why did you hide your hands in the photo?" Beritan asked. Even at the cafe, he wore a glove over his missing hand. "I don't want you to see me like this," he said. Beritan nodded: "How I wish I could give you your hands."

They had already discussed their latest plan by phone. Haroun would get his more damaged hand repaired by a reputable doctor in Jordan so that he would be suitable for Beritan's mother. If he could fix it, they would get married right away. Beritan would leave the YPJ for an administration or police job. "Inshallah it will work," Beritan told him at the cafe. "You mean like it won't work?" he asked. "No, why would I say that?" She looked hurt. *Sorry*, he shook his head. The wind picked up the grasses in the distance and spun them like a whirling dervish. They were both just anxious the plan wouldn't work out.

But by the end of the hour at the cafe, they were laughing. Haroun leaned over to say something in Beritan's ear. They took selfies in front of the view and leaned in close. Beritan did not tell Haroun that she still visited Shiar's grave and took off her glasses to cry. They did not have time for long stories like that. Instead, she reassured Haroun that they would overcome their remaining obstacles. "I'm still with you," she said, meeting his eyes.

After it was over, Beritan questioned herself and us for a long time about how the meeting with Haroun had gone.

In January 2022, ISIS staged a large-scale prison break in Al-Hasakah. The militants used a truck bomb to blast a hole in the prison wall, whose prisoners—all of them former ISIS militants—streamed out. The Syrian Democratic Forces responded to the scene, but the militants used boys detained in the prison as human shields, so the prison riot and street skirmishes were difficult to get under control. Despite being based in Al-Hasakah, Beritan was not called to fight, but she went with her camera to the prison to document what was happening. She was a fighter and could not bear to stand idly by. At the scene, she watched Kurdish fighters stop a man on a motorbike who was believed to be ISIS but wasn't, and saw another man who was ISIS jump from one roof to another and get caught.

In Tal Tamr, just a forty-five-minute drive from the prison, Cicek watched the prison break on television. She was ready to assist if needed, but she was not her old reckless self who joined any battle without reason. *Take care of yourself, Cicek. Don't do stupid things.* Also, she had the other hevals in Tal Tamr to protect.

There were some ten days of fierce fighting in Al-Hasakah, but it took a month before the Syrian Democratic Forces finally regained control of the prison. By that time, scores or even hundreds of ISIS prisoners had escaped. Some foreign policy experts warned it could be the beginning of the resurgence of ISIS, but Cicek was certain their war was largely with Turkey now.

Amid all the chaos in northern Syria, local journalists began complaining that the self-administration was trying to squash dissent. From 2021 to 2022, nearly a dozen local journalists were suspended or arrested in Rojava, often after they published a report critical of the revolution or the self-administration. The administration claimed it was just trying to license everyone. At the same time, Khalil's leading Democratic Union Party was accused of eliminating rival figures by forcing them into exile, and also of setting the offices of an opposition group on fire. Khalil denied both allegations, saying that some people had invented stories about his party to gain asylum elsewhere, and that "you can't control the angry young who sometimes break the laws individually."

But Syrian journalists remained skeptical of the administration and the major Kurdish political parties, including one journalist who did not want to be named for fear of reprisal. "They say they are not the PKK. But your father is in your blood, and you cannot stay away from your father," he told me. Another local reporter said he saw the Rojava revolution as similar to George Orwell's *Animal Farm,* in that the animals who rebelled for a better society ended up in just as troubled a state as before.

However, there was no doubt that Rojava was effectively transforming the lives of its women, more radically perhaps than the KRG in Iraq, where only some women could dress as they liked and few participated in the labor force. In both places, traditional roles for women were still entrenched in many households. In July 2021, two honor crimes against women in northern Syria made headlines, one of which was videotaped. The video shows three men drag a girl into an abandoned house and shoot her to death for the crime of refusing to marry her cousin and falling in love with another man. Days later, in a second incident, a father strangled to death his sixteen-year-old daughter after a relative raped her. Crimes like these, ostensibly to protect a girl's honor, had been happening in the region for centuries, but advocates said they were often dismissed as unimportant before the Rojava revolution. This time, women filled the streets in Al-Hasakah and Raqqa, enraged and demanding justice. They held signs that read "Stop killing women" and "There is no honor in murder."

According to the staff of the Mala Jin, or Women's House, in the city of Qamishli, women from conservative communities were increasingly speaking up about issues at home. The Mala Jin had not systemized their data collection, but anecdotally, this seemed to be true. Safaa Noori, a YPJ fighter I met who had grown up in a traditional Arab community, said she felt another path was possible after she saw women wielding guns. "I learned how they were fighting for women's rights, and I thought I, too, should play a role in freeing the woman," she told me. After years of an abusive child marriage, including being locked at home "like a bird in a cage," she said, she fled the marriage and then her village for the YPJ.

In the YPJ, a woman could smoke, drive, wield a weapon, and sleep under the stars. Safaa hoped to learn to use a DShK, rocket-propelled grenades, and a BKC. She wanted not only to fight but also to transform Syrian society. "We have learned that equality between men and women will free both of them. Because not only have the women been enslaved but the man has also been enslaved by this masculine mentality," she told me, quoting from her jineology classes. She paused to think, then said, "I think it is only together that we will build a new society."

On International Women's Day in March 2022, Cicek got an unexpected call from her senior hevals. They told her that she had some surprise guests, and to meet them in a nearby Christian village in Tal Tamr. Cicek heard the sound of women ululating as she entered a house inside the village. Then she saw her mother and father standing there, grinning, as her hevals called out wails of joy on her behalf. Cicek cried and hugged her parents. "International Women's Day was already a special day for me, but now it is doubly special," she told them.

When Cicek asked her parents how the situation was at home, they told her that Turkish and proxy forces occupied the entire region of Afrin. They described regular shelling and some fighting, and said that the Syrian National Army, a Turkish-backed militia, had taken over Dream Mountain. "Will Afrin ever be liberated?" her mother asked anxiously, meaning back in Kurdish hands. Cicek nodded, trying to project confidence for her family. "For sure, one day we'll return to our homes."

The next day, Cicek took her parents to the office building in Tal

Tamr where the drone strike had killed Sosin. She showed them the garden planted in Sosin's name after her death, and told them all about her beloved commander, as well as Zeynab and the other hevals at her base—her two worlds meeting at last.

That spring, Cicek was named commander of her base at Tal Tamr. She wondered what Sosin would think of that. For the first time, she was not just a driver or fighter. Her job was to train new YPJ fighters in political sessions and military operations. When they were deployed on the front lines, she would assign their positions. She was twenty-four, which seemed to her like an old woman for Rojava, though the hevals said she still seemed young. Many commanders were older.

Cicek cut a striking figure as commander of the base, with her strong facial features, broad shoulders, and boxy camouflage uniform. She rarely ate or slept because there was always too much to do. She signed up for a two-week training for herself on thermal weapon sights, which she had used only briefly to target Turkish-backed tanks in the black of night. It would hurt her stomach to hold the heavy weapon, but she could not always listen to Sosin. *If I connect my situation with my wounds, I will do nothing,* she thought. Buhar would approve.

Cicek's legs and hip still bothered her, especially when she ran, walked long distances, or rode a motorbike. Kobani had damaged one leg, while Tal Tamr had damaged the other. Both places, and Afrin, were responsible for the mess she'd made of her stomach. The hevals had started calling her "The Terminator," after the cyborg assassin in the movie they'd seen on Turkish TV. Cicek laughed at the nickname. Maybe it had been difficult for the enemy to kill her, but it had also been difficult for her to stay soft. Since Sosin's death, she had been gradually finding room for joy again. Whenever she walked in Tal Tamr, she remembered her days with Sosin. Sosin, the smartest woman, the greatest love she'd ever known.

When she saw Sosin's picture on the wall, "I tell myself that at one point we were talking and walking with each other, and now she has turned into a picture," she said. "Many hevals have turned into pictures on the wall. Every street I walk down, I see friends I used to eat, play, walk, and joke with. You cannot prevent these kinds of feelings; we are human beings. But these feelings affect even our thinking—my think-ing." She stopped herself, then tried to downplay her grief with her usual show of bravado. "But what can I do? This [hardship] is what makes me courageous." She laughed.

Whenever Cicek drank coffee these days, she turned the cup over and let the grinds spill out like a fortune, as Zeynab used to do.

While Haroun worked on getting to Jordan for surgery, Beritan left the YPJ for a job in Rojava's internal security, or police force. Beritan's com-mander in the YPJ had been transferred to a different unit, so Beritan decided it was the right time to try something different. Her job was to monitor the work of other police officers, which required her to sit in an office for hours. Every day was filled with paperwork, protocols, and bureaucracy. Beritan very quickly grew bored. She was used to being outside, amid the action, and at the front line. Before she had left, she killed a venomous desert cobra at her base with a garden trowel. She did not know how long she'd last at a desk.

Soon after Beritan quit the YPJ, Haroun ended their relationship. It turned out that his mother did not agree to him marrying Beritan either. Many Syrian mothers did not look kindly upon women who had been to war. It was said that they did not make good mothers and that they would be assertive instead of deferential in the home. It was said that they had seen too much, that they were no longer tender. The same judgment was made after World War II, as a junior sergeant and medical assistant described in Svetlana Alexievich's *The Unwomanly Face of War*. During the war, the soldier said, she was referred to as "dear nurse" and a her-oine, but afterward she was seen as damaged goods. When the former junior sergeant married a commander she knew from the fighting, "his mother took [him] to the kitchen and wept, 'Who have you married? A frontline girl . . . You have two sisters. Who will want to marry them now?'" Haroun's mother felt similarly of Beritan. She was such a strong fighter that she would make a poor wife. Haroun chose not to defy his mother.

Beritan could not believe the news at first. Once she accepted it, she found herself overwhelmed by emotions, each one crowding out the next: disappointment, then anger, sorrow, and, most damaging of all, disillusionment. She told herself that time would heal the particular wound of Haroun cutting her loose. But she was not sure her faith in relationships or society would recover. She was too confused and hurt to talk to anyone about it. When I first asked Beritan about what happened with Haroun, she cried and turned her head. "It is better not to speak of these things," she said.

Within months, Beritan rejoined the YPJ. She followed her old commander to a new, high-level position at the YPG-YPJ command center. She was grateful to be back in the militia, in a high-risk, high-secrecy, and high-action role. At thirty-four, she was considered a senior heval, and people looked to her for leadership and guidance. Back home, her friends were confused at how torn up she seemed over Haroun as she returned to the YPJ. "Our friends look at us as soldiers and fighters. They think that we think only of weapons and fighting, or if we go to the doctor, we will not feel pain," Beritan said, her voice as measured as ever despite the tumult she felt. "But we are human beings, we feel passion and emotions and pain. We feel everything."

Beritan felt everything, every day, for months. She carried her mobile phone with her, but Haroun did not call. Another male YPG fighter who had a crush on her tried calling to ask her out, but Beritan swiftly blocked him. She was not interested in any more romance. At least her relationship with Shiar had been pure, even if her relationship with Haroun had turned out otherwise. Shiar had never discarded her like an old coat. She still went by the name Beritan Shiar, and she always would. Şehîd Namirin. *Martyrs never die.* She had her memories of Shiar, and she had herself. That was enough. Enough for now.

In May 2022, Turkey threatened to invade northeast Syria with troops on the ground. Turkish president Erdogan said his forces planned to complete a "thirty-kilometer-deep safe zone" inside the country that they failed to establish in 2019 and before. A U.S. State Department spokesman said America was "deeply concerned" by the threats, which, if enacted, would be tantamount to the invasion of a country. Around the same time, the U.S. announced it was lifting economic sanctions on northern Syria—but not the rest of Syria, whose regime it wanted to keep the pressure on—which could help relieve the area's severe economic crisis.

But the Syrian Kurds weren't relying on the U.S. to save them or Rojava anymore. They had been buffeted and betrayed by the world's superpowers for decades, and they knew better. The self-administration declared a state of emergency to mobilize its forces, and Cicek activated her soldiers in Tal Tamr. Amid all of it, ordinary Syrians continued to try to carve out a space for themselves and their families for a better future.

Turkish drone strikes were picking off YPJ fighters all the time now. In April of that year, Turkey took out three YPJ members, and in May, one more. Then, in July, drone strikes killed three YPJ women, including a prominent commander, while they were leaving a women's conference. The American media, which had largely stopped covering the YPJ since it defeated ISIS, was suddenly interested again. "Female Kurdish commander who 'saved American lives' killed by Turkish drone strike," an NBC headline read that summer.

Also in July, the Syrian Democratic Forces announced it had arrested three spies it said were involved in the drone strike that killed Commander Sosin and wounded Cicek. According to them, the spies—one man and two women, whose names were not released—had confessed to receiving their orders from Turkish intelligence and said they had plans for other attacks.

Perhaps Cicek should have been unnerved by the reports of double agents. But it was like that famous line from Kurdish activist and politician Leyla Zana: "Kurds are like fire, if approached kindly they will warm you, if approached badly they will burn you." Cicek was confident the Syrian Democratic Forces, which encompassed the YPJ, would root out any spies, just as someday they would expel Turkey's forces from their land. "There is no more risk than the beginning with Turkey, it is the same as it used to be," Cicek said, channeling Sosin's resolve. "When they shell, we respond. When they attack, we respond. We expect everything because we know Turkey wants to invade our lands."

Although Cicek spoke with all the authority and composure befitting a commander, her old reckless ways still occasionally got the best of her. When she heard that comrades from her base were wounded from an attack on a position in Tal Tamr, she jumped on a motorbike and went to rescue them herself. She sped through the shelling and ignored the sound of drones, not considering the risk. *Whatever will happen, will happen, here or there,* she thought. *I do what is true to me. Wherever there is war, I should be there.*

After nine years of war, after all her dead comrades, the bullets, drone strikes, and everything she'd seen, Cicek had nights of feeling hopeless and embittered. She could not help feeling that nothing was the same since Sosin died. Images played in her mind of comrade after comrade, all pictures on the wall, and her commander was not there to remind her of the bigger picture. *Have less cigarettes and coffee, make sure not to stay isolated.* But those things didn't really work. At moments, she would even forget the grand ideals for which they were fighting. Many days now, she felt herself teetering between grief and disillusionment, and finding comfort in the importance of the cause. She wanted to regain her old enthusiasm, but all she really wanted was Sosin.

Still, she hadn't gone numb yet. Recently, she had become close with a woman named Arjin, who had been transferred to another base but had given her a bracelet before she left. It read, *I love you,* and Cicek wore it around her wrist. Arjin was also from Afrin, and Cicek sometimes talked to her over the radio at night before bed. Cicek found it reassuring that she could still form relationships—that she had not become too hardened. She saw connection as essential and only possible if you loved yourself and held on to hope.

She told herself she still had hope, even after Sosin's death. It was her duty to avenge Sosin, secure Rojava for her family and all families, and ensure that every woman could live freely. Cicek knew that women all over the world were fighting their own battles. On a YouTube channel dedicated to jineology, some free verse was posted linking women's struggles in different countries: "We are Kurdish guerrilla fighters / We are . . . Indian woman warriors / . . . We are the struggling mothers." Women were fighting everywhere, but her fight was here in Rojava.

"As long as there is the YPJ, there is Cicek," she said. "There is me."

And as long as she is alive, there are the memories of the time spent with her hevals. The women had spent so many long, drawn-out evenings together at the base, when they were all restless and anxious to fight. One night played again and again in her mind. It was before she met and lost Sosin, and before she lost Buhar. Cicek had found a water bucket to use as a drum and sang for her hevals, who stomped and danced in unison, as she alone kept time.

EPILOGUE

In March 2022 in Stevenson, Alabama, Brittany was arrested for falsifying a drug test after relapsing on methamphetamine. She said she asked the judge if she could attend a rehabilitation program, telling him she needed help after multiple relapses. Instead, the judge ordered her to spend nine months behind bars, and she was sent to Julia Tutwiler Prison for Women in Wetumpka, Alabama. She would be out by December, in time for Christmas with her kids. Over the jail phone, her seven-year-old daughter asked her mom why she was in jail again. "I think we need to talk about it when you're a little bit older, sis," Brittany told her. When her baby girl was old enough, she would tell her everything: about bringing them into the world, their angel brother, Will, her struggles with addiction, and how she got hurt but fought back. Later, I messaged Brittany over the jail messaging app to ask her why she had told me everything, both for this book and a documentary I produced on her case (*State of Alabama vs. Brittany Smith*). "So many women give up on their goals and on their lives after abuse," she wrote back, and said she didn't want that to be her story's ending. Once her life stabilized, she hoped to be an advocate for other women. "The time has come to be loud, to stand tall, to stand firm, to stand together and be heard. To have a voice," she wrote. "Because consequences be damned." She added: *Always stand your ground*. As of this writing, in January 2023, Brittany is out of prison and, by all accounts, ten months sober.

Some 8,000 miles away in Tirwa, India, Angoori returned to activism after the pandemic receded. She sent me a video over WhatsApp of her and dozens of others—members of the Green Gang, along with other Tirwa residents—protesting the unsavory depiction of a former king of Kannauj in a new Bollywood movie. The movie depicted the king as a traitor and villain even though he had been a hero in Kannauj. Angoori knew what it was like to be a heroine painted as a villain. It felt good to her to be back on the streets, leading chants with her fist in the air, as men and women followed behind her. Every time I asked Angoori why she wanted to talk to me, she evaded the query. Finally, she said she hoped the government would recognize her in some belated way for all the work she'd done to help women. It was a lonely lesson to realize that the Green Gang had left her broke and, if not powerless, not powerful either. Still, years after our last in-person interviews, she kept WhatsApping me photos and videos of her occasional continued activism—her forcing a recalcitrant man to wear a mask, or shouting slogans to hang the murderer of a local woman—proof that she had not stopped fighting.

The last time I saw Cicek, we sat in YPG-YPJ headquarters in a small room with coffee-colored couches, saying a prolonged goodbye. She told me why she'd wanted to participate the first time we met at her base in Tal Tamr. The other hevals told her she was "like a witness" for Rojava—to the revolution from inception, to all the big battles with ISIS, and now to Turkey's incursions. Commander Sosin also said her story was crucial for the record. Still, Cicek was antsy through many of our interviews because she wanted to get back to the fighting. In my final week in northeast Syria, as tensions with Turkey escalated, even patient Beritan was anxious to attend to more urgent work. On that last day with Cicek, she urged me to hurry up with the book because she worried that she might be killed before getting to read it. She shared a dream she'd had the night before, that someone would bring the book to her base when it was finished, and "learn that Cicek has just been martyred."

As I finished this book, however, I received news that Cicek had abruptly retired from the YPJ. She said that her "soul was tired" and she needed rest, to find a life beyond war. She moved home to her family's residence in Shahba, where she spent most of her days holed up in her room, talking to Commander Sosin's photo. "I don't talk to my mom or sisters, only Sosin's picture," she said. "She was part of me, I lost the best part of myself, so some days I feel I can't go on." Cicek said she considered throwing herself from the roof, but that she didn't think she had the right to take her own life. The stress and trauma of war had finally caught up to her, replacing her bravado with a kind of madness— the madness of having fought and fought and fought, and lost so much in the end.

And yet, that same month, women across Iran took to the streets and burned or refused to wear their headscarves, in response to the in-custody death of an Iranian-Kurdish woman who had been arrested by the country's morality police. Iranian women soon rallied around a Kurdish slogan I knew well: "Women, life, freedom." And Cicek's battles lived on.

After years of reporting on Brittany, Angoori, and Cicek, I saw how their violent actions had both helped and harmed them, and others around them. Brittany likely saved her own life. Angoori altered the course of her destiny as a Dalit woman. Cicek escaped the mini prison she so dreaded. They all found agency, a voice, and an identity beyond how the men in their towns saw them. But they got no perfect, happy endings. Their individual failings—Brittany's addiction and habit of obscuring, Angoori's quest for power, and Cicek's blind acceptance of Ocalan's propaganda—caught up to them and complicated their stories. They sought to change the status quo, yet never fully escaped the oppressive systems they grew up in and continue to live under. I believe their failings are, in part, a response to living within damaging cultures of honor.

Importantly, all three women's actions led to change not only in their own lives but also larger change within their communities. Brittany, imperfect victim as she was, forced police to respond to more complaints of abuse in her county. Angoori could not fully reimagine power for herself, but she did so for so many of her women. And Cicek, idealist until our final interview, became disillusioned but not before inspiring many young hevals to live as liberated women. Ultimately, their acts of violence added up to something worthy, setting events into motion that very well may change the world after them.

Three women—three furies—fed up with a world of injustice, fought for something different. If only we could all fight so hard.

ACKNOWLEDGMENTS

Every book takes a village, but this one seemed to take a small nation. Immense thank-yous are in order, to:

My editor at Harper, Jenny Xu, who shepherded this book with immense intelligence, insight, and kindness; my agent at WME, Suzanne Gluck, who first believed in this subject; Jennifer Barth, who trusted and pushed me to develop my thinking on it; and Emily Graff and Emily Griffin, who brought it across the finish line with care. Elizabeth Wachtel and Addie Poris, who helped me tell these stories in other mediums, plus everyone at HarperCollins and WME who touched this book.

Local journalists Kamiran Sadoun, Obeid Sheikhi, and Majd Helobi, who showed me Syria and whose work was crucial to this project. Solin Muhammed Amin, who instantly understood this book and reported beside me from day one. Saurabh Sharma, whose work with his late wife, Dipa, helped me better understand a country I am forever getting to know. Ashley Remkus, whose reporting on Alabama is worthy of her Pulitzers.

Tenzin Tsagong, whose fact-checking and research was invaluable and greatly fortified this book; any remaining errors contained herein are mine. Pooja Salhotra, the trustiest research assistant, and Kimon de Greef, Robin Visbal, Matt Nelson, and Jeongyoon Han, for essential editorial help.

My NYU family: Rob Boynton, Ted Conover, Brooke Kroeger, and Katie Roiphe, for teaching me (all over again) how to write. My *PBS NewsHour* colleagues, the *New Yorker*, the *California Sunday Magazine*, the *Economist*, the *Guardian*, *Foreign Policy*, and Lemonada Media for supporting these kinds of stories, with particular gratitude to Willing

Davidson and Raha Naddaf, and Tripod Media for the care it took with the documentary on Brittany's story.

The International Women's Media Foundation, for crucial and generous financial support to report in Syria, plus the Pulitzer Center on Crisis Reporting for early support to report in Alabama. PEN America and especially Caits Meissner, for a compassionate fellowship that deepened my understanding of America's criminal legal system.

Miranda Lambert, Heather Little, Sony Music, and Nashville Star Music, for lending me the powerful lines of "Gunpowder & Lead." Marge Piercy, for imparting your radical writing on Inez Garcia.

Lance Richardson and Daniel Stone, my brilliant and supportive writer family. Tania Rashid and Glenna Gordon, beloved friends and the most impressive journalists I know. Jon Gerberg, who kept me safe.

My friends whose existence made this book better: Charlotte Grubb, Katie Reisner, Em Brush, Arathi and Aswathi Jayaram, Bianca Elder, Reilly Nelson, Alexshea Conn, Miles Hall, Swati Sharma, Ali Withers, Hayley Harper, Lisa Levy, Jennifer Olson, Rita O'Connell and Siobhan Bonny-O'Rourke, Sonia Paul, Marie Elizabeth Oliver, Antanas Petkus, Beth Rehn, Joon Soo Song, Meredith Stoner, Adam Dolezal, and Lily Trienens.

Charles, Willow, and Teddy Frye; Marina Gearhart; and the whole Gearhart and Rubin clan. Pete Janos and Bruce Fine. The Ramos family, my home away from home.

My mama, a fighter in her own right, cheerleader, and fierce protector. My father, who gave me a superpower: his unflagging support. My sisters, Jane, Lucy, Claire, and Emily, who are my north, south, east, and west. Liz and Rob, who make hard things possible. Wendy, for your quiet and steady love. Bob, who teaches us to the see the stars. The ones who live in me: Chuckdad, Gretchen, and Vicki. Chaz, Romy, and Neza, the next generation of warriors.

Dago, my love and my heart's home, who talks with me about writing over breakfast and on dog walks and in the dark, whose steady love buoyed me to see this through.

And finally, to all the incarcerated women, experts, activists, organizers, fighters, and other women who spoke to me. Thank you. I hope this book does the subject justice.

REFERENCES

I consulted many books in the writing of this one. Here is an incomplete list:

Alderman, Naomi. *The Power*. Boston: Little, Brown and Company, 2017.

Alexievich, Svetlana. *The Unwomanly Face of War: An Oral History of Women in World War II*. Translated by Richard Pevear and Larissa Volokhonsky. New York: Random House, 2017.

Anand, Mulk Raj. *Untouchable*. London: Penguin Classics, 2014.

Beard, Mary. *Women & Power: A Manifesto*. New York: Liveright, 2017.

Brown, Elaine. *A Taste of Power: A Black Woman's Story*. New York: Anchor Books, 1993.

Çağlayan, Handan. *Women in the Kurdish Movement: Mothers, Comrades, Goddesses*. London: Palgrave Macmillan, 2020.

Campbell, Anne. *Men, Women and Aggression: From Rage in Marriage to Violence in the Streets—How Gender Affects the Way We Act*. New York: Basic Books, 1993.

Cansiz, Sakine. *Sara: My Whole Life Was a Struggle*. Translated by Janet Biehl. London: Pluto Press, 2018.

Carter, Angela. *The Bloody Chamber: And Other Stories*. London: Penguin Books, 1990.

Covington, Dennis. *Salvation on Sand Mountain: Snake Handling and Redemption in Southern Appalachia*. Boston: Da Capo Press, 2009.

Cudi, Azad. *Long Shot: The Inside Story of the Kurdish Snipers Who Broke ISIS*. New York: Atlantic Monthly Press, 2019.

Deacy, Susan. *Athena*. Abingdon-on-Thames, U.K.: Routledge, 2008.

Devi, Phoolan. *I, Phoolan Devi: The Autobiography of India's Bandit Queen*. London: Time Warner Books U.K., 1997.

Devi, Phoolan, Marie-Thérèse Cuny, and Paul Rambali. *The Bandit Queen of India: An Indian Woman's Amazing Journey from Peasant to International Legend*. Guilford, CT: Lyons Press, 2006.

Dirik, Dilar. *The Kurdish Women's Movement: History, Theory, Practice*. London: Pluto Press, 2022.

Estés, Clarissa Pinkola, Ph.D. *Women Who Run with the Wolves: Myths and Stories of the Wild Woman Archetype*. New York: Ballantine Books, 1996.

Fraser, Antonia. *The Warrior Queens: The Legends and Lives of the Women Who Have Led Their Nations in War*. Toronto: Penguin Canada, 2009.

Gidla, Sujatha. *Ants Among Elephants: An Untouchable Family and the Making of Modern India*. New York: Farrar, Straus and Giroux, 2017.

Gilbert, Paula Ruth, and Kimberly K. Eby. *Violence and Gender: An Interdisciplinary Reader*. London: Pearson, 2003.

Gillespie, Cynthia. *Justifiable Homicide: Battered Women, Self-Defense, and the Law*. Columbus: Ohio State University Press, 1990.

Gómez-Cano, Grisel. *The Return to Coatlicue: Goddesses and Warladies in Mexican Folklore*. Bloomington, IN: Xlibris, 2010.

Goodmark, Leigh. *Decriminalizing Domestic Violence: A Balanced Policy Approach to Intimate Partner Violence*. Oakland: University of California Press, 2018.

Gowrinathan, Nimmi. *Radicalizing Her: Why Women Choose Violence*. Boston: Beacon Press, 2021.

Greenberg, Imogen. *Athena: Goddess of Wisdom and War*. New York: Harry N. Abrams, 2021.

Guha, Ramachandra. *India After Gandhi: The History of the World's Largest Democracy*. New York: Ecco, 2008.

Hansen, Ann. *Direct Action: Memoirs of an Urban Guerrilla*. Oakland, CA: A.K. Press, 2002.

Homa, Ava. *Daughters of Smoke and Fire*. New York: The Overlook Press, 2020.

Kaba, Mariame. *We Do This 'Til We Free Us: Abolitionist Organizing and Transforming Justice*. Chicago: Haymarket Books, 2021.

Knapp, Michael, Anja Flach, and Ercan Ayboga. *Revolution in Rojava: Democratic Autonomy and Women's Liberation in Syrian Kurdistan*. Translated by Janet Biehl. London: Pluto Press, 2016.

Lemmon, Gayle Tzemach. *The Daughters of Kobani: A Story of Rebellion, Courage, and Justice*. London: Penguin, 2021.

Light, Caroline E. *Stand Your Ground: A History of America's Love Affair with Lethal Self-Defense*. Westport, CT: Praeger, 2002.

Mahmoud, Houzan, ed. *Kurdish Women's Stories*. London: Pluto Press, 2021.

Malcolm, Janet. *Iphigenia in Forest Hills: Anatomy of a Murder Trial*. New Haven, CT: Yale University Press, 2012.

Marcus, Aliza. *Blood and Belief: The PKK and the Kurdish Fight for Independence*. New York: NYU Press, 2007.

Markandeya. *Devi Mahatmyam*. Translated by Swami Jagadiswarananda. Los Angeles: Vedanta Press & Bookshop, 1953.

Miller, Susan L. *Victims as Offenders: The Paradox of Women's Violence in Relationships*. New Brunswick, NJ: Rutgers University Press, 2005.

Monroe, Rachel. *Savage Appetites: Four True Stories of Women, Crime, and Obsession*. New York: Scribner, 2019.

Morford, Mark, Robert J. Lenardon, and Michael Sham. *Classical Mythology*. Oxford, U.K.: Oxford University Press, 2013.

Nisbett, Richard E., and Dov Cohen. *Culture of Honor: The Psychology of Violence in the South*. Abingdon-on-Thames, U.K.: Routledge. 1996.

Ogle, Robin S., and Susan Jacobs. *Self-Defense and Battered Women Who Kill: A New Framework*. Westport, CT: Praeger Publishers, 2002.

Ovid. *Metamorphoses*. Translated by Anthony S. Kline. Ann Arbor, MI: Borders Classics, 2004.

Palani, Joanna. *Freedom Fighter: My War Against ISIS on the Frontlines of Syria*. London: Atlantic Books, 2015.

Pearson, Patricia. *When She Was Bad: Violent Women & The Myth of Innocence*. New York: Viking Adult, 1997.

Porath, Jason. *Rejected Princesses: Tales of History's Boldest Heroines, Hellions, and Heretics*. New York: Dey Street Books, 2016.

Roiphe, Katie. *The Power Notebooks*. New York: Free Press, 2020.

Rumore, Kori, and Marianne Mather. *He Had It Coming: Four Murderous Women and the Reporter Who Immortalized Their Stories*. Evanston, IL: Agate Publishing, 2020.

Sabio, Oso. *Rojava: An Alternative to Imperialism, Nationalism, and Islamism in the Middle East (An Introduction)*. Morrisville, NC: Lulu, 2015.

Shekhawat, Seema, ed. *Female Combatants in Conflict and Peace: Challenging Gender in Violence and Post-Conflict Reintegration*. London: Palgrave Macmillan, 2015.

Shukla, Shrilal. *Raag Darbari*. Translated by Gillian Wright. London: Penguin, 2012.

Sjoberg, Laura, and Caron E. Gentry. *Mothers, Monsters, Whores: Women's Violence in Global Politics*. London: Zed Books, 2007.

Snyder, Rachel Louise. *No Visible Bruises: What We Don't Know About Domestic Violence Can Kill Us*. London: Bloomsbury Publishing, 2019.

Solnit, Rebecca. *Men Explain Things to Me*. Chicago: Haymarket Books, 2015.

Soundararajan, Thenmozhi. *The Trauma of Caste: A Dalit Feminist Meditation on Survivorship, Healing, and Abolition*. Berkeley, CA: North Atlantic Books, 2022.

Spyer, Jonathan. *Days of the Fall: A Reporter's Journey in the Syria and Iraq Wars*. Abingdon-on-Thames, U.K.: Routledge, 2017.

Strangers in a Tangled Wilderness, ed. *A Small Key Can Open a Large Door: The Rojava Revolution*. New York: Strangers in a Tangled Wilderness, 2015.

Tatar, Maria. *The Heroine with 1,001 Faces*. New York: Penguin Press, 2021.

Tax, Meredith. *A Road Unforeseen: Women Fight the Islamic State*. New York: Bellevue Literary Press, 2016.

Thuma, Emily L. *All Our Trials: Prisons, Policing, and the Feminist Fight to End Violence.* Champaign, IL: University of Illinois Press, 2019.

Wolkstein, Diane, and Samuel Noah Kramer. *Inanna, Queen of Heaven and Earth: Her Stories and Hymns from Sumer.* New York: Harper Perennial, 1983.

Woodfin, Byron. *Lay Down with Dogs, The Story of Hugh Otis Bynum and the Scottsboro First Monday Bombing.* Tuscaloosa, AL: University of Alabama Press, 1997.

Zengel, Carolyn. *Immediate, Direct, Explosive! Basic Self-Defense for Women and Girls.* Kettering, OH: Asian Arts Center Press, 2005.

ABOUT THE AUTHOR

ELIZABETH FLOCK is an Emmy Award–winning journalist whose work has been featured in *The New Yorker*, the *New York Times*, and *The Atlantic*, and on *PBS NewsHour* and Netflix, among other outlets. She is the host of *Blind Plea*, a podcast about criminalized survival from Lemonada Media. Her reporting is supported by the Pulitzer Center, PEN America, and the International Women's Media Foundation. Her first book, *The Heart Is a Shifting Sea*, won a Nautilus Book Award for books that inspire and make a difference. She lives in Chicago.